Shadows of the Rising Sun

SHADOWS OF THE RISING SUN

A Critical View of the "Japanese Miracle"

Jared Taylor

William Morrow and Company, Inc.
New York   1983

Library of Congress Cataloging in Publication Data

Taylor, Jared.
Shadows of the Rising Sun.

Includes bibliographical references and index.
1. Japan—Civilization. 2. National characteristics,
Japanese. 3. Social values. I. Title.
DS821.T275 1983   952   83-9915
ISBN 0-688-02455-6

Printed in the United States of America

First Edition

1 2 3 4 5 6 7 8 9 10

BOOK DESIGN BY LINEY LI

❀

TO MY PARENTS,

with love and gratitude

✿

PREFACE

Those old enemies, the Germans and the Japanese, seem to be the people we have the most trouble fitting into a system.

We know how we feel about most countries. We feel close to the English. The French may do the most maddening things, but few Americans think that there is the smallest possibility of going to war with them. The Italians move from crisis to crisis, so that crisis comes to be the usual thing. It may not be what we want, but we accept it. We know too well how we feel about the Russians. In Asia we have been too quick to think of the Chinese as new friends. They have been at some pains to inform us that it is not necessarily so.

But the Germans and the Japanese. It is almost forty years since Japan and Germany ceased being our enemies, but still we do not quite know what to make of them. A noisy and rather scruffy little party gets a few seats in the German Bundestag, and we have nightmares about a recurrence of the old German insanity. The United States may not worry about a revival of Japanese "militarism" as some of the nations of Asia do, but Japan seems to spawn half-truths and untruths as does scarcely another country in the world. While it was weak it was for Americans a place of exquisite sensibilities and of Zen. Now that it is strong it is a place that grinds, operates with great cunning, and is devilishly clever at keeping others from playing the same game. That is one view, the hostile one. The views and the writings of those friendly to Japan have succeeded in building up a myth of Japanese invincibility.

It is good to have a book which is not hostile but which sees the Japanese for what they are. As the treatises on Japanese managerial methods and the Japanese genius for organization have poured forth, the need has grown for something that gets it right—or, since no brief statement can encompass so complex a country, gets it with a closer approximation to rightness.

Mr. Taylor has given us such a book. It is well informed and dispassionate, and it is not hostile to the Japanese, though some will doubtless think that it is. Equally important, it turns a cool eye on American attributes and capabilities, and tells us what we should *really* be learning from the Japanese. This has little to do with Japanese organizational and managerial methods, and a great deal to do with our own traditions.

Treatises that seem to inform us that there is something remarkably effective, almost magically so, about Japanese methods, and that we should therefore be imitating them, do great mischief. They seldom say explicitly that that is what they are about, but when they inform us that we have much to learn from Japan, and then proceed to describe, with some accuracy and some inaccuracy, how the Japanese do things, it is hard to know what else they can be about.

That the most widely read of them has sold far more copies in Japan than in the United States tells us something about the mischief that is done. Professor Ezra Vogel's book with the catchy title, *Japan as Number One*, has had Japanese sales in the high six figures, and probably readers in the seven figures. These huge numbers give evidence of the Japanese capacity for self-deception. It is there and it has long been there, and it is dangerous. Most if not all of those Japanese readers ought to know that things are not quite as described. The psychology is of course universal. We enjoy being described as different than we are, if the direction is toward making us seem better than we are. I love being asked if I have not lost weight, even though I know perfectly well that I have been putting it on steadily. The difference is that I do not take the question seriously. I accept it as a pleasant kind of flattery and like the person better for having asked it. There is a disturbing possibility that all those Japanese do take flattery seriously. They come to think of themselves as more handsomely endowed than they had always seen themselves to be, and indeed than they are.

Back in the years after the war the Japanese sense of inferiority was so painful that one wanted to tell them to be quiet about it at least, if they could not overcome it. By way of compensation, all manner of silly notions were prevalent, such as that Japan would be a moral example for the world (as if the world would pay much attention), or that Japan would be a bridge between the East and the West. It was hard to imagine in those days that there could be a return to the arrogance of which the Chinese and the Koreans liked to talk.

There may not be arrogance exactly, today, but there is something that may properly be called overconfidence. Assured that their methods are superior, the Japanese become inclined to think that these are what the world needs and that Japan, having them, needs nothing more. They forget that the world is a tough and dangerous place.

Arguing with them, one feels like Clark Gable, in the famous scene from *Gone With the Wind*, arguing with all those southern gentlemen at Fair Oaks, or whatever it is called, as news of Fort Sumter comes in. Gable says that the South, without resources and without factories, has done a foolish thing. The gentlemen heatedly reply that the southern spirit will overcome.

One cannot make precisely the Gable argument, of course, since the Japanese have the best factories in the world; but half of the argument does apply, and the response tends to be very much like that of the gentlemen. The overconfident view seems to argue that, like the southern spirit, the Japanese spirit will overcome.

We have heard much of the Japanese spirit before, and it has brought disaster upon the land. It may not have been believed the land over, but certainly it was believed by many Japanese, including those who led the way to the disaster, that America was a land of sloppy materialism which could not prevail over that highly honed entity, the *Yamatodamashii*, the Japanese spirit. It is an expression that has been with us for a thousand years and more, and has always indicated, though not always with the same virulence, the superior attributes of the island nation.

Not long ago I heard a reporter for an important Japanese newspaper tell an audience largely of American students that the biggest difference between Japanese and Americans is that Japanese are realists and Americans tend to be dreamers, idealists. If Americans did not soon wake up to the facts of the world, they would find that they had lost Japan, which had gone over to the Chinese. American student audiences are usually critical of the American government and its policies, but this one questioned him sharply as to the kind of realism that led to Pearl Harbor, and asked without avail for a concrete description of the devices by which the transfer to the Chinese would be accomplished. The questions were very much to the point, for all of this is a part of the same syndrome. The Japanese have a penchant, a very ancient one, for thinking that singleness of purpose, the Japanese spirit really mustered up and concentrated, can accomplish anything. People who encourage them in this view and lull them into forgetfulness of the toughness and the dangers of the world do them no service.

A part of this exaggerated and simplistic view is all the same correct, and from it emerges the most significant matter for Americans—what they should do about the Japanese "threat." The Japanese do enjoy a certain spiritual and moral superiority, and from it derives most of their success. This does not mean that there is anything unique about the Japanese spirit, except perhaps its remarkable tenacity in clinging to old moral and ethical patterns. It does not mean what is demonstrably untrue from any reading of recent history—that the Japanese spirit will prevail over everything, and therefore that the Japanese have nothing to worry about. It does mean that a similar fidelity to our own moral and ethical traditions will do more for us than all manner of attempts to imitate Japanese managerial methods.

This I take to be the central message of Mr. Taylor's book. It is a message that is made eloquently and well. The description of the Japanese is good, and the description of what America seems on the way to losing is good too.

Ryōkichi Minobe, governor of Tokyo for a dozen years, used to lecture us on morals. It is all a matter of morals, he liked to say, using a word from a European language—it is hard to know which, since the key word is virtually identical in several of them. I thought him the worst kind of governor, but some of the things he liked to say were interesting and to the point.

"Morals" may be understood in a very broad sense, applying to the acceptance of principles that have prevailed for a very long time and supply the fabric that holds a nation together. The principles are not of course the same for every society, and there is no need for them to be the same. Japanese morals come no more easily to us than American morals do to them. What is important is the acceptance, and what the acceptance comes down to is almost universal recognition that no one can have things entirely his own way. If the fabric is not to be torn apart, everyone (or almost everyone) must accept principles which by their nature mean sacrificing a part of his or her individuality.

Mr. Taylor does not put the matter in quite these words, and certainly he does not have Governor Minobe's fondness for the word "morals," which, used too often, comes to have a preachy quality about it. (Perhaps the governor avoided this unpleasant aspect by using a foreign word.) Yet I think that he is saying essentially this, in what seems to me the most important part of his book. It is a book meant for Americans, and the heart of it is his advice to them on how to look at the Japanese and themselves.

"Individually," he says on page 171, "none of the management techniques we have seen is of earthshaking importance. . . . What, then, is the secret of Japan's climb to the top?

"Deceptively simple as it may sound, *the single most important ingredient in Japan's success is the Japanese attitude toward work.*"

Anyone who has seen how they mop a floor or man a garbage truck must see great truth in this. The matter concerns not only high technology but the most menial and lowest-regarded of pursuits. There is an ancient expression, moral and philosophical in its implications, which indicates pride in doing it well, and a determination to do it well, whatever it may be. The expression is "the way." It is related to the *tao* of Taoism, and it means many things, but this is among the important things which it means. The Japanese janitor or garbage man is concerned with doing it well—he has a sense of personal accountability—as the American, and doubtless also the European, does not. It is a matter of morals, in the very general sense in which I have used the expression. It is a willingness to subordinate oneself to abstract principles.

Mr. Taylor is right in pointing out that the United States goes on being a more inventive country than Japan. Now that the Japanese have taken over so many of our inventions, perhaps they must become more inventive themselves if they are to stay ahead. We will see whether they do or not, but their record thus far has not been brilliant. From transistors to semiconductors, the inventions have been ours.

They have excelled in production. They have excelled, in other words, in the realm in which their more perdurable moral fiber stands them in best stead. So we should obviously look to our own fiber, and not let our attention be distracted by their productive and managerial techniques. Our own primitive virtues—and the adjective is not here used in a deprecatory sense—have served us very well. We should look to them in the endeavor to get ourselves out in front once more.

"For solutions to American problems," says Mr. Taylor on page 294, "we will have to look elsewhere [than to Japanese techniques] for inspiration—perhaps to our own tradition, to the values that shaped America's own achievements."

That "perhaps" might well be removed. Our "traditions," which word might be redone as "moral patterns," may have had their greedy and ruthless side, but if our concerns are production and economic competition, then it seems hardly possible to deny that they once worked astonishingly, breathtakingly well. The trouble is that they have decayed. Americans seem to think more and more all the time about leisure and "gracious living" and that sort of thing. Somewhat grudgingly they put in their time, and if they leave a mess behind, it will be cleaned up somehow—by recalling the automobiles, or something. Japan may be moving in that direction, but its competitive edge at the moment derives chiefly from the large emphasis that its moral and ethical patterns place upon work.

"Deceptively simple" things are sometimes very complicated. It may be easy enough to diagnose the ailment, and to isolate the virus; but to cure it is another matter. What is needed is a return to our own old values, and not the importation of someone else's; but of course moral revolutions, or revivals, as called for here, are among the most difficult of changes to accomplish.

Correct diagnosis, however, has the huge virtue of preventing incorrect treatment. If the myth of Japanese invincibility is allowed to swell and swell, and our awareness that the remedies suggested by the management specialists do not work grows with it, then frustrations will build up. There are always extraordinary measures one can take against a seemingly invincible adversary, provided one has the weapons: Squash him. If the danger on the one side of the Pacific is overconfidence and a dulled sense of ugly realities, on the other side the danger is in seeing things as more sinister and formidable than they are. We do have the weapons. We are more important to the Japanese than the Japanese are to us. We can take extraordinary measures, if we are sufficiently frustrated.

It may not always be the case that the truth will be our shield and buckler, but it sometimes is. Both departures from the truth are dangerous. Since Mr. Taylor has in mind chiefly an American audience, and refrains from giving good advice to the Japanese, the main danger is that America, frustrated in its attempts to follow all the good advice of the managerial experts and under the illusion that it faces an adversary beyond quelling otherwise, will run amok.

Moral revolutions may be difficult to accomplish, but they are not as difficult as imitation of someone utterly alien. If the Japanese have been so successful at imitating us, it may be asked, why should we not be as good at doing it to them? The answer may be that in moral matters they have not imitated us at all, and perhaps, indeed, they have not even understood us. That is essentially their business; and while they are deliberating upon it they might wish to ask themselves whether they would want to become like us in every respect, moral and cultural and ethical. The reverse is among the most important questions that we should ask ourselves, and it is a question that seems to get left out of all the disquisitions about Japanese organizational and productive methods.

Would we wish to be like them and do things as they do them? For me the answer is very clear. I have spent a third of a century studying Japanese culture. Admiration for the Japanese has not diminished, nor has fascination with their culture. I think that there is something wrong with the person who wearies of it. Yet I have spent much of my time being glad that I am not Japanese.

I can think of few things worse than being a "salaryman," as they are called, for a big Japanese company. I am not sure that I would like the American equivalent either, and I spend some time rejoicing that I have escaped that fate as well. Yet the life cycle of the American office worker would be far easier to put up with than that of the Japanese. There would not be that utter conformity and that lack of anything but the company and work. I know of large Japanese companies that frown fiercely upon having wives and mothers call salarymen during office hours, unless the baby is choking to death. I know of salarymen who detest golf but spend long hours in a reasonable pretense at enjoying it, because it is what must be done by way of "keeping company," so essential to *the* company.

I am *so* glad that I am not one of them! I do not presume to judge, of course. I would not wish to be understood as saying that their way is wrong and mine is right. The matter has to do with feelings and emotions, and I feel very strongly that I would find the Japanese salaried life next to intolerable. Nor do I think that I am peculiar in this respect. I think that most Americans, or English or French, would find it so too.

If I am right, then the effort to become like the Japanese has little chance of succeeding. A moral restoration, a return to our own best ways, would be easier than the attempt to take on alien ways. If a departure from our own best ways is at the heart of the problem, then how happy we must be not to have to make the more difficult effort.

Mr. Taylor will probably be accused of being anti-Japanese, certainly by comparison with the authors of those other books. I am sure that he will deny the charge, and he should. His book quite overflows with affection for and understanding of the land in which he grew up. It may be unrealistic to offer a hope that his book will, like its famous predecessor, sell almost a million copies. I hope all the same that it will, and that, besides the Americans for whom it is chiefly intended, numerous Japanese will read it and think upon it, and not be misled into thinking it hostile. The truth is too important that anything less should be allowed to control the field.

—EDWARD SEIDENSTICKER
March 1983

ACKNOWLEDGMENTS

I would like to thank all those who generously read portions of the book in manuscript and whose comments were of great help to me: Tom Andrews, Malcolm Meldahl, Ruth Stevens, Shinichiro Watari, and Suzanne Wittebort. I am also grateful to Professor Yasuo Nakazono for long, illuminating conversations and for sending me important material from Japan, and to Byron Walker who has been a constant source of encouragement and information. I would also like to thank Mark Weber, who first urged me to write this book.

My greatest debt, however, is to the scores of people, Japanese and American, who shared their lives and insights with me. This book is, in large measure, nothing more than a compilation of their wisdom and experience.

ACKNOWLEDGMENTS

CONTENTS

INTRODUCTION

The history of postwar Japan has been one of the most astonishing success stories of the century. From the rubble of defeat Japan has built an economy that is an inspiration to the developing world and a formidable competitor for the industrial world. During the twenty-five years that ended with the first oil crisis in 1973, Japan's real per capita GNP increased *tenfold*, and Japan pulled ahead of West Germany to become the most productive nation in the world, after the two superpowers.

Since the oil crisis Japan's economy has slowed but still outpaces its rivals. It has taken a world recession to drag Japan's growth rate down near the level of its major trading partners. Japan dominates the markets for cameras, motorcycles, and stereo equipment. It produces one-quarter of the world's television sets and automobiles and half the world's ships. When the yen is strong, Japan's GNP per capita is equal to that of the United States. Throughout most of this remarkable period of growth, Japan has kept its inflation and unemployment rates at levels that are the envy of even the best-managed economies.

Japan has more than just its economy to be proud of. At nearly 100 percent, Japan has the highest literacy rate in the world. Japanese have the longest life expectancy of any people, and their infant mortality rate is well below that of the United States. Social harmony, as measured by crime rates and working days lost to strikes, is the highest in the industrial world. In the 115 years since feudalism was abolished, Japan has made such strides in social equality that 90 percent of the population now considers itself middle-class. Recent cross-cultural tests have even suggested that the Japanese have a mean IQ that is ten points higher than the Western average.[1]

At one time all these achievements were menaced by the world's worst pollution; fifteen years ago Japan was on the verge of smothering itself in industrial blight. However, it rose to the challenge and, through massive investment in antipollution equipment, restored the quality of its environment. On a clear day Mount Fuji can once again be seen from downtown Tokyo, and little boys now fish in rivers that were once open sewers. According to all the standards by which nations are judged, Japan has been extraordinarily successful.

Specialists have followed Japan's steady progress over the years, but the world at large has discovered its achievements as suddenly as if they had appeared full-grown in the 1970s. What began no more than a few years ago as a trickle of admiring articles has now swollen to a flood of news items, television specials, magazine cover stories, editorials, and even entire books praising a society that seems to work so well. We learn that in fact, Japan works too well, that the success of its exports is jeopardizing the livelihood of Americans and Europeans. Trade problems are now the focus of attention on Japan, and admiration for its economic prowess has in some cases changed to fear and resentment.

Many Western businessmen continue to accuse Japan of protectionism and unfair government support for exports, but more and more have begun to realize that most Japanese successes are entirely legitimate. Japan has learned the rules of business so well that it can beat the West at its own game. The idea that Japan's management techniques may be superior to our own has struck a painful blow to the West's corporate manhood, but chastened executives from around the world have now beaten a path to Japan to study the secrets of its productivity. Books that claim to reveal the art of Japanese management have become best sellers.

It is good for Americans to study Japan. No nation has a monopoly on excellence in any field. It is a sure sign that America's pompous postwar sense of supremacy has come to an end when Americans ask to learn from their former enemies. Nevertheless, any attempt to borrow from a nation so different from ours as Japan must be made with caution. Without a doubt, there is a great deal we can learn from the Japanese, but we must not forget that their methods are rooted in a distinctive culture. That culture, in turn, is a dense mixture of values and behavior that Americans might not care to adopt.

Japanese society was built over the centuries by Japanese and is well suited to them. Americans, of course, are not Japanese and have built their own successes on different conceptions of the state, the group, and the individual. Americans and Japanese differ in many ways, and the values, behavior, and expectations of daily life reflect these differences.

It is meaningless to describe one society as "better" or "worse" than another. Each responds to the needs of its members. In passing judgment on other peoples, we only reveal our own prejudices. Nevertheless, what is good in one society may not be good in another, and from an American or Western perspective, Japanese society is riddled with defects. Some of the national characteristics that make Japan different from the West, and some that have contributed to its successes, are not models that the West would wish to imitate. Once a foreigner has become accustomed to the charm and efficiency of modern Japan, the closer he looks, the more he is likely to find that is confusing or even repugnant.

The aspects of Japanese society that Westerners may find disagreeable exist side by side with all that Japan has achieved since the war. For the most part they are perfectly compatible with economic growth and social harmony. Perhaps this is one reason why they have been largely ignored in the chorus of voices that has risen in tribute to Japan. Another reason is the complexity of modern Japanese society, in which behavior from an inscrutable past coexists with all the trappings of modernization.

Language is surely the most daunting obstacle to understanding Japan. GNP and infant mortality rates can be measured with statistics that translate perfectly into all languages, but the texture of life and the forces that move people must be felt firsthand to be understood. Journalists seldom have the time to master Japanese and are ill-prepared to delve beneath the shiny surfaces of achievement. Academics are better able to give thoughtful, evenhanded accounts of what is both good and bad about Japan, and a few have done so. However, they may pass in squeamish silence over some of Japan's more lurid habits.

If only by accident of birth, I am qualified to fill in a few of the gaps. I was born in Japan and attended Japanese schools for eight years. My Japanese is so fluent that over the phone I am mistaken for a native. I have taught Japanese at university. I have done business with the Japanese both in the United States and in Japan. I have lived a total of sixteen years in Japan, both in the countryside and in the great cities. Nevertheless, my perspective is firmly American.

The purpose of this book is twofold. First, I would like to offer a counterpoise to the tendency to portray Japan in exaggeratedly favorable terms. A nation cannot be known only by its successes. A realistic portrait of Japan must include a glimpse of what lies in the shadows of success. However, what lie in those shadows are not necessarily failures; they may be only differences.

It is in describing the Japanese as entirely like us, but somehow more successful in all the ways that matter, that commentators create a false impression of Japan. In important ways the Japanese are different from us, and though they have been very successful in ways that can be measured, they have not been successful in all the ways that matter, at least to us. Many of their successes are based on what makes them different from Westerners and have been achieved at a psychological cost we might not be willing to pay.

Japan has not prospered merely by borrowing Western principles and applying them more effectively. Western principles have been grafted onto an unmistakably Japanese consciousness, and it is this extraordinary combination that has driven Japan to the heights of achievement. Despite their video games, tennis togs, skyscrapers, and rock and roll, the Japanese are not Westerners. They have reached goals that all societies work toward, but they have arrived by different routes.

My second purpose derives from the first. I would like to caution those American and European managers who hope to learn the business secrets of the East and apply them to problems back home. Some secrets may not travel well. Many are nothing more than adaptations of corporate strategy to distinctive features of Japanese society and may not work as well elsewhere.

This book is, therefore, a book about differences. At work, at play, and in the home, life in Japan is different from life in the West. Only by coming to terms with those differences can we begin to understand Japan. This book is also a guided tour of the back side of the Japanese personality, a critical look behind the accomplishments, at how the Japanese think and behave. It may seem unfair to concentrate on those aspects of Japan that the Japanese might be least eager to publicize. However, of all the writers who have reflected on the Japanese, none have been such harsh critics as the Japanese themselves. Often, to make a point, I have only to borrow their own words.

This book is in two parts. In the first five chapters I have tried to grasp those elements of Japanese thinking that seem most different from ours. Sometimes what at first seems contradictory or mysterious can be explained in satisfying, consistent terms. There are patterns to Japanese behavior, and I have tried to describe them. The second part of the book focuses on specific areas of contemporary Japanese life. I have tried to relate those activities to the patterns of the first part, but the Japanese do many things that do not fit into neat patterns. Sometimes the best I can do is describe what I have seen.

The strongest temptation and greatest danger in writing on a subject like this are to wrap up an entire nation with facile generalizations. In his excellent book *The Japanese*, Edwin Reischauer points out: "Almost anything that might be said about the Japanese in general would not be true of many and might be flatly contradicted by some."[2] This realization did not stop Reischauer from going on to make many convincing generalizations, nor does it prevent me from attempting to do the same. Many books would never have been written if their authors had not been ready to risk disagreement and even ridicule by taking a position. Nevertheless, I have often felt humbled by the audacity of the task I have set myself and can only apologize for the errors of judgment I have inevitably committed.

As one long-term student of the Japanese has said, "In order to understand Japan, the world needs all the help it can get."[3] Yet another who devoted his life to studying the Japanese wrote, in his later years, "What a horribly difficult thing it is to write about Japan."[4] It was with the first sentiment that I started this book and with the second that I finish it.

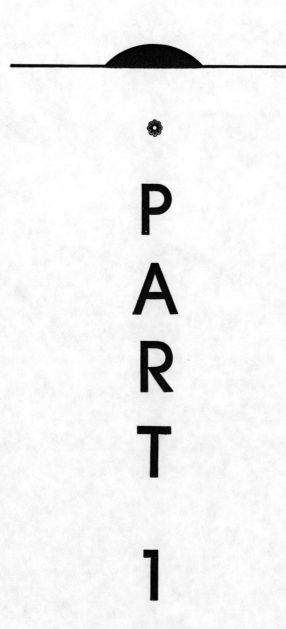

PART 1

CHAPTER ONE

❋

UNIQUENESS

In Japan there is a flourishing field of study called *Nihonjin-ron,* or, roughly translated, "theory of the Japanese." Any Japanese bookstore is likely to be stocked with such titles as *What Does It Mean to Be Japanese?*, *The Origins of Japanese Uniqueness*, *The Structure of Japanese Consciousness*, *Japanese Behavior*, *Japanese Thought—Western Thought*, *The Logic of Japanese Emotions*, *New Nihonjin-ron*, *The History of Nihonjin-ron*, and on and on. A recent *Nihonjin-ron* best seller that should soon appear in English is *The Brain of the Japanese*—a scientific treatise that claims to show that the Japanese brain processes data differently from the brains of all other people.

An author does not have to be Japanese to write *Nihonjin-ron*. Americans, Australians, Chinese, and Israelis have written *Nihonjin-ron*. Japanese are especially interested in what foreigners think about them and take an outsider's "theory of the Japanese" just as seriously as they might take their own. Probably no other people in the world have such a voracious appetite for books about themselves.

These books, and the entire field of *Nihonjin-ron,* stem from the widespread conviction among the Japanese that they are a unique people. Are they? Without a doubt, Japan is a place where visitors soon learn that people behave differently in different cultures. Many a Westerner has been charmed, mystified, or infuriated by unexpected behavior that he later learned was typically Japanese. However, what Westerners may come to feel about the Japanese, the Japanese feel much more strongly about themselves, for what perhaps *most* distinguishes them from other people is their profound, agonizing sense of just how different they are.

This feeling of uniqueness, which one Japanese author has likened to the Jewish sense of being a people apart,[1] colors all relations with other peoples. The Japanese are fascinated by foreigners but repelled by their foreignness. They long to be loved and accepted but feel threatened when they are understood. Their sense of separateness gives them a reassuring sense of community while it isolates them psychologically from the other nations of the world.

At the most basic level the Japanese react with vivid, visceral astonishment to the physical differences between themselves and Westerners. The Japanese look upon Caucasians with such wonder that they sometimes seem to think of them as members of some other species.

The American scholar Edward Seidensticker writes about a conversation he overheard in Japan some years ago. He was touring one of the southern islands where about 1,000 monkeys live in the wild but are tame enough to be visited and observed by tourists. A guide was explaining the ins and outs of monkey society and mentioned that he knew every one of the 1,000 monkeys by sight. A skeptic spoke up and wanted to know how anybody could really tell 1,000 monkeys apart. As Seidensticker reports the conversation, "'Oh, it's very easy,' said the guide, 'it's just like telling foreigners apart.'"[2]

Though perhaps not so amusing as 1,000 tame monkeys, Caucasians, or *gaijin* as they are most frequently called, attract a lot of attention in Japan. Outside the major cities a foreigner rarely ceases to be a spectacle.

Recently I visited beautiful Ritsurin Park in the provincial capital of Takamatsu. It is one of my favorite places in all Japan, and I had carefully juggled the tight schedule of a business trip in order to savor it for the first time in many years.

As it happened, that was also the day when hundreds of local junior high school students had scattered through the park to sketch it for an art class. Not long after I entered the grounds I was sighted. It was like Moby Dick breaching off the *Pequod*'s bow. The cry went up: *"Gaijin!"* and *"Haro! Haro!"* ("Hello! Hello!"). Wherever I turned, a new group of students took up the cry. Some began to imitate my walk and to jabber nonsense in pidgin Japanese. There was no escape. I quickly fled the park.

Where do Japanese children learn to act like that? A Western woman who has lived for several years in one of Japan's regional capitals suggests an answer. "I often see Japanese parents teaching their children to point and say *'gaijin'* . . . in the same way that they teach them to point and say 'panda' or 'monkey' at the zoo," she says.[3]

In fairness to the Japanese, I should describe another experience of my own. I grew up just after the Second World War, in a country village where foreigners were extremely rare. One day, when I was six or seven, an American came to visit my father. All the way from the train station to my house he was followed by the usual band of fascinated urchins shouting, *"Gaijin, gaijin."* I was one of them. Twenty-five years ago, in rural Japan, a fair-haired, light-skinned giant was as eye-popping a sight to me as he was to my playmates.

As the years go by, Japanese are learning to restrain their glee, but not fast enough for most foreigners. They get very tired of being followed around by children who point and yell, *"Gaijin."* One American reporter did not realize the effect this unwanted attention was having on his own children until he took them to Hawaii for a vacation. There they reportedly took revenge by running along the beach shouting, *"Gaijin,"* at all the Japanese children they could find.[4]

Even for adult Japanese a gangly Caucasian can be a merry sight. Occasionally they will point and make faces for all the world as if a dancing bear had just waltzed by. Several American businessmen stationed in Japan have come to me in frustration for a good idiomatic insult for such boors.

Sometimes the Japanese really seem to think *gaijin* are a separate species. Japan is one of the few countries in the world that do not accept the results of foreign drug tests. For a drug to be approved for sale in Japan, it must be tested in Japanese laboratories, even if this means needless duplication of research. This practice has been attacked as a trade barrier by companies trying to sell drugs in Japan, and international pressure has wrung a few recent concessions from the Japanese authorities: early in 1982 they agreed to accept foreign drug-testing data so long as the tests were run on Japanese living abroad.[5] Test subjects cannot be Westerners or even other Asians; they have to be Japanese.

I will never forget a conversation I once had with a middle-aged Japanese woman about Japanese-American marriages. "It has always surprised me that those couples could have children," she said.

"What do you mean?" I asked.

"The parents are so different physically. After all, Japanese have a lower body temperature and a longer gestation period than Westerners.* It really is a wonder they can have such sweet children."

I insisted that we all were the same. If there had been a thermometer handy, I would have taken my temperature for her. There wasn't one, and I walked away from the conversation baffled. Since then I haven't met a Japanese who thought his body temperature was different from mine. However, I have met a few who say they have elderly relatives who still think so.

Many Japanese continue to believe that a heavy diet of animal protein makes Westerners excitable and prone to various diseases and gives them a peculiar odor. "Stinking of butter" is how the feudal Japanese described their early, unwashed visitors, and the phrase is still used to mean "Western" or "Western-influenced."

To the Japanese, eating habits are powerful proof of fundamental differences. In 1981, during an assignment to Japan with my company, I applied to attend a weeklong finance seminar put on by a large Japanese bank. The seminar was to be conducted in Japanese, and no other foreigners had asked to participate, so the seminar director invited me to come by his office for a little chat.

I was fortunate in learning Japanese just as effortlessly as I learned English, so a few minutes of conversation was all it took to dispel his worries about language. Still, he was clearly reluctant to let me join his seminar, and I gently began to probe for the reasons. Finally, he

---

*Japanese think of pregnancy as lasting ten months rather than nine. This is not because they stay pregnant longer than Westerners but because they calculate the time in lunar, or menstrual, months of 28 days rather than in months of 30 or 31 days. Ten 28-day months actually come closer to the human gestation period of 280 days than nine 30- and 31-day months. Nevertheless, when Japanese hear Westerners talking about nine-month pregnancies, many assume that the difference is physiological rather than cultural.

explained to me: "Taylor-san, every day we fix a Japanese-style lunch for the seminar participants, and I just don't see how we could arrange beefsteaks specially for you."

That man was genuinely concerned that I might be so dismayed at the prospect of doing without my midday beefsteaks that I might drop out of his seminar. It made no difference to him that I have lived longer in Japan than in America. For him, Americans eat beefsteak and Japanese eat raw fish; there could be no variation from so basic a truth. Only after I had repeatedly assured him how gladly I would eat Japanese lunches did he finally agree to let me attend his seminar.

Many Japanese are convinced that their food—like their culture—is so unique that only Japanese can enjoy it. They are astonished to see foreigners gobble it as if it were really no different from Italian, Chinese, or Indian food. Sometimes they are also a little disappointed: they and their food are somehow not as unique as they were before.

Japanese are just as conscious of cultural differences as they are of physical differences. They are painfully aware of how much their customs differ from those of other countries and seem to think of them as inevitable extensions of physical or psychological differences.

Generally Japanese expect foreigners to be utterly ignorant of their culture or language, and many take wry pleasure in finding their expectations frequently justified. This only confirms the impenetrability of Japan's unusual consciousness. There is a certain level of acquaintance with things Japanese to which foreigners are encouraged. Japanese are pleased to meet *gaijin* who are struggling with the language or who have a simple admiration for kabuki or tea ceremony. However, most Japanese find protective satisfaction in wrapping themselves in a mantle of Japanese mystery and are unnerved by foreigners who know enough to penetrate it.

After all the years I have lived in Japan, it is perfectly normal that I should speak the language and know a little about the country. But to the Japanese, it is a near miracle to hear their language flowing from the lips of a white man. Granted, it is statistically an unusual phenomenon, but the fact that I grew up in Japan does not temper their astonishment. It seems preposterous to them that a Caucasian should speak fluent Japanese no matter what his background. They seem to feel that their language does not "take" with anyone who has blue eyes.

This is an ancient conviction. In 1858 the British and the Japanese had to decide on an official language in which to conduct their newly established diplomatic relations. According to the British envoy, Laurence Oliphant, he was told by the Japanese, "You had better make English the official language: there is no telling how long it will be before you will be able to write a dispatch in Japanese; but give us five years and we shall be quite competent to correspond with you in English."[6] Clearly, there was no hope for the benighted *gaijin* to master so unique a tongue as Japanese.

In 1904 another Englishman wrote, "Seeing that you speak Japanese, they will wag their heads and smile condescendingly, and admit to each other that you are really quite intelligent—much as we might do in the presence of a learned pig or an ape of somewhat unusual attainments."[7] Any Caucasian who is comfortable speaking Japanese is still practically a sideshow act. I once met a man who manages performers for Japanese television. He told me he would have no trouble getting me on talk shows.

When I meet a group of Japanese for the first time, they may turn to each other and joke nervously about my fluency: "Well, here's one foreigner we can't keep any secrets from." Japanese think of their language as a secret code, a sign of the brethren. Their language is vital to their image of themselves and is an essential ingredient in their sense of uniqueness.

In a recent book entitled *New Nihonjin-ron*, one author warns that the code has been cracked and that Japanese should think twice before they sit down to write books about themselves: "If we go on writing books about how strange we are, more and more foreigners who are learning Japanese will read those books and decide that we really are strange. Until now, we could get away with writing about how strange we are because no one else could read Japanese. Now that's no longer true. . . ."[8]

For a *gaijin* to know a few unusual facts about Japan is faintly disturbing—just as it is for one to enjoy raw fish or speak Japanese. To a casual explanation about some aspect of the history of the part of Japan with which I am most familiar, Japanese will laugh uncomfortably and say, "My goodness, here I am learning something about Japan from a foreigner."

The conviction that whatever is distinctively Japanese must be incomprehensible to outsiders is not just a folksy superstition; it thrives in universities as well. The very idea that a *gaijin* might presume to teach Japanese literature strikes many academics as absurd. Who but a native could possibly talk sense about *The Tale of Genji* or *The Pillowbook*? A few foreigners, such as Columbia professor Donald Keene, have lectured to the Japanese about their own literature, but resistance to the idea is still strong.

There is some question as to whether foreigners can teach anything at all to Japanese. *Gaijin*, no matter how learned or clever, cannot be expected to fathom the mysteries of communicating with the Japanese mind. Thus, until 1982, foreign scholars were not allowed to hold regular faculty positions at national universities, and they still cannot be named president or department head.

The traditional arts are perhaps the final redoubt for the impenetrable essence of Japan. Robert is an American who spent eight years working with one of Japan's most prestigious pottery families. Simply being accepted as an apprentice was an achievement for a non-Japanese, for as the family told him years later, they didn't expect a *gaijin* to last more than six months. "While I was still fumbling around in the studio, it was cute," says Robert. "Foreigners aren't expected to get past the bungling stage. But when I got good, I was a threat. I didn't fit the pattern anymore, and they couldn't handle it." Relations in the studio became so poor that the intruder was forced out and eventually left Japan.

I doubt that anyone in the West is threatened if a Japanese or any other Asian wins the Tchaikovsky prize at the annual competition in the Soviet Union. The identities of Westerners are not bound up in the exclusive mastery of their own language or culture. For many Japanese, however, there remains an inner circle of mystery which can only be profaned if penetrated by a foreigner.

Where does this sense of uniqueness come from? Why has it survived for so long? The endless self-examination that has produced a raft of books on *Nihonjin-ron* has established a number of standard answers to these questions. Virtually all Japanese are familiar with them and are liable to recite a few should the conversation touch on national characteristics.

One favorite and plausible theory turns on the homogeneity of the Japanese people. Unlike Europe or the United States, Japan has never been the scene of làrge migrations. The ancestors of the present-day Japanese arrived on the archipelago from Korea in prehistoric times and have stayed to this day. The original inhabitants, the Ainu, were eventually pushed into small enclaves in the north and lost all influence on Japanese events. In the meantime, there has never been a major influx of foreigners that might have brought with it a competing culture. As a result, Japan is not a polyglot, multiracial society, and its people have not had the broadening influence of contact with immigrants. If the Japanese population has a homogeneity index of 99 percent—the highest in the world—the United States has an index of 50 percent.[9]

Another barrier to Japan's intercourse with the outside world is language. Japanese is roughly classified as a member of the Altaic family, along with Mongolian and Turkish. It has some resemblance to Korean but has no close relatives. The Japanese began using Chinese ideograms for their written language in the sixth century A.D., but the spoken language is completely unrelated to Chinese.

As one American writes, it might be convenient if we could neatly classify Japanese as, say, "four times as hard as French" or "twice as hard as Russian,"[10] but Japanese fits no pattern. It is simply an extremely difficult language for Westerners to master—so difficult, in fact, that Francis Xavier, the sixteenth-century Spanish Jesuit who was the first missionary to Japan, complained that the devil himself must have invented the language to prevent the spread of Christianity.

Of course, it is just as difficult for Japanese to learn Western languages, so not many can carry on a conversation with a foreigner. Most Japanese who travel overseas return without the broad familiarity with a foreign culture that can come only from knowing its language. Even those who have lived for eight or ten years in America or Europe have often spent so much time with other overseas Japanese that they still do not have enough language skill to establish close relations with foreigners. *Nihonjin-ron* thus tells us that linguistic isolation has kept the Japanese unique.

However, the most common explanation for Japan's uniqueness is the island nation theory, according to which geography has cut Japan off from the rest of the world—rather like it has New Guinea. This idea is so thoroughly embedded in the Japanese consciousness that even former Prime Minister Kakuei Tanaka used to refer to it to explain Japanese behavior to foreigners.[11] I have never understood how a theory that clearly begs the question can be so popular.

In the early days of ocean travel Japan's island fastness was no doubt a barrier to foreign influence. However, in the seventeenth century, as Western traders and missionaries began to call more regularly, the Japanese authorities decided that natural barriers were not enough. They added their own man-made barriers and established a strict policy of near-total isolation.

In 1635 and 1639 the shogun's government passed laws which forbade overseas travel by Japanese on pain of death and even refused readmittance to Japan of shipwrecked Japanese fishermen rescued by foreign ships. Commerce was outlawed with all nations except China and Holland, and citizens of no other country were allowed into Japan. The Dutch were confined to a small island in the port of Nagasaki, where they carried on a limited trade in guns, clocks, and other products of European science. Under no circumstances were the "red-haired people," as the Dutch were called, allowed into the rest of Japan; they were forbidden even to bury their dead on Japan's sacred soil.

Japan was shut off from the world for more than two centuries and might have stayed that way indefinitely if the United States had not decided "to engage in opening this Japanese Oyster."[12] In 1853 Commodore Matthew Perry sailed into Edo (Tokyo) Bay with a fleet of gunboats and announced to the startled Japanese that their policy of isolation was over.

Two centuries of seclusion certainly allowed a distinctively Japanese culture and mentality to flourish. During this period Japanese art and literature produced some of their finest masterpieces. But this unique culture flourished undisturbed not so much because of geographic barriers as because of a radically isolationist foreign policy. The Japanese were not victims of natural isolation; they gladly pressed it into the service of *un*natural isolation. The policies of the seventeenth century doubtless contributed to a profound sense of separateness among the Japanese, but they do not mark its beginning. That such policies should have been implemented in the first place shows only that by 1635 the Japanese were already convinced they were unique and wanted to stay that way.

The ostensible reason for shutting out the world was to protect Japan from contamination by Christianity, and in 1638 the authorities stamped out the remnants of this foreign virus by slaughtering tens of thousands of Christians who rose up against their feudal lords in what is called the Shimabara Rebellion. However, an equally important reason for isolation was protection from outside influence of any kind.

Back in the distant past, when they were learning culture at the feet of the Chinese, the Japanese were already conscious of their own special spirit. Under the slogan *Wakon kansai* ("Japanese spirit, Chinese learning") Japan tried to absorb the techniques but reject the spirit of their clever teachers. The same slogan was reborn as *Wakon yōsai* ("Japanese spirit, *Western* learning") when Japan was dragged into the modern world by Commodore Perry. Throughout its history Japan has tried to preserve its uniqueness. The fact that it was an island nation only made the job that much easier.

Clearly there is nothing fatally isolating about geography. Great Britain is another island nation just off the coast of a great continent, but geography turned it outward rather than inward. Kunitake Kume (1839–1931), who is credited with introducing the island nation theory to the Japanese, pointed that out more than 100 years ago.[13]

One foreign observer sees the modern versions of this theory as nothing more than a variant of what he calls "the principle of virgin Japan."[14] He argues that the Japanese have always seen their home islands as a holy precinct, a fortress of virtue, for which every foreign incursion was a violation. In his view, even today the Japanese have a longing for the purity of an isolated Japan and see its forced participation in the modern world as a fall from Eden. "With the phrase 'we Japanese' constantly on their lips," he adds, "they cling blindly to the myth that they are a special people, a race apart."[15]

When the Japanese talk about their island nation and their homogeneous population—and they talk about them a lot—it seems to me that they are not trying so much to explain Japanese behavior as to cite justifications for it. They are imbued with the notion that for better or worse, they are different. When they make contact with the outside world, they seem to be looking for confirmation of their uniqueness rather than for its denial. There is a pervasive, exclusive notion of "we Japanese" that draws a firm line between "we" and "they."

Americans believe, perhaps to a fault, that all peoples are basically the same and that with a little understanding and goodwill, all apparent differences can be reconciled. Few Japanese believe this. For them, cultural and racial differences are intractable; the gulf that separates one people from the next is at some level unbridgeable. The explanations they propose for Japan's uniqueness are thus important but they needn't make sense. They are used as apparently rational cover for convictions that are not necessarily available for rational examination at all.

Sophisticated Japanese are perfectly aware of this widespread form of self-deception and have begun to speak out against it. "Japanese suffer from a peculiar handicap," write the authors of a recent work of *Nihonjin-ron*, "namely, the conviction that they are burdened with a unique culture, that their thought processes differ from those of other people. They therefore believe that real communication with foreigners is impossible."[16] A longtime U.S. correspondent for the *Mainichi* newspaper warns that the Japanese must stop saying to the rest of the world, "Sorry. We're an island people and a homogeneous nation and we just can't get along with other folks."[17] A professor at Nagoya University concedes, "We Japanese are probably too strongly convinced of how radically different we are from foreigners."[18]

Language often offers insights into how the Japanese view the world. In Japanese there are at least ten different words that mean "foreigner," and all of them are pejorative. Most are antique and little-used, and many translate literally as "barbarian." Others have more specific meanings, such as "southern barbarian," "hairy barbarian," or "blue-eyed barbarian." The least offensive and most commonly used is the familiar *gaijin*, which means "outsider." During the feudal period the word meant "enemy."

Non-Japanese accept the word as a more or less neutral expression, but the Japanese themselves have no such illusions. When Japanese acquaintances begin to discover how well I know their language, they sometimes ask apologetically if I don't resent being called a *gaijin*. On reflection, this is a very curious question. The only way to cease to be a *gaijin* is to become Japanese. The question suggests that the only way to be a fully respectable human being is to be Japanese.

On several occasions, when their feelings toward me had been warmed by long association and a few drinks, Japanese friends have "comforted" me with the declaration that in spite of all appearances, I was really Japanese. I am sure that this was always meant as a sincere expression of friendship, and I was always moved by it. Nevertheless, it betrays the feeling that true acceptance is only reserved for Japanese.

In 1977 a group of Japanese radicals hijacked a Japan Air Lines plane to back their demands for millions of dollars in ransom money and the release of half a dozen jailed comrades. When a high government official raged that the criminals were "not Japanese," it was probably the worst insult he could think of.

Ever since Japan was opened to the West, foreigners have fallen in love with the subtlety and beauty of its culture and longed to be finally accepted into the circle of uniqueness. They have tried to rid themselves of their stigma, have tried to cease being *gaijin*. However, it is no mean feat to become Japanese, and deep-seated feelings cannot be changed by an act of law.

I know a woman named Shirley who is one of the very few Westerners who have taken Japanese citizenship. At the beginning she was amazed at the forms she had to fill out before immigration officials would start work on her case.

"They wanted to know the name of the kindergarten my father attended," she says, "and the date and place where my mother first got a driver's license. My parents couldn't even remember some of that stuff." The police were sent around to quiz the neighbors about Shirley's character and behavior. "They talked to the grocer, the fishmonger, the sushi shop proprietor," she says. "The police talked to people who didn't even know me. I met some of them later, and they would say, 'So you're the *gaijin* the police were asking about.' I would think, 'My gosh, not another one.'"

Shirley's case went relatively smoothly, and she was granted citizenship in less than a year. However, Shirley had a definite advantage. At the time of her application she was married to a Japanese man.

One of the trickiest requirements of citizenship is that the applicant must take a Japanese name. He may not take just any name he pleases; he must be vouched for by a Japanese citizen who in effect adopts him. The new family member is then entered on the *koseki*, or name roll of the family's village. The *koseki* is a precious legal document which records birth, marriage, death, and other vital facts about a person.

"When we first got married," says Shirley, "I wasn't a Japanese citizen, so my husband's *koseki* didn't even recognize my existence. It was duly noted that he had married, but not to whom or to what. He could have married a monkey. It was only after I took his name and became a citizen that I was entered in the *koseki* as his wife."

Jesse James Kuhaulua is a Hawaiian-American wrestler who went to Japan years ago to become a sumo wrestler. Sumo is Japan's oldest professional sport and is heavy with tradition. A wrestler's active career usually does not run very far into his thirties, so an informal retirement plan has been devised whereby outstanding wrestlers continue their career as "elders" or paid advisers.

Kuhaulua is now the oldest active wrestler in Japan and holds records for the most professional bouts and the largest number of consecutive bouts. However, he had no hope of becoming an elder because *gaijin* are not even considered. After fighting the *sumo* authorities for years, he finally took his Japanese wife's name and was granted citizenship. This is still no guarantee that he will be appointed an elder, although a native Japanese with his distinguished record would be a shoo-in. The now Mr. Watanabe expects to continue his wrestling career to age forty, so the decision is still to come.

Adoption by the family of one's spouse seems to be the least complicated way to acquire citizenship, but the head of the family has the right to refuse a foreigner the family name. Citizenship, like adoption, is by invitation only. I know of no other nation that requires a foreigner to abandon something so precious as his own name in order to become a citizen.

Citizenship is no guarantee of final acceptance. No matter how well adapted he is, a Caucasian Japanese, even with his Japanese name, will be a freak his entire life. Unlike Americans, who are accustomed to fellow citizens of all races and backgrounds, the Japanese are totally unprepared for a Caucasian who is nevertheless Japanese.

"I know I can never be entirely accepted in this society," says Shirley. "The Japanese have a little box in their mind labeled '*Gaijin*.' All foreigners they meet have to fit into that box. When they meet a *gaijin*-Japanese, they can't deal with it—it blows their fuses. If I meet someone casually and mention that I'm Japanese, it's a total conversation stopper. Suddenly he's late for an important meeting."

Lafcadio Hearn (1850–1904), the great British admirer of Japan, took his wife's name, Koizumi, and became a Japanese, but citizenship never brought the solace he had hoped for. One of the first things that happened to him was logical but unexpected: His university salary was sharply reduced from that of a visiting foreign professor to that of a Japanese. Koizumi later realized that as a foreigner he had always been treated as a guest. As a Japanese he was a misfit, a perpetual outcast; he ended his days in self-pity.

Many Westerners who embraced Japan eventually lost their love for their adopted country and went home embittered. Perhaps they had learned what one writer calls the "subtler idiom" that underlies all Japanese thought and behavior:

> No matter how well a foreigner speaks the language, the Japanese have determined that it is against nature for him to master this subtler idiom. Should he actually do so, the Japanese, whether consciously or unconsciously, will spurn him. I must warn those foreigners who wish to commit love suicide with Japan: this is a country in which a non-Japanese may stay only for a time, where he will never be more than a foreign guest. Anyone who attempts to violate this unseen principle will be spiritually and psychologically crushed.[19]

Are the Japanese unique? Or do they just think they are? The French are different from the British, the Swedes are different from the Italians, and no one is quite like the Japanese. In the sense that no nationality is exactly like another, of course the Japanese are unique. If it is possible to quantify such differences, the Japanese are probably more different from Americans than are the French, the Russians, and perhaps even the Chinese. I would not have written this book if I did not think they have qualities that set them apart from other people. However, I also think that the Japanese are excessively concerned with how they differ from other people.

Twenty years ago sociologist David Riesman was so struck by this determination of the Japanese to think of themselves as different that he suggested they should study more cultural anthropology. He said this might help them understand that despite differences in form, no culture is incomprehensible to outsiders willing to make the effort to understand it.[20] If he were to visit Japan today, he might still say the same thing.

To a large degree, works of *Nihonjin-ron* that claim to treat *Japanese* behavior or *Japanese* emotions are nothing more than sociological observations that would be generally true of all societies. Authors of *Nihonjin-ron* often write as though they assumed that what is true of Japanese society is not true of any other. If Americans assume that all people are fundamentally the same and note differences only as they appear, the Japanese assume that people are fundamentally different and note similarities only as *they* appear.

On a recent browse through a Japanese bookstore I came across a volume entitled *The Japanese Nose.*[21]* It was a pop biology book about the physiology, diseases, malformations, and functions of the nose. I have not read that book. Still, I am convinced that 90 percent of whatever it says is true of all noses. What is there to be said that is true only of Japanese noses? In any other country that book would have been called *The Nose* but in Japan it is *The Japanese Nose.*

On the same trip to the bookstore I leafed through a serious study of human evolution with the disturbing title *From the Fossil Apes to the Japanese.*[22] This, it seems to me, is going a bit far. Not even the Nazis brought out a tract called *From the Fossil Apes to the Germans.*

A well-known Japanese radio commentator puts the matter in simple terms. "I'm going to make a very blunt statement:" he writes, "the Japanese don't consider foreigners to be human beings."[23] He goes on to say that this does not mean that the Japanese despise foreigners but only that they think of them as different and unfamiliar. This is only partly true. The Japanese do despise foreigners, but they also adore them. These contradictory feelings are an extension of one of the most distinctive facts of Japanese life: hierarchy.

*This book is not quite so silly as it sounds. The Japanese pay more attention to their noses than we do. When a Japanese points to himself in a "Who, me?" gesture, he touches his nose instead of pointing to his chest. Also, nose size is one of the physical differences between Orientals and Westerners that the Japanese find most striking.

CHAPTER TWO

❀

HIERARCHY

All societies establish hierarchies. In few societies, however, are they so widespread or important as in Japan. For the Japanese, rank is so finely determined that equality is rare—everyone and everything are at least slightly above or below the nearest apparent equal. Family members, workmates, schools, companies, even nations and races all have their places. Hierarchy is inseparable from orderliness; a group is not properly organized unless its members are ranked.

Hierarchy has a long history in Japan. Philosophically it is associated with Confucianism, which arrived from China in the early fifth century. Confucius had taught that all men are morally bound to submit to elders and superiors. These teachings had a natural appeal for Japan's ruling class and were used to justify the inflexible social hierarchy of Japan's feudal period.

During the 200 years that Japan was shut off from the world, it had one of the most inflexible, inegalitarian social systems the world has ever seen. The nation was ruled by the Tokugawa dynasty of shoguns, who were at the pinnacle of a class society organized by profession. All Japanese, in descending order of prestige, were samurai, peasants, artisans, or traders.

These classes were as rigid as Indian castes and as loaded with privilege and prohibition. Peasants were theoretically just below the ruling warrior class because they grew the food that everyone had to eat. In practice, a peasant's life was constant humiliation and backbreaking toil—far worse than that of any city dweller.

The founder of the shogun dynasty himself, Tokugawa Ieyasu (1542–1616), urged the samurai to keep the peasants humble by bullying and abusing them. Peasants were forced to grovel in the dirt in the presence of samurai and were forbidden to travel on horseback. They could be cut down without warning by any passing samurai who wanted to try out a new sword.

Merchants and artisans had no such rights over the peasants but were almost as subservient to the samurai. Profession and social status went hand in hand and were passed down from one generation to the next. Intermarriage between the classes was forbidden.

Tokugawa Japan actually had a fifth class, a class of untouchables. These were the subhuman *eta*, who were as far beneath the peasants as the peasants were beneath the samurai. Some modern scholars suspect that this class was established by the shoguns in order to give the peasants an underclass on which to vent their frustrations.[1]

Thus workers in certain unclean trades, such as tanners, leatherworkers, executioners, and prison guards, may have woken up one day to find that they were stuck in a terrible new class that was to be as rigidly hereditary as the others. Their professions all fell afoul of the Shinto religion's emphasis on ritual purity and abhorrence of death. Buddhism, with its prohibition against killing or eating fourlegged animals, added to the prejudice against unclean occupations.

Hatred for the *eta* took deep root. They were hardly considered human, and the miserable villages reserved for them were not even listed on maps. If a road went through an *eta* area, that part was not even included in distance calculations! *Eta* were not allowed to wear shoes, were forbidden to leave their villages at night, and lived in terror.

In feudal Japan everyone knew his place. Even within the official classes there were further subdivisions, each with a slightly different status. Among the samurai there was a bewildering proliferation of titles that allowed more than 100 different shadings of rank. Society was static and unchanging and remained so for two centuries.

In its attention to titles and rank, Japan has hardly changed from the Tokugawa period. What *has* changed is the way hierarchies renew themselves. Very little privilege is now inherited. In the hoary old schools of tea ceremony or traditional dance, leadership may still be passed on from father to son, but otherwise almost all Japanese must now work to achieve high positions.

For a nation that is proud to claim the world's longest unbroken line of hereditary monarchs, the nobility—except for the emperor and his immediate family—have practically no special role in society. The titled classes have far greater influence in Europe, where counts and barons are still found in ministries and boardrooms.

The few descendants of samurai that I have known take a whimsical pride in their ancestry and may still have a fine old sword or two in family storehouses but they have none of the airs or pretensions of Continental aristocracy. Those who still long for the old days meet at a club in Tokyo that is a little like the DAR, but no one takes them very seriously. This transformation in a little more than 100 years from a society of strictly hereditary privilege to one where class differences now hardly exist is an astonishing achievement.

It would be tempting, therefore, to say that all Japanese are now born equal. They are not. Hierarchy begins at birth in the sense that age and sex are important determinants of rank within the family. Status differences in the home are not nearly as important as they were in prewar Japan, but they have by no means died out. According to persistent Confucian tradition, fathers outrank mothers, elders outrank juniors, and boys outrank girls.

Since the war Japan has made great progress toward achieving equality of the sexes, but in many respects society still operates according to the principle of *Danson johi* ("Honor the man, despise the woman"). An old Japanese proverb teaches that by the age of seven little boys and girls should know that their status is different. And, as a Japanese woman complained some years ago in the letters column of a major newspaper, "a woman's status in Japan is halfway between that of a bird and a man."[2]

Girls are reared to be homemakers while boys are encouraged to make their fortunes. Boys are pushed much harder than girls to succeed academically, so, especially around exam time, their needs come first. Since education is vital for boys but an ornament for girls, the best universities are still overwhelmingly male while junior colleges and regional diploma mills are largely female: Only 22 percent of the students at four-year colleges are women while 88 percent of junior college students are women.[3] "After all," says a Japanese woman now living in America, "a diploma from Tōdai [prestigious Tokyo University] doesn't help a woman find a husband."

It's not hard to tell who is important in the family and who is not. Recently I spoke with an American friend who does business with many Japanese companies. He was shaking his head over a recent conversation. "I had lunch the other day with Umezu-san, the new Mitsubishi representative, and all he talked about was his son. It was only over coffee that I found out he has a wife and two daughters. To hear him talk, you'd think he was a single parent with an only child."

There has never been anything resembling chivalry in Japan. Even after the war foreign visitors were surprised to see wives walking several paces behind their husbands and carrying the packages. Now couples walk side by side, but at table men are served before women, and they go through doors first. A Japanese man wouldn't dream of helping a woman get into her coat or holding a car door for her. Women are to serve men, not vice versa.

Seniority, the other indispensable criterion for status, is never far from the surface. When a friend introduces me to a family member, he will never say simply, "This is my brother Tarō." He will always introduce Tarō as his older brother or younger brother. By the same token, if I introduce my brother John to a Japanese, nine times out of ten, I will be asked immediately if John is younger or older. It is important to get the hierarchy straight from the start. Even in the case of identical twins, the "firstborn" is the elder and enjoys the rights of seniority.

Women do not necessarily gain seniority with age the way men do. There is still some truth in the old Japanese saying that in youth a woman submits to her father, in marriage to her husband, and in old age to her son. Women may run the household down to the smallest detail, but the final authority on important matters is always a man.

Within the family it is traditional, at mealtime, to fill each person's rice bowl in rank order. After bathing, family members take turns soaking in the same hot tub; seniors bathe before juniors so as to soak in the cleanest water. Older children have rights over younger children and will pull rank if, for example, there is a dispute over which television program to watch.

At school hierarchy is just as important. Teachers demand and get the respect of students. Students in the lower grades defer to students in the higher grades. In student-organized clubs in Japanese universities junior members do the drudge work while senior members have all the fun.

Once I was watching a college tennis club practicing and noticed that some of the members were smashing the ball back and forth while the rest did nothing but chase loose balls. I caught one that bounced my way and tossed it back to the girl who was chasing it.

"When are you going to get a chance to play?" I asked her.

"I'm a first-year student," she replied. "This is my job."

A well-known Japanese sociologist writes about how the junior members of a college mountain-climbing club have to carry the heavy loads, pitch the tents, and cook meals while the seniors sit around smoking.[4]

In class students sit quietly taking notes and almost never interrupt their professors to ask questions. I know a college professor who was so used to meek Japanese that he was badly flustered by spirited questions from American students during a year as a guest lecturer at an Ivy League university. He thought he was being picked on because he was Japanese until he learned that there was brisk discussion in all classes.

Among college professors it is very difficult for junior faculty to disagree openly with a department head, especially on academic matters. As one Japanese professor complains, status consciousness is so pervasive in university circles it "stifles the free expression of individual thought."[5]

"You'd be nuts to disagree openly with the department head in a faculty meeting," says an economics professor at a small Japanese college. "At first everybody would be so astonished they wouldn't know what to say. Later they all would gang up on you even if they thought you were right.

"No matter how good an idea is," he goes on, "it's got to be brought up by the right person to be taken seriously. The same suggestion might be acted on if a senior professor made it, but rejected if a lecturer made it. A young guy with a good idea has got to find somebody with authority who is willing to represent him. The big guy acts as though it were his own idea and people will listen to him."

In private, strong-willed subordinates may sometimes defy their superiors, but a public display of insubordination, no matter how justified, is very bad form and does not attract sympathy. In few other countries are the chain of command and proper channels of communication so important.

Sometimes respect for hierarchy gets dangerously out of hand. In 1981 Captain Seiji Katagiri of Japan Air Lines flew his DC-8 into Tokyo Bay, killing 24 of the 174 people on board. Investigations into the incident revealed that Katagiri was a borderline psychotic who probably crashed his plane intentionally. It was also discovered that his behavior on a previous flight had been so erratic and potentially dangerous that his copilot and flight engineer had agreed to watch him closely and wrestle him away from the controls if necessary. However, they had not reported his behavior or spoken to him about it. As captain of the aircraft Katagiri was a superior in the hierarchy whose authority was not to be taken lightly.[6]

Most of the time Japanese accept the authority of hierarchy far more cheerfully than Westerners do. Wives agree with their husbands, workers obey their bosses, students believe their professors, and patients follow doctor's orders without seeking a second opinion. The government, as the highest authority in the land, gets the greatest respect.

Japanese who come to America are astonished at wives who defy their husbands, students who argue with professors, and workers who joke with their bosses. It all seems terribly disorderly to them. Many Americans who go to Japan make the mistake of trying to cut across the lines of hierarchy. A comradely approach to high and low alike only embarrasses the Japanese.

In a society that values hierarchy so highly, relations of real equality are rare. Well-defined conditions must be met before two Japanese dispense with formality and treat each other as true equals: They must be the same age and sex, and they must have had some kind of long, intense experience together as classmates from the same village, privates in the same army unit, or age-mates in the same corporation. Only then can they completely relax together.

Language is a constant reminder of how few equals a Japanese has. Every time he opens his mouth he must take care to use language appropriate both to his status and to that of the person he is addressing. Japanese is built around a system of *keigo,* or rank distinctions, that are infinitely more complex than the *tu* and *vous* of French or the *du* and *Sie* of German. Verbs, pronouns, verb endings, special phrases—all must reflect the hierarchical relationship between two speakers.

The most common Japanese verbs have three completely unrelated forms: an honorific form used when the subject is a superior, a neutral form when the subject is an equal or inferior, and a humble form when the speaker is the subject and he is addressing a superior. Unusual verbs, for which there is only one form, can be dressed up with prefixes and suffixes to make them honorific or humble. There is even a special vocabulary reserved for referring to or speaking with the emperor!

Words for the subject "I" vary according to gender as well as rank. What a man calls himself when talking to his wife is not what he calls himself when he is with colleagues. Women often refer to themselves with special pronouns and, as benefits their lower status, are expected to use more honorific language than men. Female speech uses different verb endings which emphasize sex and status differences.

Forms of address are very important. Most people are addressed *in the third person* either by title or by last name: "Would Mr. Section Chief like a cup of coffee?" Use of the pronoun "you"—there are half a dozen variants according to relationship and status—is more delicate and emotion-laden. First names are reserved for close family members and those rare people who are one's equals.

One of the most important and widely used titles in Japan is *sensei*, or teacher. The word literally means "earlier-born," and the respect it evokes harks back to Confucian veneration of elders. There need be no teaching relationship between two people for one to call the other *sensei*—everyone calls teachers and professors *sensei* out of respect for their profession. *Sensei* is not a strictly academic title. Experts in all fields, from modern dance to sword appraisal, are *sensei*.

No matter how important they eventually become, all Japanese call their schoolteachers *sensei* for the rest of their lives, for the student-teacher hierarchy can never be reversed. The prime minister would call his kindergarten teachers *sensei* if they were still alive. Even a man who has gone on to become a college professor and thus a *sensei* in his own right still calls his old teachers *sensei*. They, of course, can call him *sensei* right back.

It is difficult for Americans to imagine the constant formality of Japanese speech. The tone of an American college faculty meeting would change dramatically if all the profs addressed each other as

Professor So-and-so and called the president Mr. President. A day at the office would be an entirely different experience if businessmen called each other Mr. Vice-President or Mr. Assistant Treasurer and said "yes, sir," "no, sir" to the boss. Two hundred years ago Boswell and Johnson constantly called each other sir, but today Americans recoil from the cold politeness of such elaborate speech.

In Japan language is a constant indicator of each person's place in the hierarchy and the nature of his relations with others. For the Japanese, it is second nature to keep all this in their heads whenever they speak. Foreigners not only find the honorific *keigo* difficult to master but are often dismayed by the psychology it is based on.

Susan is an American who spent several years working on a private project with a group of Japanese friends. At one point it became clear that the project would fail without outside financing, so Susan started making the rounds of large businesses in the area to ask for help. Linguistically her position could not have been lower. Both as a suppliant and a woman she had to use the most honorific language when addressing others and the most humbling language when referring to herself.

"Some days I would come home and just burst into tears," she recalls. "It was horrible to have to spend the whole day referring to myself as if I were rubbish." After nearly a decade in Japan Susan is still not sure how the Japanese handle the psychological fallout of *keigo*. "Americans usually mean what they say, and it really hurts inside to be constantly humbling yourself. I still don't know whether that kind of speech is pure hypocrisy for the Japanese or if they are so much a part of the hierarchy that humble speech reflects how they really feel. There must be a lot of both."

Younger Japanese play by the rules of *keigo* because that is how you get ahead in Japan. "Sure you don't always mean that stuff," says one, "but that's what the boss wants to hear. It's just the way you have to talk. It doesn't mean anything." Older Japanese realize that the respect shown to them in speech does not always come from the heart. Nevertheless, as a man in his late forties once told me, "honorific speech reflects the way people *ought* to feel. The young ones will understand that when they are older." I suspect that they will.

I grew up speaking both English and Japanese, so *keigo* is neither difficult nor painful for me. However, it was not until I was an adult that I realized I had two distinct personalities, depending on which language I was speaking. In Japanese I was polite, deferential, flattering, and often insincere—a description of my personality that would astonish Americans who know me. I prefer my English-speaking personality and lately have tried to bring the two closer together. Nevertheless, there are a thousand liberties I take in English that I could never take in Japanese. Disagreement, for example, is much more unpleasant in Japanese than it is in English.

Japanese sometimes find it hard to believe that English is so unconcerned with hierarchy. When they write business letters they are likely to dredge up such antique phrases as "your humble and obedient servant" and "respectfully submitted." This out-of-date language is the closest thing we have to *keigo*, and I have sometimes had trouble persuading Japanese not to use it.

Many women are convinced that there must be an English equivalent of female speech and are eager to learn it. Not long ago I ran across a Japanese book that claimed to meet that need. It urged women to say, "I haven't got a stitch to wear," and to describe things as "luscious" or "so adorable." In moments of distress they are told to say, "Heavenly days!"[7] The Japanese have a hard enough time learning perfectly ordinary English. Nothing would amaze me more than to hear a Japanese woman who had taken a pratfall say, "Heavenly days!" However, for the Japanese, female speech is important, not only because it is ladylike but because it buttresses the sexual hierarchy.

The Japanese do not reserve hierarchy only for individuals. They are quick to establish rankings for companies, universities, cities, and even nations and races. Many Japanese, even if they have no professional reason for knowing, can recite the names of the top banks or automakers in descending order of prestige. They can do this with the same confidence with which an American geologist might name the five highest mountains in North America. The rank is well established. There is similar unanimity on which government departments have more prestige, which schools of tea ceremony have the most glorious tradition, and which universities offer the best chances of success.

In this environment of undisputed rankings a man's affiliation is vitally important. The chief accountant for a prestigious company is clearly the social superior of the chief accountant of a lesser company. His social status is shared by his wife and even by his children.

Americans are far more likely to see themselves in terms of personal qualifications rather than group affiliation, whereas in Japan inequalities through affiliation can sometimes put an end to former relations as equals. I have known classmates who used to treat each other as complete equals but who drifted into an unequal relationship after one had been employed by a more prestigious company.

Hierarchy is an essential social lubricant in Japan. Japanese are so skilled at determining rank that questions of precedence almost never become a problem. Rankings can usually be established on terms everyone accepts. Thus once the appropriate hierarchy for any situation has been established, business or social relations can proceed smoothly. Roles are defined and tasks are assigned without long arguments.

A Japanese housewife once told me about a local PTA committee she had joined to look into traffic safety in school zones. Responsibilities within the committee were parceled out according to the *husband's* status. "One of the women was married to a big shot in an important company," she said, "so naturally she had to head the committee. I don't think she even wanted the job, but what could she do? She outranked everyone else." As it turned out, another committee member discreetly did most of the work, but for form's sake, rank had to take precedence over enthusiasm or ability.

An American professor who works at a Japanese college was amused to find that in faculty elections for dean or president there is no provision for cases when two candidates get the same number of votes. "I have never actually seen a tie vote," he says, "but if there ever were one, I have no doubt that the *older* man would get the job. In America there would be some kind of formal tie-breaking procedure because Americans don't have the same automatic respect for age."

Another example of unquestioned hierarchy is the well-known system of *amakudari*, whereby a group of high-level bureaucrats who all started work at a ministry in the same year will resign en masse when one of their number is finally named vice-minister. They "descend from heaven" and take jobs in private industry, so that none will have the embarrassment of having to report to a man who was once his equal.

In new situations the Japanese like to establish the right status and appropriate role for everyone. This allows them to follow protocol and precedent so that they don't have to figure out for themselves how to behave. Most Japanese are not very comfortable in unstructured social situations like cocktail parties. They prefer seating arrangements, name tags, or some other evidence of hierarchy that gives them clues to how to act. A stranger presented without context is a wild card—there is no telling what his status may be.

One Japanese puts it this way: "When the Japanese relate to each other as individuals, there is apt to be some confusion, whereas all becomes clear as soon as a person's group affiliations become known. The individual will be signaling his affiliations almost as if he believed the quality of his character depended on them. . . ."[8]

When people are thrown together with incomplete introductions, the results can be entertaining. In such circumstances I have heard Japanese carefully feeling each other out in medium-polite language until they figured out what the status relationship was. If one happened to be higher-ranking than the other had guessed, there may be a polite apology and a switch to the appropriate language level. It won't do simply to use the most polite speech until the facts are in— one runs the risk of looking ridiculous if the new person turns out to be an ex-convict.

At the national level Japan is like France, in that the capital is by far the most important city and the center of everything. The national railway system identifies its trains not as east- or westbound but as moving toward or away from Tokyo. Even in the most distant provinces a train running in the general direction of Tokyo is an "ascending" train, and one in the opposite direction is a "descending" train. Just as Mecca orients Moslems, the capital orients travelers. Lesser cities vie with each other and establish rank according to how nearly they can imitate Tokyo in cultural or commercial attractions.

This love of hierarchy extends to nations and races. Japanese rank them unabashedly according to their "superior" or "inferior" qualities, and Japan's niche in the hierarchy is carefully monitored. As one Japanese explains it: "The Japanese reflex to modify behavior according to rank . . . applies to races as well.

"For this reason Japanese have absurd, unreasoning feelings of inferiority toward Americans or Europeans, but flaunt an equally unreasoning superiority and self-importance in the face of Southeast Asians or Africans."[9]

Japan first began to modernize under the slogan *Fukoku kyōhei* ("Rich nation, strong military"), and the Japanese have continued to rank nations according to the same priorities. During the 1960s, as their economy grew larger than those of the European nations, the Japanese were probably the most GNP-conscious people on earth. In 1968, when Japan pulled ahead of West Germany and became the second largest economy in the free world, there was real rejoicing. Newspapers trumpeted the news, and Japanese discussed it proudly with their foreign friends. It must have been a trying time for Germans living in Japan. This pride in GNP often takes the form of contempt for underdeveloped nations and for those, like Britain, that have slipped behind.

The military component in world rankings is more complicated. The Japanese have a rueful respect for nuclear arms and, to a degree, rate other nations according to their military might. They have not forgotten that until they were beaten by the United States, they were the lords of Asia. Japan had a substantial empire in Manchuria, ruled Taiwan since 1895, and formally annexed Korea to the home islands in 1910. All this came to an end only in 1945.

As it built its empire, Japan's conception of international hierarchy could not have been clearer. The Japanese made no bones about subordinating captured nations to their own interests. After the war in Asia had begun in earnest, Japan imported work gangs from its overseas territories to fill jobs left by workers who had been drafted. Between 1940 and 1945 nearly 1 million Koreans were brought over practically as slaves to work in the most dangerous, degrading jobs. Many ended up in the coal mines, where they were starved and brutalized. Korean women were used for different purposes: approximately 60,000 were rounded up and sent to the front to service the imperial troops.[10]

One of Japan's important wartime objectives was the establishment of a clear hierarchy of Asian nations. The Greater East Asia Co-Prosperity Sphere was designed as a neat international hierarchy with Japan at the top. The Japanese, with their inbred sense of order, couldn't understand why the defeated nations wouldn't recognize their own inferiority and assume tributary positions. Japanese still have a distinct feeling of superiority over the peoples they overran during the war, and this attitude has been strengthened by the subsequent poor economic performance of many of them.

Since the war Japan has reconquered economically what it lost militarily. In Indonesia Japanese investment is greater than all other foreign investment combined, and Japanese control is increasing in the other countries of the area. Japanese have ruthlessly exploited the cheapest labor available and have exported part of their pollution problem by setting up heavy industrial complexes overseas.

In Southeast Asia Japanese have behaved with an arrogance that deeply offends other Asians. Their economic policies have earned them the epithet "economic animals," and their personal behavior has earned them some names that are unprintable. Southeast Asians are united in complaining that the Japanese mistrust them, feel superior to them, and give them no responsibility in business.

One sober Japanese handbook for foreign investment warns, "Overseas Japanese are criticized for creating their own separate society and for making no effort to understand the local country or learn its language. They are said to hog the golf courses, smoke only Japanese cigarettes, use only Japanese-made office supplies, eat in Japanese restaurants, patronize Japanese travel agents, and live in a separate world of their own."[11] The Japanese have hardly helped their own cause by setting up memorials in World War II battlegrounds that pay tribute to Japanese soldiers and ignore the thousands of natives who died in the fighting.

To Americans, this kind of insensitivity sounds only too familiar; the ugly American has passed on the mantle of opprobrium to the ugly Japanese. Nevertheless, in some cases the Japanese may be doing us one better. One international banker reportedly advises his men to "use the locals like cattle."[12]

Hostility to Japan burst forth spectacularly in riots and demonstrations that dogged Prime Minister Tanaka's official visit to Southeast Asia in 1974. Since then the government has made it clear to business that excesses in Asia would not be tolerated, and the worst have been corrected. Nevertheless, old habits die hard. Japanese businessmen in Asia are far more likely to be rude and domineering than those posted to Europe or America. This may be due, in part, to a tendency in some companies to send better men to Frankfurt or New York than to Jakarta, but this, too, reflects a clear conception of which countries are important and which are not.

A particularly distasteful example of how Japan views its neighbors is the sex tour. These are package tour groups of Japanese men who are flown off for a week at a time to sample the fleshpots of Seoul, Taipei, Bangkok, or Manila. Korean *kisaeng* girls, who will feed a man with chopsticks, spend the night with him, and even wash his underwear, are especially in demand. Droves of libidinous Japanese are now such a common sight in Asia that when Prime Minister Zenkō Suzuki visited five neighboring countries in 1981, he had to handle repeated complaints about them from his hosts.[13]

Asian capitals are handily located nearby, but their status in the international hierarchy makes them especially ripe for sexual plunder. Such behavior would be unthinkable in nations for which the Japanese did not feel contempt. It can hardly be a coincidence that the two most popular destinations for sex tours—Korea and Taiwan—are former colonies. Moreover, the economics of the business are strictly colonial: tours are managed and operated entirely by Japanese interests, who pay the local women a pittance for their services.

Japan's treatment of the boat people of Indochina reflects the same disdain for other Asians. The Japanese were extremely reluctant to sacrifice their national purity by accepting any of the hapless castoffs of poverty and underdevelopment. It was only in response to sharp criticism from the West that they agreed to accept 3,000 refugees for permanent settlement.

A woman who worked in the small office that was set up to run the resettlement program told me she thought the director and half his staff felt they had been exiled by their new assignments. They had no interest in the plight of the boat people and did just enough to give the world the impression that Japan was concerned about the problem.

When a housing facility was finally built and the first refugees were accepted, my informant tried to get acquainted with the new arrivals and help them adjust. She was reprimanded. "I was told that speaking to the refugees was not part of my job," she says. "Can you imagine that? I was on the staff of the office assigned to settle them in Japan, and I wasn't even supposed to speak to them!"

Ironically, Japan is not having an easy time filling its tiny resettlement quota. If they don't know it before they arrive, refugees soon discover how closed Japanese society is. Most would like to move on, preferably to the United States,[14] and the Japanese do nothing to hinder them.

Of all the nations of Asia, only for China do the Japanese seem to feel any kind of fraternity or kinship. It was from China, after all, that Japan received its writing system, the beginnings of its culture, its political administration, Confucianism, and Buddhism. In the thaw that followed President Richard Nixon's visit to Peking in 1972, Japanese executives rushed off to China in the hope of doing business. The Chinese authorities demanded—and got—apologies for the Rape of Nanking and other wartime atrocities before they would sit down and talk business. When the Chinese gave Japan a pair of pandas as a sign of friendship, the whole country nearly went crazy with delight.

Sino-Japanese relations took a jolt in 1981, when the Chinese decided to rein in their development plans and canceled seventeen large industrial projects in which Japanese companies had contracted to take part. Still, Japanese feel that there is a bright future of cooperation between the two countries.

The Japanese attitude toward the people who conquered them has been radically different from their attitude toward the peoples they themselves conquered. To the astonishment of the occupying Americans, the ferocity and hatred with which Japan did battle disappeared without a trace immediately after the surrender. The Japanese concluded that they had been beaten by a "superior" power that should be admired and imitated rather than resisted. They behaved as if their obedience and loyalty to the emperor had suddenly been transferred to General Douglas MacArthur.

Until recently this recognition of the superiority of the victor—and, by extension, the other white nations—was confirmed by America's economic might. Japan's treatment of Caucasians in distress has accordingly been in marked contrast with its heartlessness toward the boat people.

The 1977 Japan Air Lines hijacking incident shed light on this contrast. As negotiations over the hijackers' demands dragged on, the gunmen threatened to start killing the passengers one by one if their terms were not met. The government told them to go ahead. The hijackers then hauled one of the few American passengers to the door of the plane and before the eyes of the startled Japanese negotiators announced they would shoot him first. The authorities immediately capitulated.

Afterward the Japanese press wondered unhappily whether the authorities would not have lost their nerve if the first victim had been an Oriental. In the case of an American, Japan was dealing with a potential victim from a traditionally "superior" country, not a boat person. His life was valuable.

Of course, different treatment for different races does not require such dramatic circumstances. Asian exchange students to Japan complain of being snubbed and ignored while their white-skinned fellows are overwhelmed with hospitality. Even in business, where the Japanese are usually so hardheaded, race can make a surprising difference. One well-traveled Japanese businessman complains: "We Japanese seem to have a continuing weakness for white people and for English speakers. Many Japanese have the peculiar habit of assuming that a white person is likely to be as good at everything else as he is at English. However, the same Japanese may make the opposite assumption about Asians who have taken the trouble to learn Japanese. They will rate the Asian's other abilities on a par with his poor Japanese."[15]

Japanese are well aware of this "*gaijin* complex." It has been around for a long time. Near the turn of the century novelist Sōseki Natsume (1867–1916) spent two miserable years in England. He felt hideously short and ugly in the company of Englishmen and in 1901 wrote in his diary, "We are country bumpkins, nincompoop monkeys, good-for-nothing ashen-colored impenetrable people. So it's natural the Westerners should despise us."[16]

There is a Japanese expression, *Nihon-jin-banare*, which translates as "un-Japanese" or "ceasing to be Japanese." Oddly enough, it is a compliment. A woman with long, shapely legs or a man who speaks a foreign language fluently may be called *Nihon-jin-banare*. Such *gaijin* achievements go beyond the usual limitations of being Japanese.

Japan's defeat by Caucasian America gave the *gaijin* complex a terrific boost. In the immediate postwar years Japanese were desperate for any evidence that they could stand up to whitey. Rikidōzan was a Japanese professional wrestler whose exploits in the ring were a source of national pride. In the preface to his 1962 autobiography an admirer writes: "In a nation laid waste by defeat in war and in the milieu that prevailed under the occupying army, by knocking large-bodied *gaijin* around the ring and beating them to the mat, Rikidōzan vented in proxy the pent-up emotions of the Japanese people at the time. We must not forget his meritorious service in thus imparting courage to the postwar Japanese."[17] Ironically, this redeemer of the nation's manhood was an ethnic Korean who worked very hard to conceal his origins.

Watching Rikidōzan stomp on large-bodied *gaijin* was not enough for some Japanese. A bizarre self-loathing is still part of how many of the older generation see themselves. This is the opening passage of a book that was first printed in 1973 and went into its fifteenth printing in 1981:

> There is an old joke about a Japanese visiting a city in the West, who catches sight of an especially wimpy-looking man walking toward him. As the two approach each other, the Japanese realizes he is watching his own reflection in a store window.
>
> A Japanese walking the streets in the West has a forlorn, hopeless, unprepossessing look about him—and not just because he is small.
>
> Westerners, by contrast, even under a foreign sky, have a maddening kind of majesty about them. Their step is firm, their shoulders are square, and they stride forward with confidence.
>
> Not even the most sympathetic observer could think that wimp-man has half a chance against majestic-man—at least not from just looking at the two. This may be mortifying, but it's true.[18]

Some Japanese are fed up with this kind of thinking, but most still have a definite weakness for white people. They are quick to offer help to any *gaijin* who looks as if he needs it and are generous and loyal to their *gaijin* friends. Many Americans and Europeans delight in this special treatment and think that Japan is a wonderful place to live. Their children, who grow up in Japan as the center of attention, often fail to adjust to life back home, where they are not automatically special and have to be talented to attract attention.

Nevertheless, for the Japanese, the world hierarchy is not static. As Japan overtakes the United States in one area after another, the *gaijin* complex has begun to fade. Those who have long known the Japanese see a new air of confidence in their foreign and economic policies.

On an individual level as well, Japanese behavior has begun to change. A Japanese newsman has pointed out that "Japanese who work in the U.S. will bow and scrape in the presence of whites, but as soon as they are alone, they will say, 'Americans sure are stupid,' or, 'American products are junk,' and wallow in feelings of superiority."[19] I don't expect the bowing and scraping to last much longer.

In some circles the Japanese reaction to the U.S. space-shuttle program was: "If we had built it, the tiles would never have fallen off."

Before long I expect more Japanese to behave like Kakuzō Okakura (1862–1913), one of the pioneers in introducing Japanese culture to the West. Unlike his more timid contemporaries, he made a point of wearing only Japanese clothing when he traveled abroad. At about the time Sōseki Natsume was living in England and calling himself a nincompoop monkey, Okakura was in New York. Once he was stopped in the street by a passerby who wanted to know what kind of "-ese" he was, Japanese or Chinese. Okakura is said to have retorted, "Are you a Yankee, or a monkey, or perhaps a donkey?" As they begin to swagger, the Japanese will not be as pleasant to deal with, but the current change in their attitude toward whites has long been overdue.

The Haworth Country Club, in northern New Jersey, is near a community where many Japanese businessmen live when they are posted to New York. In 1981 Japanese interests bought the club and raised membership fees from around $300 to more than $5,000 a year, a figure far beyond the means of many long-term American members. Some complained bitterly. "They're trying to boot us out so they can make this an all-Japanese club," said one at the time.[20] Members are now practically all Japanese, and their employers pick up the tab.

No one can, of course, prove that the new owners meant to drive Americans out. However, I doubt that a group of Japanese would have risked even the appearance of high-handedness fifteen years ago. America is certainly not the same as Indonesia in the eyes of the Japanese, but what was once possible only in Southeast Asia is now possible anywhere.

The United States is no longer on a pedestal, culturally or economically. Not long ago, I saw an ad in a Japanese magazine for American blue jeans. The copy was simple but revealing: "What is there left to admire in American culture," it asked, "but blue jeans and great FM stations?" It was not so long ago that blue jeans were a symbol of all that was glamorously American. They promised a whole continent of excitement. Now, they are marketed as the only worthwhile product that American culture can offer to the discriminating Japanese. This is a daring, offbeat approach to America, but it is the thin edge of the wedge.

As the relative positions of strength and wealth change, Japanese behavior will change with it. For some time to come, especially in

Japan itself, Westerners will still be treated to displays of giggling subservience, but one day this, too, will stop. Americans do not keep the same watchful eye on the world hierarchy that Japanese do. They may have a vague feeling that America has declined from its immediate postwar mastery of the globe, but few realize how much a change in hierarchy means to the Japanese. In world affairs, as in Japanese society, there are very few equals—only superiors and inferiors.

Just as the Japanese rank the nations of the world, so they rank its races. Japan's reverence for hierarchy and its profound sense of uniqueness perhaps lead inevitably to racism. The Japanese are convinced, against all anthropological evidence, that they constitute a distinct race separate from all other Asians and they are, in fact, some of the most painfully race-conscious people on earth.

Within Japan's homogeneous society, Koreans have perhaps been the most visible victims of prejudice. The Japanese have considered the Koreans a beggerly, inferior people ever since the late sixteenth century, when Hideyoshi Toyotomi (1536–1598) invaded the peninsula and laid it waste. After Korea had been annexed in 1910, Japanese companies started importing cheap labor, and the resident Korean population began to grow.

These Korean laborers were the target of what was probably modern Japan's only pogrom. In 1923, immediately after the great Kantō earthquake had destroyed much of Tokyo, the Japanese rose up and slaughtered the Koreans in their midst. According to one account, "The Japanese in Tokyo went berserk hunting Koreans. They used bamboo spears to stab, clubs to beat, and bare hands to choke Koreans to death."[21] Estimates of the death toll range from several hundred to as many as 6,000. In the shock and confusion of a natural disaster the Japanese vented their rage on the nearest scapegoats.

Today about 660,000 Koreans live in Japan. Citizenship is very difficult for them to obtain, and about half do not even have permanent resident status. Every three years they must reapply for permission to stay in Japan, even if they have been born there. Those who are descended from workers brought over during the war are, by any reasonable standards, Japanese. They have lived in Japan all their lives, and Japanese is their native language. Their behavior and attitudes are overwhelmingly Japanese, and they are physically indistinguishable from the majority.

Many have taken Japanese names and try to "pass" in Japanese society. Some go to great pains to conceal their background, for they may face serious prejudice should they be found out.

Japanese seem to be always trying to penetrate their disguises. A person's *koseki*, or village name roll, is an infallible account of his background. Nowadays it is against the law to go snooping around in someone else's *koseki*, but determined busybodies still manage to do it. Some prospective employers or marriage partners will ask outright to see a copy, while others may conduct a discreet investigation. There are private detective agencies that will do the sleuthing for a fee. Koreans who have become Japanese citizens are so indicated on their *koseki*, and those who are not citizens have no *koseki* at all. There have been innumerable cases of engagements being broken and new employees being fired after a *koseki* check.

"Koreans don't even bother to apply for jobs at the best companies," says a Korean-Japanese who now lives in America. "What's the use? Either they'll be fired when it turns out they're Korean, or they'll be made to feel so unwanted they'll leave anyway. Smaller companies can't afford to be so picky." Since the economic mainstream presents so many obstacles to Koreans, many enter professional sports or become entertainers—much like blacks in America. Many Japanese claim to feel no prejudice against them but may still occasionally play spot-the-Korean around the television set. "In effect," writes one scholar, "Koreans have remained colonial subjects, exploited economically and despised socially."[22]

The approximately 2 million present-day descendants of the outcast *eta* are, if anything, worse off than the Koreans. Now renamed *burakumin* (the word "*eta*" is written with characters that mean "heavily polluted"), many deny their background and also try to pass as regular Japanese. They, too, can be found out by a *koseki* check and face rigorous marriage and job discrimination. As late as 1957 a man committed suicide because his son insisted on marrying a *burakumin* girl.

Although there is not a shred of historical evidence for it, many Japanese justify their prejudice with the belief that the *burakumin* are descendants of prisoners taken by early Japanese raiding parties on the Asian mainland. This elaborate fiction labels the *burakumin* as non-Japanese—like the Koreans—and thus inferior.

After the war public discrimination was made illegal, but in 1960 firms were still proclaiming their "no *eta* or Koreans" hiring policies.

Since then, the law has been more diligently enforced, and in 1974 the Hitachi company lost a celebrated court case for firing an employee who turned out to be Korean, so discrimination must be more discreet.

Several years later the Korean-Japanese Kim Kyong Duc successfully brought suit in the Japanese Supreme Court for the right to attend the Judicial Research and Training Institute. This is a specialized school through which all who wish to enter the legal profession must pass and, until Kim's suit, had been firmly closed to all non-Japanese. It took a wrenching act of courage for Kim to take his case before the nation. "Throughout the years of my life in Japan," he wrote, "I have hated myself for being Korean and always tried to pretend to be Japanese. I don't know how often I have trembled with fear at having my real identity discovered by my peers."[23]

Burakumin radicals have formed a Buraku Liberation League, but many of their people fear that agitation will only make the problem worse. Japanese are very hesitant to take their differences before the courts, and many cases of blatantly illegal discrimination go unchallenged. Outcasts and Koreans are slowly gaining acceptance in Japan, but social change moves at a glacial pace.[24]

Discrimination against minorities is one of Japan's most uncomfortable secrets. When books by foreigners are translated into Japanese, references to racism may be artfully edited out. One writer explains: "Some mainline presses are known to censor Japanese translations of the works of foreign scholars to give their majority readers the impression that Japan is being seen from abroad as they prefer to be seen: with no ethnic minorities beneath the cherry blossoms."[25] Edwin Reischauer's book *The Japanese* was reportedly shorn of several passages on the *eta*, and James Clavell's novel *Shōgun* appeared in Japanese with only one of its many references to them. Even that one was apparently too many—the publishers recalled the book and issued a totally pure version of *Shōgun*.[26]

Americans are no strangers to racism, but theirs is straightforward prejudice against people who are physically or culturally different. Not even the WASPiest American would break an engagement with a girl he loved simply because he found out her parents had changed their name from du Pont to Johnson or that her ancestors had been tanners. In Japan somone may seem to be a perfectly good Japanese in *every* respect yet be excluded for what Americans would feel was an abstraction or a technicality. For the Japanese, these are significant issues; purity and uniqueness are at stake.

Purity is, of course, far more threatened by outright racial differences. Even in the closed society of feudal Japan, subtle differences in skin color were very important. Long before regular contact with "blue-eyed barbarians" the Japanese had coined the proverb "With women, as with rice, the whiter the better." In premodern literary works, such as *The Tale of Genji*, beautiful women are praised for their white skin, and modern Japanese still prefer light skin. Occasionally I have praised a woman's beauty only to hear men dismiss her as "black-skinned." On second glance the woman may have been a little darker than most Japanese, but no *gaijin* would ever notice or care.

In Japan dark skin was long associated with poverty and inferiority. It was seen as a sign of having toiled in the fields under the sun, while light skin was evidence of indoor leisure.[27] Differences in skin color are one reason for Japanese feelings of superiority over their darker Asian neighbors.

Okinawans, who have darker skin than Japanese mainlanders, have always been stepchildren. Before the war, of the forty-three Japanese prefectures, Okinawa was the only one that did not even have a high school. Okinawans were so unhappy with administration from Tokyo that when the war ended, many would have preferred to attach themselves to the United States.[28] That feeling did not survive the early years of American occupation, and Okinawa was returned to full prefectural status in 1972. Nevertheless, Okinawan Japanese still face many of the prejudices that Koreans and *burakumin* suffer from.

Concern for skin color can reach obsessive proportions. A friend who has lived in Hawaii told me about an incident that came to the attention of the state's medical examiners some years ago. To their astonishment the examiners discovered a case of rickets in a young boy of Okinawan descent. Rickets is caused by a lack of vitamin D, which the human body absorbs from the sun. In sun-drenched Hawaii it is virtually unheard of. The investigators found that the boy's mother had kept him in the shade his whole life in order to keep his skin as light as possible. She hoped that this would make it easier for him to live among the prejudiced Japanese.

When, in the nineteenth century, Japanese were forced into contact with other races, their reactions were pronounced. In 1860 the government of Japan sent a delegation to the United States to ratify a treaty of commerce. One of the members of that delegation wrote in his diary his reactions to the skin color of foreigners. Of American children, he wrote ". . . their natural, beautiful complexion was whiter than snow, and more resplendent than jewels. They looked like goddesses in Paradise."[29]

Of Africans that he encountered on his return trip he wrote, "Both sexes have kinky hair, and their faces are black and ugly. . . . The grotesque way they shuffle around in the sand reminds me of the painted images of devils."[30] To the straight-haired Japanese, the curly hair of blacks looked like the fur of animals.

A strong dislike of blacks continues to this day. An American working for the U.S. government in West Africa told me about a Japanese diplomat he had known.

"The whole two years he was there, the guy didn't once try African food. At first I thought he was worried that it might not be clean, and invited him for a meal at my house, but that wasn't the problem. He didn't have to try any to be convinced that the stuff was disgusting.

"What he felt for their food, he felt for the Africans. He would say, 'These people have no culture.' *No culture!* Sometimes a conversation with him would just run into a brick wall. How do you argue with someone who says the Africans have no culture at all? And this guy was with their Foreign Service."

I have had similar experiences in America. Once I was talking with a group of Japanese about whether a Japanese-style public bath would be a commercial success in New York. I argued that there were 30,000 or 40,000 Japanese in the area and that many were probably nostalgic for a luxurious soak in a real Japanese bath.

"It would never work in Manhattan," said a young lady. "You'd have to put it out in the suburbs."

"Why is that?" I asked.

"As soon as you got a black in the place, you'd lose all your Japanese customers."

"Yes," said another with a laugh, "they'd probably be afraid they'd turn black if they got into the same water with one."

During the American occupation several hundred Japanese had babies by black American servicemen. The women, as well as their children, were practically hounded out of the country, and many emigrated to Brazil. Those who had babies with white servicemen didn't have an easy time of it either, but prejudice against them was not nearly so extreme.

Most Japanese are dismayed by racial diversity or integration when they encounter it overseas. Many who are posted by their companies to New York or Los Angeles arrive with a full-grown hatred of minorities. They have heard all about blacks and Hispanics from colleagues who preceded them. Several Japanese have told me they do not think of nonwhites as fully American. The hierarchy of apartheid strikes many Japanese as perfectly natural, and they are pleased with their status in South Africa as honorary whites.

Hierarchy is thus important to the Japanese, both at home and abroad. It can be ugly when it takes the form of racism, but it is understandable that the Japanese should try to apply to the world at large a system that provides order and social harmony at home.

Japanese society is like a formal seating arrangement. For those who know the rules of the arrangement, a glance is all it takes to know who is superior to whom and what level of politeness is called for. The whole world could be run on this system if all the nations would only agree to take their assigned places. The problem, of course, is that independent nations never agree on who should sit where.

Hierarchy is important to the Japanese because it creates order. Nothing gets done when people or nations are continually jostling each other for the top spot. At home and abroad hierarchy gives shape to a formless mass. It is an important indicator of appropriate behavior that relieves individuals of having to decide too much for themselves. Japanese society has several such indicators; an equally important one is the group.

CHAPTER THREE

❁

THE GROUP

On May 30, 1972, a Japanese terrorist named Kōzō Okamoto and two companions went on a murderous rampage in Tel Aviv's Lod Airport. In the name of Palestinian rights they opened fire with automatic weapons, killing twenty-four travelers and wounding many more. When the shooting was over, his two companions were dead, but Okamoto was taken alive. Ten years later he is still in an Israeli jail.

The world was astonished to learn that self-effacing postwar Japan could produce such a deranged killer. But the world was even more astonished by how the Japanese government reacted. Instead of sending condolences and politely disclaiming responsibility for the actions of a private citizen—as any other government would have done—Japan first sent a high-ranking official to apologize formally to Prime Minister Golda Meir for the killings. It then accepted full responsibility for the crime by making generous financial compensation to the families of the victims.

I doubt that a Western government would have gone so far even if one of its official representatives had suddenly run amok and started killing people. Okamoto was a wanted criminal. However, for the Japanese, their government's reaction was a high-level but perfectly consistent example of the importance of the group. Okamoto was a member—a family member—of the Japanese national group, and his misbehavior was therefore the responsibility of the entire nation. As a member he was expected to fly group colors at all times. He not only committed an outrage against innocent people but betrayed and shamed the Japanese group.

One of Japan's most prominent national characteristics is the individual's sense of the group. At every level of society the Japanese have a very strong sense of who is on the inside and who is not. The group draws firm boundaries between "us" and "them" and, like hierarchy, is an essential guidepost to proper behavior. Group ties can be so close that members feel collective responsibility for each other's actions. Loyalty to the group and a willingness to submit to its demands are thus key virtues in Japanese society. It is the values of the group, rather than abstract principles, that serve as morality for many Japanese.

No one knows how the group came to be so important to the Japanese, but some historians see its origins in Japan's wet rice farming methods. Paddy fields require a complicated system of irrigation and drainage ditches that can be built and maintained only by the village working together. Thus, it is said, the Japanese peasant learned early that if the village was to have enough to eat, everyone had to cooperate.

There is no doubt that the village was the primary focus of loyalty in rural Japan. Unlike American farmers who lived in isolated homesteads surrounded by their fields, Japanese villagers clumped their houses together practically gable to gable. One Japanese author points out that not only did villagers cooperate on public projects, such as roads and irrigation ditches, and on preparations for festivals, but they became very closely involved in each other's personal lives as well. Weddings, funerals, and care of the sick were the affair of the entire village, and neighbors were expected to help each other plant, build houses, and harvest crops.[1]

Service to the village was enforced by the terrible threat of *mura hachibu*, or ostracism. The law of the land took care of villagers guilty of such crimes as theft, rape, or arson, but the village itself disciplined those who broke its own unwritten law. The community would ignore the very existence of a family that had failed to show loyalty to the group. It did not matter if only one member of the family was guilty; the village as a group froze out the family as a group. Victims of *mura hachibu*, who had only the slimmest chance of being accepted into another community, often committed suicide.

Mura hachibu sputtered on until not long after the war, and one of the last occurrences was reported in the early 1950s. A young girl, who had just learned in school about Japan's new, American-inspired democratic system, denounced a case of vote buying to the authorities. Her family was promptly frozen out of all contact with the rest of the village.

Many Japanese see their own group consciousness in terms of an agricultural heritage as opposed to what they think of as a hunting and herding heritage in the West. They see farming as a settled, cooperative way of life in contrast with the mobility and individuality of hunters. One author fancifully likens Japanese society to a community of plants and Western society to a community of animals. Plants grow up harmoniously with each other, without the conflict that gives rise to individuality. Animals roam about, fight each other, and develop a strong sense of self.[2]

This explanation for how Japanese and Westerners differ is surprisingly pervasive. In the summer of 1982 employees of Hitachi Ltd. and the Mitsubishi Electric Corporation were caught in an FBI entrapment operation and were charged in U.S. courts with conspiring to steal IBM trade secrets. One of Japan's best-selling newspapers, the *Mainichi*, editorialized sagely on the case:

> Imagine . . . the U.S. Federal Bureau of Investigation . . . and its cover-up [*sic*] agents licking their chops as they snare their targets. The recent FBI "sting" operation . . . is illustrative of the traits of the hunter races. The way the Japanese involved in the case huddled themselves up at the frightening prospect of their "master's house" [their employer] being plunged into a crisis is typically the reaction of the agrarian races. Blood will out even in the field of high technology.[3]

Whether or not it is due to thin, paddy field blood in their veins, group loyalty begins at home. The family is the first group any of us joins, and here children first learn the value of belonging. Sociologists have long been aware of differences in Japanese and American child-rearing practices. In Japan the baby is considered an independent organism that must be drawn into the bosom of the family in an increasingly dependent way in order for it to mature. In America the baby is seen as a dependent creature that must be taught to stand alone. Studies claim to have found that Japanese mothers encourage a passive, yielding attitude toward the environment, while American mothers encourage exploration and interaction.[4]

Japanese children often sleep in the same bed as their parents until the age of five or six. They may then get beds of their own, but may continue to sleep in the same room as their parents until puberty. This is partly because of Japan's cramped living conditions but also because Japanese feel it is cruel to make young children sleep alone. Even adults can feel lonely without someone else sleeping in the same room. Japanese are shocked to see American mothers putting infants to bed in little rooms of their own.

At bathtime Japanese babies are taken into the tub with their parents rather than put into bassinets and washed from outside. Also, some expectant mothers still ask their obstetricians to save the umbilical cords when their babies are born. The cord is taken home and preserved as a symbol of how closely the child was attached to his mother. Finally, Japanese parents are more likely to discipline their children by excluding them from family activities than by punishing them physically. All these practices encourage group ties rather than a strong sense of individuality.

Some Japanese argue that the very architecture of their houses helps suppress individualism. Traditional houses do not block rooms off with solid walls the way Western houses do. Instead, one large interior space can be cut up into changing patterns of smaller spaces with screens or sliding paper doors. There is no consistently private area where a person can shut himself off from the rest of the family, and what may have been a small, personal space yesterday could be a large, public space today. Sound, of course, travels easily through paper doors. Privacy has not traditionally been of much interest to the Japanese, and the language does not even have a word for it.

Often the Japanese seem to prefer the company of others when Westerners might prefer solitude. Tourist brochures show beaches crowded with bathers and mountains thronged with hikers; the press of humanity is reassuring to Japanese vacationers, who might otherwise feel lonely. The appeal of the herd also helps explain why Japanese cities are so crowded. There is often plenty of hilly land outside Japanese towns, but even in the age of the automobile it remains uninhabited because Japanese would feel uneasy without the crush of neighbors.

An American couple who live in southern Japan have built a house on a small hill that is only a few minutes' drive from town. They report that many of their Japanese friends admire the hilltop view but confess that they could never live in such a place because it is "too lonely."

Westerners, of course, value human contact as well, but Japanese often establish groups when we would operate as individuals. A Japanese professor who recently came to the United States to participate in antinuclear demonstrations saw typical differences between Japan and America in the way the antinuclear movement was organized. In Japan, he pointed out, the movement has generally been run by political interests or other organized groups, such as labor unions or consumer unions, which do grass-roots organizing through their local chapters.

"In America," he told me, "there are plenty of demonstrators who don't represent anybody—they're just citizens opposed to nuclear weapons. A Japanese who takes part in a demonstration almost has to be part of a group delegation, but Americans can join in entirely on their own."

Groups come in all varieties in Japan, but most Japanese seem to focus their lives around one central group. This is usually a work group, such as a university department, a faction within a political party, a subsection at the office, or a unit in a factory. Japanese who are not part of a tight group at work may become active in one of Japan's new religions or join a local consumer union or political association. The members of this group are a person's *nakama*, or buddies, and can easily become more important to him than his family.

Groups command undivided loyalty; political apostasy and job-hopping are extremely rare. In return for his dedication the individual receives a strong sense of mission and personal identification. The more of himself he devotes to the group, the more meaning he finds in it. A man's professional affiliations can be so strong that it is difficult to tell where he draws the line between his public and private lives. Almost a cliché example of this is the way a Japanese introduces himself as an employee of such and such a company rather than as a welder or personnel manager. The group affiliation is more important than the individual profession. The values of the group become the individual's values, and a large part of his leisure time is spent in the company of colleagues and other group members. Just as the Japanese tend to travel overseas in groups rather than as individuals, so is each Japanese sustained through life by his group.

Westerners value their affiliations as well and may also be extremely loyal to their work groups. Nevertheless, they tend to have many competing loyalties and to build up a network of loose associations. They may well be on close terms with many people who do not even know of each others' existence. Some of their friendships may be in clumps, but others can be strictly one to one.

Recently, when I was transferred to Japan by my company, one of my good customers in New York urged me to look up one of his close colleagues in Tokyo. I saw the man socially several times, but never alone. He always brought with him several of his closest co-workers— that is to say, his *nakama*. Another man I met during that assignment was posted to the United States not long after I returned. I entertained him at my home soon after he arrived, and he reciprocated by inviting me to dinner. By American standards, it was an unusual invitation: he asked me to bring four or five of my best friends—that is to say, my *nakama*. Between Westerners both those friendships probably would have first grown up between individuals. In Japan a group can quickly get involved.

Close Japanese friendships occur within groups that see each other often. It is among *nakama* that they are formed and thrive, and without regular doses of contact they wither. One Japanese author writes enviously of other cultures in which friendship can remain strong in spite of long separations.[5] Unlike the Japanese, Westerners are seldom so caught up in one or two groups that their lives revolve around affiliations. Groups of buddies are seldom so tightly bound as *nakama*.

In the West there is usually a clear distinction between functional groups and communities, or kinship groups. Functional groups are made up of people who come together on a more or less contractual basis to accomplish a specific task. Corporations are a perfect example of this kind of group. Communities, however, may not have any *specific* function but exist to support individuals through ties that are emotional rather than contractual. Families operate this way.

The Japanese commentator Shichihei Yamamoto has pointed out that this distinction is much less clear in Japan. I believe he is right when he says, "[in Japan] a functional group can only begin to function once it has become a community, and any group that is forced by circumstances to assume a function quickly turns into a community."[6] A business or committee, which in the West would simply be a number of people assembled for a specific purpose, would, in Japan, turn into something Yamamoto calls a virtual blood-kin group.[7] If it did not take on this flavor, nothing would get done.

When a worker joins a company, he must be trained to become a member of the family before he can function effectively. Thus, as Yamamoto explains, "It is improper under any circumstances to fire an employee from the company seen as a functional group. The only exception to this rule is the expulsion of an employee who has besmirched the good name of the company seen as a community.

"In this case, it is his expulsion from the community that results in his being fired from his job, and not the other way around."[8]

This is reminiscent of *mura hachibu*. The Japanese villager would not be expelled from the community for anything so general as breaking the law. It would be for violating the community spirit that he could be ostracized.

The "family" character of Japanese organizations is well known. The ideal relationship between superior and subordinate is one that most closely resembles that of parent and child.[9] "The workplace is no exception," writes a Japanese scholar. "The boss is 'Dad' and a trusted lieutenant is 'his better half.'" More experienced colleagues are "older brothers," and to the middle-aged men who run the company, young female employees are "our cute daughters."[10]

In a burst of affection over after-hours drinks a young Japanese worker may call his kindly boss *otōsan* ("father"). For both men, this is as it should be: One has found a concerned protector who will look after his interests both on and off the job; the other takes satisfaction in his role as guide and mentor and is flattered by the younger man's loyalty.

Family analogies occur in the Western corporate world as well. A company that establishes smaller companies in which it has a controlling interest is called a parent company. The Japanese not only use the term "parent company" but refer to the resulting subsidiaries as "child companies."

The most extreme form of surrogate family group identity is found in underworld gangs, whose members pride themselves on being the only modern Japanese to keep alive the spirit of the samurai. Crime bosses are called *oyabun* ("parent figure"), and their henchmen are *kobun* ("child figures"). *Kobun* are supposed to be ready to lay down their lives for their *oyabun* or to mutilate themselves in atonement for any violation of the code of loyalty.

Loyalty, once given, is for life. The word for the passion a *kobun* feels for his *oyabun* is *horeru*, the same word used to describe erotic love betwen men and women. In return for his *kobun*'s love and loyalty, the *oyabun* is sworn to care for and look after his dependents, just as a father would cherish his sons.

In the arts as well, loyalty to one's teacher is so great that it would be an insulting breach of etiquette to seek additional instruction from a different master or a different school. It would be like chucking one father and taking up with another. The same feelings, to a lesser degree, are found in other groups. Loyalty is personal and durable and frequently translates into very effective group performance. Many groups in Japan elicit the same gung ho enthusiasm found in the West only in athletic teams or crack military units.

It is not just Westerners who have been struck by the Japanese ability to work together. The Koreans, who have had more than enough reason to brood over the Japanese national character, have a quaint way of describing it. One on one, they say, a Korean can whip a Japanese every time, but pit three Japanese against three Koreans and the Japanese are sure to win.

Japanese group consciousness results in a sense of collective responsibility that is alien to Westerners. If a family member commits a serious crime or causes a scandal, the rest of the family may suffer the modern equivalent of *mura hachibu* and be deserted by all their friends. In the late summer of 1981 a Japanese was arrested in the Philippines after having fled Japan in the wake of a spectacular bank swindle. The fact that the criminal was young, a woman, and pretty guaranteed loads of media coverage. As a result, her parents were viciously snubbed by their community, and her father soon died—of mortification, it was reported.

Back in the 1970s, when Japan's radical Red Army Faction was throwing bombs and hijacking airplanes, at least one parent was driven to suicide by remorse and social stigma. Japanese feel more responsible than Westerners for the behavior of family or group members and, by the same token, are held responsible by society. Americans have a more individual sense of responsibility. John Hinckley's parents were grieved by their son's behavior, but they were not ostracized by their community or deserted by their friends.

Individuals have an equally excessive sense of shared responsibility with their virtual blood-kin groups. A few years ago prestigious Keiō University was pilloried in the news because of a scandal involving the advance sale of entrance exam questions. While the bad publicity was raging, Keiō professors dropped their usual proud style and started slinking around the campus as if each were directly to blame for the scandal.[11]

This is the attitude that Japanese expect from group members, and a case involving the Mitsui industrial group was no exception. In 1980 and 1981 it began to look as though a huge petrochemical complex it had started with the Iranian government might never be completed. The Khomeini revolution, the Iran-Iraq War, and other misfortunes had bedeviled the project from the start. The group had hundreds of millions of dollars tied up in the complex and appealed to the Japanese government for a partial bailout.

When Mitsui and the government finally began dickering over terms, Mitsui employees started getting phone calls at home from angry strangers denouncing the company's recourse to taxpayer money. Even the children of employees were sneered at by schoolmates. In America the Chrysler Corporation was actually granted more than $1 billion in government loan guarantees, but I have never heard of private employees' being taken to task for risking the loss of taxpayer dollars.

In 1975, when it was revealed in U.S. congressional hearings that the Lockheed Corporation had been bribing Japanese airline executives in order to make sales, the Japanese investigation into the affair was almost as much a media event as Watergate was in America. Lockheed's sales agent, the Marubeni Corporation, was implicated in the payoffs and suffered as a result. Several municipal and prefectural governments suspended contract talks with the tarnished company, and the city of Sapporo decided that Marubeni was no longer fit to act as contractor to build its subway. The people who build subways have nothing to do with the people who sell airplanes, but they all were guilty by association.

Lockheed, of course, did not escape the wrath of the Japanese. At the height of the scandal, the widows of two Air Self-Defense Force pilots killed when their Lockheed-built F-104 fighters crashed announced they were suing Lockheed. One claimed, absurdly, that her husband had died as "a victim of graft."[12]

The affair taught the Japanese that American employees do not have the same kind of personal identification with the firm that they do. A newsman sent to visit Lockheed installations at the height of the hysteria was amazed to find that employees did not show the slightest sign of embarrassment about the case.[13] The reporter expected even low-level employees to share the shame of the "family." He didn't realize that there is no such thing as a Lockheed community in the sense that there is a Mitsui or a Marubeni community.

In Japan identification with the group is so strong that it may sometimes outlive its usefulness. Corporate mergers, for example, are very delicate operations. In 1971 the Dai-Ichi Bank and the Kangyō Bank merged to form the Dai-Ichi Kangyō Bank, Japan's largest. A decade later loyalties to the original banks are still so strong that management must go to great lengths to see that power appears to be shared equally between former Dai-Ichi men and former Kangyō men. If the chairman of the board is from one bank, the vice-chairman must be from the other. If the manager of the prestigious London branch is a Kangyō man, the New York branch manager must be a Dai-Ichi man, and so on down the line.

One young employee told me, "When I joined the bank not long after the merger, there was real tension in the air. You had to be careful not to get too chummy with the Kangyō men, or the Dai-Ichi men might not like it. Now there are ten years' worth of new employees who joined after the merger who obviously don't have any former loyalty, but the higher-ups still haven't forgotten where they came from. There's still some animosity. But if you think it's bad at Dai-Ichi Kangyō, I hear they're still at daggers drawn over at Taiyō Kobe." Taiyō Kobe Bank, which merged a few years after Dai-Ichi Kangyō Bank, is a competitor.

Another notable merger was that of the Mitsui Shipping Line and the OSK Line. It was a foregone conclusion that the name of the new company would contain the names of the two original companies, but there was a serious wrangle over which name would come first. A compromise was finally reached: The company's name would be Mitsui OSK Line in English but OSK Mitsui Line in Japanese!

In cases like these, each original company has established itself as something approaching a blood-kin group as well as a functional group. It is not easy suddenly to expand that family devotion to take in a large number of strangers, all of whom have a competing sense of devotion to their own group.

At its best the Japanese sense of group identification can be credited for the country's remarkably low crime rate. In any other society Tokyo would surely be a terrifying, dangerous place. It has grown rapidly since the end of the war, and with a population of more than 10 million, it is one of the most densely populated cities in the world. It grew largely because of wave after wave of newcomers from the countryside, who left home to find work in the capital. This rootless labor force should have been ripe for the alienation and frustration that lead to urban crime. It was not. Burglary is a rare event in Tokyo, and muggings are virtually unheard of. Unescorted women can walk freely at all hours of the night in practically every neighborhood.

Collective responsibility keeps Japan safe. Even when they leave their families behind in the countryside, Japanese who come to the big city soon establish close ties with new groups, usually at work. They have learned from childhood that a member's disgrace is shared by all. Criminal behavior will not only result in exclusion from the group but also cover the whole group with shame. Thus the group has strong reasons to prevent its members from misbehaving because it will share in the disgrace. At the same time the individual is reluctant to risk personal disgrace because he knows that the entire group will suffer. These two forces seem to be strong enough to keep Japan's murder rate at one-sixth, and its larceny rate at one nine-hundredth, of the equivalent rates for the United States.

When a Japanese is arrested by the police and marched off to headquarters, he is likely to hide his face in his hands or pull his shirt over his head in shame. If the crime is important enough to bring out the news- and cameramen, the criminal will almost invariably hide his face. He is shamed in the eyes of society, and his shame will be shared by any group of which he is a part.

The group that shares in its members' shame also takes credit for their success. At home or on the job the group counts for more than the individual. Matasaburō Maeda, who designs automobiles for Mazda, points out that there are no prima donna designers in his company. "In Japan we don't generally produce such extremely talented people," he explains modestly. "We have, instead, many individuals who have reasonable capacity. Based on this reality, teamwork makes quite good sense."[14] Even newspapers, which Americans think of as dependent on each reporter's pluck and initiative, rarely run by-lines. Attributing articles to individuals would violate the principle that the group as a whole is responsible for success.

In the group, no one may stand out too far. Even what is clearly the success of an individual must always be described as *okagesama-de*, or thanks to the help of the others. This is a requirement that annoys Westerners. "I got awfully tired of *okagesama-de*," says an American woman who lived for several years in Japan. "Sometimes things clearly got done because *I* had made them happen, but that didn't mean I could take the credit—it was always *okagesama-de*."

The same phrase has another common use that throws light on how the Japanese view the individual. It is the stock reply to an inquiry about one's health and means, "Thanks to you, and the gods, and everybody else, I am in good health." At some abstract level Japanese even share responsibility for whether they are sick or healthy! To Westerners, this kind of thinking seems to ignore the boundaries between individuals.

The Japanese have a loose attitude toward intellectual property that seems to reflect this dim notion of where you end and I begin. Westerners think of a person's ideas as valuable assets and have set up elaborate copyright and patent laws to protect them. When American scholars refer to the work of others, they take pains to cite their sources correctly. Japanese scholars appropriate each other's ideas without so much as an attribution or a second thought. They rarely footnote and, when they do, almost never include a page reference.

I know an American who worked for an English-language publishing house in Tokyo, whose job was sometimes complicated by this problem. "We once did an English translation of a book on Middle Eastern art by a famous *sensei*," she says. "We had given the text to a very capable translator who read some standard English-language works on the subject as background for the job. She was shocked to find that the distinguished *sensei* had lifted whole chunks out of these books without a line of attribution. Believe me," she says, "the English version had a few footnotes by the time we were through with it."

My friend George runs a small consulting firm and has worked with several Japanese companies. He points out that one of the problems in getting new business is that before a customer signs a consulting contract, he must be convinced that the consultant can deliver the goods. Sometimes the only way George can convince a customer is by explaining his approach and some of his insights beforehand.

"Americans understand that," he adds. "They know that they haven't paid for that information yet and that it isn't really theirs. If they like what they hear, they'll sign you up for the job."

The Japanese apparently behave differently. "They don't have the same view that ideas are valuable and should be paid for," says George. "They will pump me for as much information as they can and then say, 'No, thanks. We're not signing.'"

I do not think that the Japanese are being sneaky. I think they just don't have the typically Western notion—perhaps exaggerated—of the individual origin of ideas.

Photo images are sometimes treated with the same nonchalance as intellectual property. Japanese laws governing the commercial use of photographs are much less strict than in the United States. Clearances are seldom required, and private citizens may find their pictures in a magazine without warning or compensation. Neither privacy nor individual contributions have much place in a context of collective responsibility.

One of the worst by-products of intense group consciousness is an exaggerated sense of "we" versus "they." People outside the family—whether real or surrogate—are *tanin* ("outsiders"), the opposite of *nakama*. As foreigners have discovered to their surprise, Japanese who can be elaborately polite with friends and *nakama* can be recklessly rude to *tanin*. "The Japanese have two faces, like Jekyll and Hyde when it comes to distinguishing between *nakama* and *tanin*," writes a Japanese scholar.[15] This is what gives rise to the question in the title of a recent *Wall Street Journal* article, "Are the Japanese the Rudest People or the Most Polite?"[16] The answer is that they are both, depending on whether they are dealing with *nakama* or *tanin*.

What often makes Japan a delight for travelers is the Japanese attitude toward customers. Customers are temporary *nakama*. The very word for "customer"—*okyaku-san*—means "guest," and patrons of hotels or restaurants are usually treated with impeccable courtesy. However, once this artificial relationship comes to an end, and one faces the Japanese behind the wheels of private cars or as part of an anonymous crowd, they switch into their Hyde personality. Japanese drivers from north to south have the graciousness of New York City cabbies, and the larger the vehicle they drive, the more aggressive they are. Truck drivers, who in America are often the gentlest drivers on the road, are the most ferocious in Japan.

Bus, train, and subway crowds bring out some of the worst Japanese behavior. Pushing, elbowing, and cutting into line are all normal crowd behavior. On the sidewalk two people have to slam right into each other before they will acknowledge a collision. Japanese who travel abroad are surprised at the behavior of Western crowds, where the slightest brush between two people can bring a simultaneous "excuse me." One writer laments over the "giant, wordless human moles" that burrow their way through a packed subway car to reach the door. "Why can't they say, 'Getting off, please'?" he asks, rather than grimly muscle their way out of the car.[17] I believe it is because anonymous subway riders are simple *tanin* to whom it is useless to speak and who can be elbowed with impunity.

The Japanese proverb *Tabi no haji wa kakisute* roughly translates as "The traveler's shame can be brushed off." All people away from home are tempted by indiscretions they wouldn't normally dream of, but the Japanese are more tempted than others. Foreigners, after all, are the ultimate *tanin*. Japanese atrocities committed in Asia during the war were partly explained by this attitude, and the leering men who fly off on sex tours seem to brush off their shame without a trace.

Back home, there used to be clear evidence of traveler's license in the piles of garbage the Japanese would fling about, especially at famous tourist sites. A national cleanup campaign seems to have entirely cured this habit, but resident foreigners wait in vain for a national campaign to promote decent behavior on subways.

The powerful Japanese sense of "we" versus "they" hampers the development of the secondhand business. Japanese have a visceral dislike for goods that still have the "dirt" of strangers on them. Thus Japan's castoff clothing and furniture end up in the trash barrel rather than at the thrift shop. Tokyo trash is a bonanza for impecunious foreigners, who may furnish an entire apartment with *objets trouvés*. For similar reasons, public libraries have never been popular in Japan. The Japanese are voracious readers but far prefer to buy their own copy rather than paw the pages of a book soiled by strange hands. Few libraries even have a subject index, and every year the average

American borrows eight times as many library books as the average Japanese.[18]

A Japanese graduate student at an American university told me of his surprise at finding common washing machines in the basement of his apartment building. "At first I had to get used to the idea of doing my wash in the same machines as everyone else," he told me, "but it soon made perfect sense. It now seems ridiculous to me that Japanese apartment dwellers all seem to feel they have to have their own, tiny, personal washing machine. It's a great waste." Needless to say, laundromats have never been a success in Japan, where people either do their own washing at home or send it out to professionals. There is no telling how much anonymous dirt might be floating around a laundromat.

The intensity with which Japanese distinguish their *nakama* from the rest of society has important implications for their conception of morality. Ruth Benedict is justly famous for characterizing Japan as a shame culture as opposed to the guilt cultures of the Christian West. The distinction she drew in 1946 still rings true.

She argued that in Japan morality is a function of the demands of the group, that the Japanese are so attuned to the opinions of others that shame is the strongest psychological sanction and the key to morality. She contrasted this with Western culture, in which each individual absorbs universal, usually religious principles which become a person's conscience. Thus Westerners can feel guilty for having violated a universal principle, even if no one else knows of the violation. Shame, on the other hand, requires an audience. Benedict, therefore, held that the Japanese need the group and its sanctions in order to feel they have done right or wrong. Westerners carry around their consciences and their universal principles wherever they go, but Japanese morality is more fluid and dependent on context.[19]

Benedict was, of course, simplifying in order to make a point, and her clear dichotomy was probably more accurate of both cultures thirty-five years ago than it is today. In the meantime, the voice of Western conscience has lost some of its authority and the Japanese are moving toward a more personal and independent sense of morality. Nevertheless, the distinction between guilt and shame cultures is useful in understanding the Japanese.

Shame can be an important social sanction because Japanese are deeply concerned about the opinions and feelings of others. The interpersonal sensitivity that is necessary for smooth behavior within the group leaves the Japanese vulnerable to the threat of shame. Universal principles, on the other hand, do not allow enough room for human relations. Japanese may thus sacrifice abstract morality in order to preserve close group ties. As a former American ambassador to Japan puts it: ". . . the Japanese on the whole do think less in terms of abstract ethical principles than do Westerners and more in terms of concrete situations and complex human feelings. To the Westerner the Japanese may seem weak or even lacking in principles; to the Japanese the Westerner may seem harsh and self-righteous in his judgments and lacking in human feelings."[20] It is shame, based on human feelings, that replaces abstract principles.

Another writer notes that the Japanese language has eleven different words to describe different kinds of shame.[21] He also points out that the most common word that means to feel shame—*hajiru*—comes from the word *hazure*, which means "detached," "out of line," or "contrary."[22] Shame comes from being out of step with the group, and *nakama-hazure*, or falling out with one's group, is both lonely and shameful.

The nature of apology reflects the importance of shame. The Japanese apologize not necessarily because they have done something evil in itself but because they have violated the norms of the group. An apology is thus a plea to be spared the worst possible punishment: expulsion. It is a request that one's shame be overlooked, that one be readmitted to one's *nakama*.[23] ". . . the goodwill of the group comes first, and truth or justice only afterward," says a Japanese professor.[24]

This kind of thinking makes it difficult to get to the bottom of corporate or political scandals because very few people will come forward to betray the group. During the war crimes trials conducted by the American occupation forces, lower-ranking soldiers almost never tried to blame their superiors. To the consternation of American prosecutors, they often took the blame so that their superiors might be let off. When they could not plausibly take on their superiors' guilt, soldiers simply refused to cooperate in identifying those responsible for atrocities. No matter how abominably the military had behaved, each soldier's responsibility was to its group; its honor and reputation came before morality.

The honor of the group was the paramount concern for the defendants during investigations into what the Japanese call the Lockheed scandal. When the U.S. Congress looked into Lockheed's unsavory overseas business practices, it discovered that All Nippon Airways (ANA) was one of the companies that were offered fat kickbacks in return for buying Lockheed equipment.

The Japanese authorities immediately undertook their own investigation, which involved testimony by a number of ANA executives. As the story began to unfold, it became clear that several were lying through their teeth in order to conceal ANA's wrongdoing. In particular, the president of the company, Tokuji Wakasa, stoutly denied ANA's involvement, even in the face of overwhelming evidence. However, his behavior was by no means universally condemned. His unflinching loyalty to the group and his readiness to commit perjury in order to protect its good name won the grudging respect of many Japanese.

Although Wakasa was eventually convicted of perjury and violation of foreign exchange laws, his judges officially recognized the parallel morality of his behavior. In passing sentence on him, the court stated: ". . . we recognize the main motive [for the defendant's false testimony] as an attempt to protect the honor and trust of All Nippon Airways. . . . We cannot help but understand that notwithstanding the impropriety of his actions, the defendant's feelings were such as to make it very difficult to speak the truth while under the public scrutiny of the nation. These factors must be considered in a manner favorable to the defendant."[25] Wakasa received a suspended sentence. American courts also take notice of extenuating circumstances, but a defendant's illegal attempts to protect the honor of his group would certainly not win the same sympathy as in Japan.

Whenever there is a spectacular scandal in the United States, insiders practically race each other to the publishers with books on the inside dope—even if it means staining the reputations of the group or of their superiors. Nothing would seem more shameful to the Japanese. When former Prime Minister Tanaka was investigated for suspected involvement in the Lockheed affair, his chaffeur committed suicide rather than admit to investigators where he had driven the boss on certain crucial days. In Japan anyone who goes public about a scandal within the group is "a great criminal."[26] I doubt that any of the Japanese involved in what is known as the IBM scandal will ever act in a way to implicate the senior management of their companies, even if it means that they must take the blame themselves. They are even less likely to rush into print with the inside story.

The bonds of the group and the flexibility of principles that may be required to meet its changing demands are well illustrated by the saga of Lieutenant Hirō Onoda. Onoda was a Japanese soldier in the Second World War who was in the Philippine jungle at the time of Japan's surrender. According to the morality of the time, surrender was the most shameful thing a soldier could do. When he left for the front in 1944, his mother reportedly said to him, "When you die, die gloriously. The worst thing you could do to me is to let yourself be captured. You will serve the emperor by dying gloriously for your country."[27]

Although most Japanese soldiers did give themselves up when they learned the war had been lost, Onoda, and many like him, decided to obey their final orders to fight on until death. Inevitably many lost their resolve, and during the rest of the 1940s, the '50s, and early '60s, Japanese soldiers continued to trickle out of the jungles of Asia. Onoda was at war until 1974—*at war*, not just camping out. In 1972 he lost his last comrade, Corporal Kinshichi Ozuka, in an ambush on Filipinos. Onoda was finally tracked down by a Japanese tourist but refused to leave his post until ordered to do so by a military commander. The Japanese Air Self-Defense Force had to fly an officer down to the Philippines to relieve him officially of his previous orders. Only then would Onoda return to an astonished Japan.

Back home, Onoda was like a ghost from the past. His military bearing and deep reverence for the emperor seemed impossibly antique to the Japanese of the seventies. But to the surprise of his countryman, this man, who had carried on the war in the Pacific for twenty-nine years, melted quickly into the patterns of contemporary Japanese life. Some even ridiculed his transformation. But for more thoughtful Japanese, his actions were to be expected. The wartime group of which he was a part no longer existed. He had upheld the ideals of that group until ordered to abandon them. Once so ordered, he left those ideals behind in the Philippine jungle. He adopted the morality of the new group.

As one Japanese author points out, the entire nation gave up those old ideals when ordered by the emperor to lay down its arms. Onoda was only doing twenty-nine years later what the rest of the nation had done in 1945.[28] When the group that upheld a certain kind of behavior was discredited, that behavior disappeared.

Japanese student radicals went through a similar transformation. Successive generations of chanting, helmeted activists carried the fight against business and the conservative government well into the seventies. However, as each class of students was graduated, its members cut their hair, bought suits, and turned over a new leaf. They proceeded to devote themselves to the corporate world just as ardently as they had attacked it. This kind of conversion was so dependable that it became something of a standing joke to the Japanese.

A great many of the student radicals in the West also ended up "selling out" to the establishment. However, for them it was often the result of a long, psychologically wrenching journey that took them to communes and public interest groups before finally setting them down on Wall Street. Abbie Hoffman spent six years in the wilderness before he went straight and turned himself in. For the Japanese, it seems to have been a less individual and soul-searching process. They quickly left behind one group and its values to embrace the next.

Japanese emigrants to the United States have also shown the same adaptability to the demands of a new environment. Once they decided to transfer their loyalties, they fled the shelter of their sense of uniqueness and opened their souls to a new way of life. For the most part, they absorbed the values of their new homeland more quickly and thoroughly than other immigrant groups. They left behind their culture, their religion, and their language and deliberately made a clean start. This ability to become wholehearted Americans, without constantly looking over their shoulders to the mother country, has certainly helped make them one of the wealthiest, most successful ethnic groups in the country.

Japanese affiliations show another kind of flexibility: they can expand to include former competitors whenever a general threat appears. As in any society, former antagonists join forces if their common interests are at stake. Group affiliations quickly expand in concentric circles from one's officemates (nakama) to the corporate division, to the company as a whole, to the industrial group, to the whole economy, and finally to the nation itself.

If the threat comes from beyond their borders, the Japanese are particularly quick to drop internal differences and close ranks. In late 1981 it was perfectly normal for the Japanese steel companies to come together like old friends and screw the lowest possible price out of Australian ore producers. They showed a remarkable degree of cooperation that American steel companies rarely approach in their campaigns to keep foreign steel out of the United States.

Japanese auto companies that battle over domestic market share cooperate admirably when it comes to pressing the Ministry of Foreign Affairs to argue the merits of free trade to the Europeans and the Americans. In such cases, loyalty to the company becomes loyalty to the industry, which quickly becomes loyalty to Japan.

In fact, the Japanese group consciousness that foreigners are most often aware of is this affiliation with the largest meaningful group, which is the nation. Foreigners quickly get wind of this instinct for national solidarity and soon discover how intensely nationalistic the Japanese are.

Curiously, Japanese do not think of themselves as nationalistic or patriotic at all, and superficially they appear not to be. American flags dot the U.S. landscape, but in Japan flags are a rare sight. On national holidays the red and white may flutter over public buildings, but private citizens almost never fly the flag. Japan has no equivalent of the American pledge of allegiance. The Japanese probably like to sing more than any other people on earth, but they have no popular patriotic songs like "America the Beautiful" or "My Country 'Tis of Thee." They do have a national anthem, which is sung before baseball games and at the beginning of professional sumo wrestling tournaments. However, until recently it was almost never sung otherwise, and many Japanese children thought the song had something to do with sports.

Before the war the Japanese used to celebrate Empire Day as a patriotic holiday, but the American occupation abolished it. Thus for twenty years Japan had no "national day," like France's Bastille Day, our Fourth of July, or the independence day that other former colonies celebrate. In 1966 the government finally filled that gap by resurrecting Empire Day and renaming it National Foundation Day. Celebrated on February 11, it commemorates the first mythical emperor's accession to the throne in 660 B.C. It is a very small-scale holiday; hardly anyone thinks of it as anything more than a day off.

There are two reasons why the Japanese do not wave the flag. The first is that strident patriotism was the hallmark of Japan's wartime chauvinism. Many older Japanese have an instinctive revulsion for nationalistic symbols of any kind. The other reason is that they do not need rousing patriotic paraphernalia. Nothing could be more obvious to them than the fact that they are Japanese, not Chinese, Koreans, or Hottentots. Being Japanese is as natural as breathing. There is no need to shout about it.

By contrast, the United States is a nation of great diversity and centrifugal loyalties; it needs the flag and other national symbols. The same is true of the Soviet Union and many other European countries. The new nations of Africa and Asia are painfully trying to overcome tribal and ethnic divisions by stressing national unity. Japan can do without all that. Its sense of national cohesion is a built-in extension of group loyalty.

With loyalty to the national group comes a broad and touching sense of responsibility. A few years ago an American journalist wrote: "If the theft of a camera from an alien is reported in the newspapers, the amazed foreigner may find himself presented with several replacements by Japanese who are complete strangers but who feel that the stain caused to the community reputation must be erased."[29] Even a thief is part of the national group; his actions implicate all Japanese.

This sense of the group is a potent source of nationalism. When the Japanese find themselves face-to-face with other nations, they discover how profoundly patriotic they are. During the years of extraordinary GNP growth the Japanese were bursting with pride as they pulled ahead of one European economy after another. Japanese eyes are the first to moisten when they see their flag rise over an Olympic medalist.

As a businessman I used to capitalize on this latent patriotism that can take the Japanese by surprise. Whenever an important customer called on my company's headquarters, I found that it was good tactics to fly a Japanese flag in front of the building. If the visitor was not a frequent traveler and was not comfortable in America, the flag could make a huge impression. Some guests nearly embraced me with the joy of seeing their flag, and others made a point of having their picture taken with the flag in the background. It was an overwhelmingly favorable way to begin a business discussion.

The Japanese sense of national solidarity flows naturally from a sense of national uniqueness. The resulting capacity of the Japanese to pull together in the interests of the nation is probably one of its greatest strengths. The nation's postwar achievements now win our admiration, but its prewar record is just as impressive. Between the two world wars Japan increased its manufacturing output sixfold, while the United States grew only by about two-thirds. Nor was Japan starting from a dead stop. In 1905 it already had the industrial might to thrash the Russians.

Japan's first modern leaders could never have put through the *fukoku kyōhei* ("rich nation, strong military") program with such speed and success had the people not been willing to set aside their differences and put their shoulders to the same wheel. If postwar Japan has an equivalent motto, it is *Oitsuke, oikose* ("Catch up and pass [the West]"). The Japanese are vividly aware of their destiny as a national group and have worked like slaves to bridge the gap between Japan and the other advanced nations. "There are probably no other people in the world who are so well trained in group thought and behavior as today's Japanese," writes one observer. "They link their fate to that of the nation, the corporation, or the group and therein find a peculiarly Japanese reason for living."[30] A sense of national destiny is nothing more than group consciousness writ large.

The Pacific war was, of course, the most terrifying manifestation of Japan's sense of destiny and of the ability of its people to band together against the outside. The nation was one great underworld gang, with the emperor as its *oyabun*. Millions of *kobun* died for their *oyabun*, and none so proudly or with a greater sense of fulfillment as the kamikaze pilots. The *kobun* were getting ready to defend their turf with sharpened bamboo sticks when the *oyabun* finally ordered them to surrender.

Every nation rises to the supreme challenge when its very existence is threatened, but Japan is able to enter the psychological state of war even in times of peace. In spite of their awesome successes, the Japanese still have not freed themselves from the gnawing fear that destruction may be just around the corner.

"We Japanese," a trading company executive once told me, "have a crisis consciousness that keeps us going full tilt all the time. I don't know where it comes from; but we have it, and you Americans don't."

"You gave us a nasty crisis at Pearl Harbor," I pointed out.

"Exactly," he said. "And look at what an aroused America was able to do. Since the war America has gotten fat and lazy, while Japan has stayed lean and anxious."

A former Japanese politician writes of Japan's "hunger mentality," which he sees as the driving force behind 100 years of Japanese progress.[31] I believe Japan's sense of crisis carries back at least to the thirteenth century, when the Mongols assembled a gigantic fleet to invade Japan. Doom seemed certain until, at the last moment, the Japanese were saved by a great storm that destroyed the Mongol fleet. This was the original kamikaze ("divine wind"), from which the suicide pilots took their name. The Japanese were convinced that no human power could save them.

Although the attempted invasion took place 700 years ago, the terror of that event is seared into the national memory. Isshō Yada, the nineteenth-century artist, devoted his entire career to painting scenes from the invasion. The town in southwestern Japan where the Mongols actually landed has celebrated the great victory every 50 years. Since that time only America has stamped the sacred soil of Japan with the invader's boot.

It was fear, as well as a sense of uniqueness, that drove the Japanese to seal off their country from the rest of the world in the seventeenth century. When Japan was brought face-to-face with the power of the Occident in 1853, the temples of the capital were filled with people praying for another divine wind. Japan subsequently modernized with a haste born of fear. With so many willing colonizers waiting in the wings, the nation's independence was at stake. After the devastation of the Second World War Japan bent the same survivalist zeal to the task of reconstruction.

Even today many Japanese have a dark sense of foreboding about their country's dependence on imported resources. Before the war schoolchildren were taught that the necessary elements of a great nation were lots of land, rich resources, and a bountiful agriculture. Japan had none of these, so went out and seized them. Now it is back where it started, a small country without resources that cannot feed itself. Japanese sometimes joke about how they are not interested in running Manchuria anymore.

"What we'd really like," they add with a smile, "is California."

Japan's natural poverty makes it uncomfortably dependent on trade and on the stable international relations that permit trade. The Japanese would starve without trade, for America alone grows more food for Japan than the Japanese grow for themselves. Trade war would seriously inconvenience the United States, but it could destroy Japan.

Japan has always had a demon's pantheon of forces beyond human control, and trade war is only the newest member. The bombings of Hiroshima and Nagasaki ushered in nuclear holocaust as a new menace to Japan's existence, but the traditional threats were foreign invasion and natural disaster. For generations the Japanese built houses of sticks and straw which could be thrown up again in a week after an earthquake or typhoon. The city of Tokyo conducts serious earthquake drills in the hope of limiting the damage should the great Kantō quake of 1923 repeat itself.

Japan's major insurance companies maintain enormous unused lines of credit with foreign banks for fear that some great catastrophe might strike Japan and force them to pay out every policy on the books. This is not as superstitious as it sounds. One of every ten recorded earthquakes is felt in Japan, and in the summer of 1982 torrential rains and flooding killed several hundred people and left 32,000 homeless in southern Japan.

The 1973–74 oil crisis thus evoked centuries-old fears and inspired new visions of catastrophe. Apocalyptic movies and novels flooded the market. They foretold the destruction of Japan by trade war, tidal wave, earthquake, nuclear war, or the usual monsters from space. This craze has died down, but the sense of vulnerability remains. Many of the dangers that menace the Japanese cannot be foreseen or controlled, but any that can be defused through human effort are attacked head-on.

In the common struggle against the forces that threaten Japan, each individual is first of all a Japanese, and Japan has had little experience with citizens who shirk their duty. This is why Okamoto's senseless killings at Lod Airport so shocked the Japanese. Americans are more used to seeing their fellow citizens behave in divisive, even repulsive ways. Their ties to the group are weaker, and their norms of behavior less rigid. If an American commits a shameful crime against foreigners, it is regrettable, to be sure, but Americans do not feel as though the nation's name has been dragged through the mud. A deviant who massacres innocent passersby is a madman first and a citizen of his country a distant second.

For the Japanese, Okamoto was first of all a Japanese. He was "one of us," and his act implicated all Japanese. This we/they split can result in remarkably decent behavior, such as the unsolicited compensation of the victims' families or the gift of a camera from a stranger. But it also shows the sharp distinctions Japan draws between itself and the rest of the world. Though it may be meanspirited to say so, restitution to foreigners stems from the same corner of the Japanese mind as the Rape of Nanking. In 1937 Japanese troops could slaughter hundreds of thousands of civilians because they were not Japanese, not members of the national group. Forty years later the Japanese government generously made amends for the actions of one of its citizens, once again because the victims were not Japanese. The two events were mirror-image opposites, but both reflect the same reality: an abiding sense of separateness from all other peoples.

Thanks to Okamoto, all Japanese suddenly felt their national affiliation with uncharacteristic intensity. But group affiliation in Japan ends at the nation's borders. It does not go on to embrace mankind as a whole.

Japan's consciousness of itself has a dark, exclusive side that occasionally hits an individual with the full force of its ugliness. An American friend named Ellen once told me about her experience as an exchange student in Japan. She arrived hardly knowing a word of Japanese and lived with a Japanese family for a year. During that time she made rapid progress in Japanese and was received like a daughter into the bosom of her adopted home.

"Near the end of my stay," she says, "the family sat me down for a little talk. They said to me, 'Ellen-san, it's been wonderful to have you with us. We've learned so much about America, and you've learned so much about Japan. We hope you will go back to America and be a bridge of understanding between our two countries. But one thing we must tell you: We would never forgive you if you married a Japanese. We would never forgive you for spoiling the purity of Japanese blood.'

"I was shocked," says Ellen. "I was flabbergasted. Maybe they thought that they had led me too deeply into Japanese life, that they had to draw the line somewhere. But my feelings for those people never recovered."

Japanese can exclude foreigners so casually that it almost seems second nature to them. A few years ago, in Japan, I remember hearing reports about an airplane that had crashed in South America. There were several Japanese surnames on the passenger list, and the media were following developments closely. A day or so later a television newsman reported that the victims were not Japanese, but Brazilians of Japanese descent. The nation immediately lost interest. Japanese-Brazilians may be racial brothers, but they have changed camps, committed national apostasy, and are no longer part of the group.

Japanese do not care very much about disasters that occur far from home or that do not have Japanese victims. Admittedly the Western press carries only pro forma accounts of Indian bus accidents or Mexican train wrecks. Nevertheless, it is a little subtler about its lack of concern than the Japanese are. When, in June 1975, an Eastern Airlines plane crashed at Kennedy Airport, killing 110 people, all three major Japanese dailies led with the headline "No Japanese on Board."[32]

Japanese realize perfectly well that their survival depends on peace and international cooperation, that the welfare of Japan depends on the welfare of the world. Yet the idea of solidarity with all peoples—admittedly a difficult concept for anyone—remains more remote for them than for other people. The Japanese have great difficulty showing enthusiasm for any group that stretches beyond the shores of Japan to include Turks, Malays, and Argentines.

The Japanese are in the world, but not of it. They are a people with an isolationist soul and an international economy, an insular clannishness and a worldwide impact. It is this paradox that a recent article in a well-known business magazine was wrestling with when it urged the Japanese to please join the human race.[33]

Edward Seidensticker was wrestling with the same problem in a column he wrote some years ago for one of Japan's English-language newspapers. He had been living in Japan for fifteen years and was a recognized expert on the country. He had finally decided to go home to America but found himself besieged by friends and acquaintances who wanted to know why. In his column he explained his decision: "The Japanese are just like other people . . . but no. They are not like other people. They are infinitely more clannish, insular, parochial, and one owes it to one's self-respect to preserve a feeling of outrage at the insularity. To have the sense of outrage go dull is to lose the will to communicate; and that, I think, is death. So I am going home."[34]

CHAPTER FOUR

❁

CONFORMITY

Perhaps the insular Japanese are particularly conscious of how different they are from foreigners because they are used to being so similar to each other. The shock of foreign diversity is heightened by uniformity at home.

There is a proverb that neatly summarizes the Japanese attitude toward individualism: *Deru kugi wa utareru* ("The nail that sticks out will be pounded down"). Japan is a dangerous place for standouts. Once I gently taunted a Japanese friend with this evidence of how much his country values conformity. He replied that he was sure there was a similar proverb in English which proved that Anglo-Saxons could be just as conformist as Japanese. I told him I couldn't think of any, but he promised to track one down.

When I saw him several days later, he smugly announced that he had found an English proverb that praised conformity. He took out a piece of paper and, to my amazement, wrote the words "The squeaky hinge gets the grease."

"Look at that," he said. "If an American squeaks and is different, he gets covered with grease. It's just like the Japanese nail that gets pounded down." My friend's triumph turned to chagrin as I explained that the two proverbs were exact opposites, that for the squeaking hinge, the grease is a symbol of reward, not punishment. Westerners think that there is everything to be gained by standing out, that by screaming loud enough, they may even reap undeserved rewards.

With uncharacteristic tact, I did not tell my friend that in the meantime, I, too, had found another proverb: *Kiji mo nakazuba utaremai* ("The pheasant that keeps silent escapes the hunter").

It is impossible, of course, to say which came first: a society that values conformity or institutions that encourage it. The two have grown up together, while Japan's isolation from cultural competition made it easy to hammer out rigid standards of behavior. Group and hierarchy write the rules for the Japanese: The group offers meaning and identification, while hierarchy within the group dictates proper behavior.

The resulting conformity is one of the most striking aspects of life in Japan. At home and in school Japanese children are taught to fit in rather than stand out, and the habits of intellectual submission that they learn as students follow them into adulthood. As consumers the Japanese are easy prey to fad and fashion and in all that they do are careful not to violate the dictates of proper form. Since they are so accustomed to the comfortable predictability of their homeland, they often band together in groups to brave the jolts and shocks of overseas travel. However, it is in the *nakama* group that the forces of conformity are strongest. The ties that bind a member to his group can also smother him.

As the Japanese become more familiar with how Westerners think and behave, many have begun to wonder if their groups have not robbed them of individuality and creativity. For increasing numbers of intellectuals, subordination to the group has ceased to be an unqualified virtue. The pages of recent *Nihonjin-ron* are spattered with the tears and torment of the individual's struggle for autonomy.

In Japan it is possible to distinguish between nationwide uniformity and the more immediate kind of conformity required by the *nakama* group. In addition to the pervasive sameness at the national level, small groups establish their own internal demands for sameness. Thus, even in the case of clearly opposed groups, such as warring political parties, the uniformity that may have disappeared at the aggregate level is replaced by predictable behavior at the group level. An opposition group is still a *group*, and its behavior may be as similar to the group it opposes as its views may be different. The lone wolf, the solitary battler of windmills, is very rare in Japan, and the word "individualism" itself has connotations of selfishness.

The institution that is probably most responsible for uniformity at the national level is the Japanese school system. Since the end of the nineteenth century, when it was patterned on the Prussian system, it has retained many of its authoritarian qualities. From the first grade through high school, it is a common, nationwide network directed from the Ministry of Education in Tokyo. The curriculum is thoroughly vetted by the ministry, and only officially approved textbooks may be used. There are a few private and parochial schools with slightly different curricula, but their numbers are insignificant. Consequently, through age eighteen practically all Japanese learn the same material, from the same textbooks, taught by teachers accredited by the same ministry.

In Japan schools are in full partnership with parents in rearing children. Teachers often shepherd the same class through several grades, so they can become close to their students over a period of years. For many Japanese, teachers are memorable, influential figures, with whom they stay in touch as adults.

Sensei's influence is so great partly because Japanese children are in school for many more days out of the year than American children. Japanese have a half day of classes every Saturday and at least a month less vacation each year. The academic year is also broken up differently, beginning in April and ending in March. This means that the longest school vacation—the summer holidays—occurs within school years, not between them. Teachers assign mountains of homework to do over the summer and don't expect their students to have forgotten anything when they come back in the fall. Children never get the sense of total release from schoolwork that makes summer so magical for Western children.

For many Japanese, their most vivid summer memory is of plowing through piles of homework. On Japanese television there is a word associations game show, in which the players try to help their teammates guess a specific word by giving them one-word clues. On one show the designated word was "homework." The player thought for a minute and then gave his clue: "Summer vacation." His teammate immediately answered, "Homework."

In school Japanese children are taught to conform rather than innovate. School uniforms—black for boys, navy blue for girls—are still required in the lower grades and, in some areas, are worn all through high school. Children carry their books in identical book bags and eat lunch out of identical lunch boxes. There are still many schools that require *nafuda* ("name tags") that specify grade and name.

An American friend once told me of the care with which her Japanese neighbor prepared his child for school in America. "The night before school opened," she told me, "he brought all of his daughter's school supplies over to my apartment for me to look at—notebooks, pencils, lunch box, everything. He wanted my assurance that everything was absolutely normal. He was worried that if he sent his daughter to school with some strange item, the other children would laugh at her."

Until recently left-handed school children in Japan were forced to write with their right hand, so as to be just like everyone else. Now teachers have been warned of the psychological damage this can do to a child, and the pressure to switch is not so strong as it used to be. However, since the schools can no longer be counted on to stamp out left-handedness, many parents take on the job themselves. For many Japanese, a southpaw is too glaring a deviant to have in the family.

The Japanese also keep all age-mates in the same grade. No matter how bright or how stupid, children never skip grades and are never held back. The group stays together. Children in the same grade cannot even be put in different classes according to ability. In the spring of 1982, when a junior high school in a Tokyo suburb tried to do that, it had to switch back to the old system after only a month. The parents complained that separate classes for the high and low achievers "hurt the children's feelings and fostered prejudice."[1]

When I was attending Japanese schools—admittedly sometime ago—insistence on sameness occasionally went to absurd lengths. My brother, who went to the same school and was always good at math, once amused himself by solving test problems in imaginative ways of his own devising. He never did it again. His answers were right, but his methods were wrong, so he lost credit for the problems. The way we arrived at the solution was as important as the right answer.

In those days a teacher's authority was absolute and discipline was strict. Grade school had something of a boot camp flavor to it. We all learned basic military commands like "ten-hut" or "right face," and we practiced precision drill on the playing field. By the time we graduated my class could do a very snappy column left.

Naturally we didn't act like little soldiers all the time. We cut up and carried on just like kids everywhere. But anytime a teacher wanted our attention, all he had to do was shout, *Kyotsuke!* ("Ten-hut"). What might have been a mob of screaming brats a split second earlier instantly became a group of very worried fourth graders standing stiffly at attention. If we disobeyed orders, we knew we could get whacked.

Japanese schools are no longer run as strictly as they were fifteen or twenty years ago. Physical punishment is dying out, and students aren't marched around in formation as much as they used to be. However, today's adults were educated with a firm hand, and parents who are nostalgic for the old days can always send their children to boarding school at Nissei Gakuen, in the Iga area of southern Japan. There 4,000 junior high and high school students get a strict, militaristic education that starts at four-thirty every morning. All twenty-four hours of the day are accounted for in a curriculum that includes ascetic exercises and physical conditioning. When the students go for their daily run, they run in groups and they run *in step*.

The school's motto is: "Do your best, train yourselves in utilizing every single moment, overcome your selfishness, respect your parents and teachers, observe good manners, obey regulations, and be the light of society."[2] Nissei Gakuen claims to be flooded with applications, no doubt for good reason. Its regimented approach is perfect preparation for Japan's notorious college entrance examinations.

These exams are the culmination of secondary education. Since Japan's national mania for ranking has clearly defined which are the best colleges, and since the best colleges practically guarantee access to the best jobs, competition for college entrance is ferocious. The battle fever to get into college cascades down to the lowest levels of the education system. Although grade schools and secondary schools teach the same curriculum, some are known to teach it better than others. Certain high schools have the best records of getting their graduates into the right colleges, and certain junior high schools manage to get more of their graduates into the right high schools, and so on down the line.

Local competition to get into these preferred schools can be just as grueling as the fight to get into college. In Japan there are now many high-powered kindergartens that have competitive entrance examinations. The rat race begins at age five! Some of these kindergartens have such a backlog of applicants that only a few children have a chance even to take the exam, much less be admitted. For the very best in preschool education, parents are advised to put in an application for their child *as soon as he is born*.

At every step of the way the less bright are sluiced out of the elite channel by an unending series of tests. By the time they reach high school students who want to go to college are so busy studying they have no time for anything else. Children who are really interested in sports, for example, end up going to vocational high schools that make no pretense of preparing students for college. Unfortunately for the rest, since college entrance exams demand a knowledge of facts rather than the ability to think, high school is one long cram session.

Many children trudge off to private coaching sessions after normal class hours for another go at the materials. These cram schools, or *juku*, are big business in Japan; once a few college aspirants started attending, all the rest had to go out of self-defense. Most *juku* are general college prep programs but some are meant to groom children for specific careers. One scholar describes a specialized medical cram school:

> This pre-doctor *juku* attempts not only to provide its charges with the knowledge it [sic] will need to pass the exams but also with the mannerisms appropriate to the profession. Thus, each day the young students, many of whom are still in primary school, wash their hands upon entrance to the *juku*, don white robes and a stethoscope, and proceed through a routine. . . . The typical *juku* session ends at eight in the evening with the young trainees tired and hungry, just as they can expect to be a few years later if they succeed in becoming interns at medical school.[3]

At *juku*, as in class, the emphasis is on brute memorization. What the teacher and the textbooks say is not to be doubted. Rather than formulate an opinion of their own, students look for the "right" opinion. There is no room for innovation or love of learning. Knowledge is a purely practical matter that should bring tangible rewards—namely, high test scores.

The final examination period in January and February is called examination hell. Every year it drives enough hapless students to suicide to give Japan one of the highest child suicide rates in the world.

Paradoxically, after the long, hard slog to get into college, the next four years are practically a vacation. Many students, even at the prestigious institutions, throw themselves into extracurricular activities and study as an afterthought. Professors are only incidentally available to the students and show little interest in their progress.

Tōdai (Tokyo University), direct descendant of the feudal period's Institute for the Study of Barbarian Books, is Japan's oldest university and unquestionably its most prestigious. Recently I spoke with one of the very few Westerners who have even attempted its grueling entrance exams. She told me that she nearly went out of her mind memorizing the answers to essay questions that might appear on the exam but, after a Herculean effort, passed her tests and was admitted to the graduate school.

"Once I was in," recalls Elizabeth, "my reaction was, 'My God, is this all it is? Is this what people are killing themselves for?' An American graduate school would have given me an education that was ten times better."

Her classwork was utterly undemanding. "All you had to do was show up. Period." She recalls one seminar, given by a famous professor, who handed each class over to a student to speak on any subject he liked. "The famous professor slept through every class," she adds. "He might as well have been a piece of furniture.

"At Tōdai," says Elizabeth, "there was no such thing as the free exchange of ideas you expect at an American university. The students were afraid to ask questions. They were afraid someone might ridicule them for not knowing the answer. They were Tōdai students and thought they had to know everything."

Elizabeth's professors were busy writing for slick publications and working as business consultants. "All they seemed to be interested in was making money," she says. "The students were their lowest priority. Only one of my professors even posted office hours, but that turned out to be a lie. I had to make an appointment three weeks in advance to see him."

Elizabeth spent five years at Tōdai, where she earned a master's degree and did most of the course work for a Ph.D. After she discovered how unchallenging her class work was, she took a full-time job with a Japanese company. Essentially Elizabeth attended Japan's top graduate school in her spare time. "And you *know* how hard they work you in a Japanese company," she adds.

If anything, undergraduate school at Tōdai is probably worse. One evening, over dinner with a businessman I knew to be a graduate, I asked him what he had majored in.

"Economics," he replied.

I had studied a little economics myself and was curious to know how it was taught at Tōdai. "What did they teach you?" I asked.

"What do you mean?"

"Did you study mostly macro or micro? What do they think of Marx at Tōdai?"

"Wouldn't you really rather hear about the glee club?" he said after a pause. "I never learned much of that stuff." I am not sure I believe this man learned as little as he claims. Still, it is hard to imagine an economics graduate from Harvard or Yale frankly admitting how little he remembers or even cares about the subject.

Most Japanese nonacademics seem to have retained only the vaguest notions of whatever they studied in college and have no interest in discussing it. Once I met a steelman who had studied French literature and was eager to talk about it, but he was a refreshing exception. For most Japanese, serious schoolwork ends in high school.

Oddly enough, the nation takes a benign view of its layabout college students. The period between examination hell and entry into that other great pressure cooker the corporation is the only chance many Japanese will have to relax until they retire. They can cut classes, sleep late, grow beards, or play Mah-Jongg all day. For many, this is the first time since age five that they don't have to put on a school uniform every morning. It may be their only chance to dabble in the arts, try a little political activism, or experiment with nonconformism. The Japanese speak of the "moratorium" of the college years, and all but the most determined goof-offs get their diploma. At graduation time the holiday is over, and former hippies join the corporate lockstep.

Americans who teach in Japanese colleges are disappointed by how little work their students are willing to do. They are also dismayed by the intellectual habits left over from high school. "They could learn all right," says a teacher who has returned to America, "but they couldn't think. They could take tests, but they couldn't write papers. I used to try to make them write essays; but their ideas were flabby, and they couldn't develop their opinions."

Another American who ran into the same problem told me how he once singled out a student for special praise. "The boy had written an original, insightful essay," he says, "and I asked him to read it out loud to the class. He got partway through and stopped; I couldn't make him read any further. After class he came up to me privately and told me he appreciated the praise but didn't want to be singled out again. 'I have to live in Japan,' he said." Japan is not an easy country for standouts. Originality and unpredictability are suspect traits, and being singled out from the crowd—even for praise—can be painful.

Recruits from Japanese colleges make good corporate soldiers; they enter the company without rough edges. They have gone through a relentless series of tests and eliminations that is perfectly designed to winnow out the brightest, most pliant young men in Japan and funnel them straight into government and business. They arrive with much the same body of knowledge and experiences and a proven ability to conform to the demands of an inflexible system. They are perfect material for on-the-job training and can be molded readily to fit the company image.

Graduate school is preparation only for an academic career. Japan has no such thing as a master's degree in business administration, and Japanese companies do not have the sprinkling of M.A.'s and Ph.D.'s in their ranks that American companies do. Thus, in most fields, Japanese college graduates bring to their jobs little more than the dusted-off remnants of a superintensive high school education—the same standardized package that emphasizes memorization rather than originality or synthesis.

Recently the Japanese education system has come under increasing criticism, and not just from Westerners who are used to something different.[4] Even the influential *Asahi* newspaper has written, "It is now clear to everyone that what has stopped our education system dead in its tracks is the scourge of conformity."[5]

Many Japanese also deplore the intense pressure and ugly competition that flourish in their schools. Even young children go to depressing lengths to trick and bring down their rivals. Recently a friend spoke to me of the damage he thought the system might be doing his child. The day before an important exam he overheard his grade-school son tell a playmate about a particularly good television show that was to be on that night. The son had no intention of disturbing his own study schedule but hoped that his rival would be tempted to watch the program rather than study.

There are other countries that have examination problems too. In France the *grandes écoles*, a handful of prestigious institutions, are outside the regular university system and are entered by competitive examination. However, the French have a disparaging expression for students who have their eye on a *grande école* and are always studying. They are *bêtes à concours* ("examination animals"). Japan brings up practically all its little boys to be examination animals before they mature into economic animals.

There is increasing concern among the Japanese over how grim their children's lives have become. What one reviewer calls "the biggest best-seller in postwar Japanese publishing history"[6] is a novel that is roundly critical of Japan's education system. The book, titled *Totto-chan, the Little Girl at the Window*,[7] throws a harsh light on Japan's present system by evoking the author's own remarkably liberal and individualistic education. The same reviewer concludes ". . . Japan's postwar educational system is a disaster. It, like the society which has supported it, is authoritarian to a degree unexampled in any non-totalitarian country."[8] More and more Japanese are beginning to agree.

There has long been talk of relieving the pressure on students and somehow doing away with examination hell. Nevertheless, exams have been an important rite of passage in Japan since before the war, and those who have already suffered through them would think less of their juniors if this obstacle to adulthood were removed.

There is another important reason why Japan has no way out of this system: Success and the route to success are too rigidly defined. A career in a ministry or in a topflight corporation is what all Japanese parents want for their sons, and a degree from the right college practically guarantees such a career. Both in college and in the best jobs the Japanese can look forward to virtually automatic promotion. Therefore, getting into the right college can be the most important move in a man's entire career. Success or failure in life can hinge on a series of exams taken at age eighteen.

Muffing them once can be forgiven. Every year many Japanese

high school graduates who failed to get into a good school don't go to college at all. They enroll in private cram schools and take the exams again the next year. Still, there is a limit to how many tries a disappointed student gets. The ministries and corporations hire only young men right out of college, who have passed their exams at about the right time every step of the way. At a certain age, around twenty-three or twenty-four, the door to success slams shut. The Japanese get just a lap or two around the field, and in this race it is devil take the hindmost.

Americans not only have broader notions of what constitutes success in life but have more ways of achieving it. A good college education and a good job may be the safest route, but it is only one of many. Americans can change careers at forty, go back to school at thirty, or goof off in high school but redeem themselves in graduate school. Japan does not give many second chances. Those who jump the tracks haven't much hope of climbing back on. The risks of non-comfority are far greater.

Even after they have left the school system, most Japanese remain under the spell of academic authority. Many never shake off their high school admiration for unquestioned truth and love to be told what to think by experts. As it happens, the experts are the same people who run the education system—university professors—as well as scholars affiliated with private research institutes. They are Japan's intellectuals, or *interi*, and are addressed by everyone as *sensei*. It is important to remember how much respect this title commands in Japan. It is the same title by which all Japanese, as terrified first graders, addressed the first real representatives of the adult world.

Interi have a lot of clout in determining how the Japanese think and behave. In few other countries do academics have such a stranglehold on *the* authoritative point of view, and any recognized *interi* gets a respectful hearing on almost any subject he chooses to carry on about. Japanese TV talk shows are full of physics professors explaining how leisure time should be spent and linguists discussing the balance of trade.

By the same token, someone who is not a professional *interi* may have trouble getting a hearing. An American with long experience in Japan recently said to me, "It's a good thing you're not writing this book for the Japanese market. Since you're not a *sensei*, you probably wouldn't be taken seriously."

Americans seem to think that movie stars have the opinions most worth listening to, but no group in America has the monopoly on wisdom that the *interi* do in Japan. *Interi* can maintain such a position because Japanese are taught in school that there is one right answer or point of view and that time spent examining alternatives is time wasted.

I have always thought that the Japanese love of proverbs comes from the same respect for established authority. A deft epigram is colorful in any language, but it is also an appeal to the hoary authority of tradition, an appeal that soon loses credence in an environment of intellectual dynamism and creativity. In the English-speaking world the seventeenth century was "the heyday of the proverb as a vehicle for then unquestioned truths."[9] Now we generally associate proverbs with oral cultures, with pretechnological, tradition-bound peoples. They are also common currency in Arabic-speaking countries, where frequent references to the Koran reinforce a religious and basically static view of the world. Bible quoting played the same role in some early American communities by reinforcing the one accepted view on all things.

I know of no other industrialized nation where aphorism has anything like the authority it does in Japan, where a sage proverb, properly quoted, can end an argument. Many common proverbs are borrowed from Chinese and are cryptic nonsense without an explanation—which makes them especially effective intellectual ammunition. This antique wisdom is appealed to so often that no *interi*'s library would be complete without a good proverb dictionary. I have only a popular pocket-size edition, but even it has more than 2,000 entries. A sure way for a foreigner learning Japanese to dazzle anyone within earshot is to trot out an ancient elegant proverb at just the right moment.

Conventional wisdom is the refuge of people who prefer not to think for themselves. Japanese are usually careful to take their cue from the crowd before they make a move of their own, and nowhere is this clearer than in consumer behavior. Here the need to conform is heightened by the fact that Japan is, in effect, an entire nation of nouveaux riches. After all, Japan has increased its production tenfold in real terms in *one generation*. Flush with cash and unsure of their tastes, the Japanese behave the way one might expect the newly rich to behave: they worship brand names. Brand names are the perfect solution in a society where individual preference is muted. Once a designer, say, Yves Saint Laurent, catches on, the scramble begins. As soon as consumers are confident that YSL means prestige, they will snap up anything that sports the reassuring logo.

This kind of goggle-eyed consumption goes on all over the world, but nowhere as avidly as in Japan. Even before designer products became readily available domestically, boutiques in London, Paris, and New York quickly learned what the Japanese craved. They hired Japanese-speaking salesgirls, advertised in Japanese, and made a killing with their appeal to brand and status consciousness. Designer goods are now sold in Japan, so a Gucci lighter is no longer proof of a trip overseas, but it is still just the thing to wave in the boss's face whenever he reaches for a cigarette.

"Until five years ago," writes the *Economist*, "one of the daily curiosities of the Paris fashion scene was a queue of affluent Japanese businessmen and tourists at Vuitton's sober store near the Arc de Triomphe." They were standing in line to buy Louis Vuitton luggage, then and still a very hot item on the Japanese consumer scene. The Vuitton people eventually got the message and in 1977 opened their first store in Japan. Now nearly half of their thirty stories worldwide are in Japan, and they are planning to open four more there in 1983.[10] The yellow LV logo was already a recognized status symbol even before Vuitton products went on sale in Japan. Flooding the market seems only to increase the Vuitton appeal.

Recently Japanese consumers have gotten a little cagier. They no longer rush out and buy just any recognizable brand. Instead, they buy glossy publications filled with photographs of acceptable brand name products, from English shotguns to Italian purses. Before making a purchase, the with-it consumer now consults a reference work to be sure of his choice.

Sadly, it may be just as well that the Japanese have sacrificed their judgment to the likes of Gucci and Pucci. Except for clothes, their taste in Western furnishings is dreadful. Western-style Japanese homes are often a gruesome mismatch of ugly furniture and knick-knacks. This is at first surprising for a people who have such a refined and delicate aesthetic of their own; but Western taste is still a foreign idiom for many, and it is natural that they should flounder in it at first.

Designer logos are part of the Japanese mania for hierarchy. They are a sure sign that one product is "better" than another, and this calms the anxious consumer. An American friend, who is a diamond wholesaler, once described to me a similar phenomenon in his trade.

"The classification system for diamonds wouldn't be anything like what it is today if it weren't for the Japanese," he says. "They want detailed standards and rankings even when they don't *mean* anything. They don't want to have to judge each stone on its individual merits. They want to put it in a class, a group."

I asked how diamond dealers operate in other countries. "Everyone else just works in a few broad categories," he said. "They know each stone is different and don't hesitate to judge it individually." The Japanese accept the significance of a meaningless classification of diamonds, just as they submit to the tyranny of a logo or the authority of an expert.

Not surprisingly Japan is a nation of fads, or booms as the Japanese call them. One of the most spectacular in recent years was the bowling boom. In the late sixties and early seventies bowling alleys appeared all over the country. People thought it might be a sport to rival baseball in popularity. But in a few years, for reasons no one has yet fathomed, bowling lost its sparkle. Bowling alleys went out of business one after another. In land-scarce Japan many were converted into supermarkets or movie theaters, but some still stand forlorn, theii giant rooftop tenpins visible for miles around as memorials to a sport that came and went.

Booms can suddenly go bust, and anyone left out in the cold must scramble for the safety of a new norm. Tennis and golf are now the new sporting norms, with golf well entrenched as the businessman's required sport. Lately jogging has arrived from America, although no one knows if it will be as permanent as golf or as fleeting as bowling.

For seven years Japan went through a nonstop panda boom. When relations with China were normalized in 1972, Zhou Enlai gave Premier Tanaka a pair of pandas as a goodwill gesture. The Japanese went wild with delight. Suddenly panda decals, panda dolls, and panda decor were everywhere. Panda madness was actually the closest many Japanese got to the real thing because there was always an enormous line of people waiting to get into the panda house at the Tokyo Zoo.

When Lan Lan, the female, took sick in 1979, a team of veterinary surgeons—from Tōdai, naturally—worked around the clock, trying to save her. The hourly bulletins on Lan Lan's condition were the lead stories on TV and radio news. When she finally succumbed, the prime minister expressed his personal concern at the tragedy, and a solemn memorial service was held for the dead animal. Concern was so great that a TV commentator, in a slip of the tongue, referred to the panda's death in honorific language that is reserved for highly re-spected humans. An official from the Peking Zoo remarked at the time that he thought Lan Lan might have died from "too much atten-tion and care."[11]

A more recent sensation among the young has been the Gundam boom. Gundam is the name of a TV-series robot that is operated by a seventeen-year-old computer whiz kid. Together they routinely save the world from the forces of extragalactic evil. When a movie version of Gundam was produced, a line began to form in front of the theater four days before the film was released. In early 1981 nineteen children were injured in a wild stampede at a department store when plastic models of Gundam first went on sale. Entire shops sprang up to sell nothing but Gundam T-shirts, Gundam dolls, Gundam posters, and other Gundam accessories.[12] The boom has now gone bust, and the Gundam stores have fallen on hard times.

The fashion industry is, of course, built on fads and booms, and the Japanese market is perfect for it. A Korean-Japanese now living in America says, "Fashions may not change any more often in Japan than in the West, but when they do, everybody falls in line. When miniskirts are all the rage, you can't buy anything else in the stores. Everybody from students to secretaries to housewives wears the same thing. Fashions change in America," she adds, "but more people have the confidence to ignore them."

Japan is a nation where there is a "right way" to do all things: greet a minister, solve an equation, tie the belt of a kimono, carve a fish, swing a bat. Form comes first, and function a distant second. Much of Japanese teaching, especially in the traditional arts, is con-cerned almost exclusively with form. Several years ago this approach cost me a moment of considerable embarrassment.

One summer, during a lengthy stay in Japan, I enrolled in an adult brush-writing course. As a child I had learned basic calligraphy and have never lost my love of Japan's beautiful script. I had gone for years without practicing and hoped to regain some mastery over the brush. My class met in the evening at the town hall, and the princi-ples of instruction were extremely traditional.

The teacher would begin every session by writing several model characters for all the students to copy. The students' work was to look as much as possible like the teacher's. Every so often *sensei* would come by our desks and observe our strokes. If a student were not imitating *sensei*'s brush movements precisely, he would stand over the student, wrap his hand around the student's hand, and write the characters while the student held the brush. This way we could feel every movement that *sensei* made. It was a technique that would never have worked on left-handed students, so we all were glad to have been cured of that bad habit back in grade school.

I was at the bottom of the class, so it was a rare session that *sensei* did not take me by the hand at least once. At the end of class all the students would bring their best copies of the characters up to *sensei*'s desk, where he would comment, and make corrections with a special brush and vermilion ink.

At the end of one session I shuffled through my twenty or thirty copies and found one that looked uncommonly good. I brought it and a few others up to the teacher for correction, but he just stared at my characters. The class was always interested in seeing what the lone *gaijin* could turn out, and two or three of my fellow students drifted up to the desk to have a look.

"Hey, not bad," said one. "Taylor-san, you're making progress."

"Thank you," I said. I thought so, too.

"Well, *sensei*," said another, "aren't you going to go over his copy?"

Sensei seemed lost in thought. "This," he said finally, "is the one I wrote when I took his hand. I'm not going to correct my own calligraphy."

Not even my polite classmates could hold back their mirth—they howled with laughter. It took courage to show my face in that classroom again.

Other Americans have been caught short by the Japanese conviction that there is only one right way to do something. Professional baseball teams in Japan are permitted by regulations to keep two foreign players in the lineup. These are almost always aging American major leaguers who are rounding out their careers. They may never have been stars, but they have played a lot of ball in America, where eccentric playing style is perfectly all right if that's how a man plays best. Many have been astonished to learn from their new Japanese batting coach that their form is all wrong and that they are going to have to change.[13]

The concern for form in sports is partly an inheritance from the martial arts. There is a right way to deliver a kick or dodge a blow, and all students diligently copy the master. A large part of the training in many schools is the memorization of elaborate shadow-fighting routines. These choreographed sequences, called *kata*, are mastered by precise imitation of the teacher's every move. Form comes first, and if the student can match the master, he should soon match the master's ability.

There is a right way to compliment a foreigner on his attempts to speak Japanese. One American has marveled:

> Why is it, for instance, that *all* Japanese say to the stammering, stumbling *gaijin:* "You speak Japanese better than we do?" How and where did they all learn that it is the thing to say? Do mothers advise and caution their little ones: "My dear, we all of course hope that it will not happen, but still you must be prepared. Some day a strange, ugly creature known as a *gaijin* may come slouching up. You must tell it that it speaks Japanese better than we Japanese do. That will please it, and soften its erratic impulses." [14]

The same author goes on to say, "The Japanese are among the most conformist of all peoples, but some of their conforming ways seem rather eccentric, and inquiry into the process of eccentric conformity would be more interesting than a great many of the things that occupy social scientists." [15]

Whether or not their standards seem eccentric to us, they exist to be adhered to, not violated. Japanese are bewildered by the constant choices that Westerners make as a matter of course. For example, in Japan there is only one right way to serve coffee: with cream and lots of sugar. It wouldn't occur to most Japanese that a guest might prefer it black. "When I get on that Pan American flight for Los Angeles," says the president of Nomura Securities International, "and the stewardess asks me if I want coffee or tea and if I want cream or sugar in it, I know I'm back in the world of instant decision making. Just to order a meal in America takes fifteen or twenty decisions: hors d'oeuvres, wine, salad dressing, rare or well done—there's no end to it. In Japan I can just ask the chef to bring me what's best that day. Frankly we Japanese find all this decision making quite exhausting." [16]

There is even a right way to use a sit-down toilet. Step-by-step instructions, complete with stick-figure drawings, are posted in some Western-style hotels. No doubt they are meant to protect the customers from unnecessary and exhausting decision making. Twenty years ago a bumpkin from rural Japan who had used squat toilets all his life might have had a moment's hesitation about how to relieve himself. Nowadays only a nation obsessed with good form would think such instructions were in anything but comical bad taste.

However, it is for just such encounters with the mysterious Occident that the Japanese wish to be perfectly prepared. This is why the variety of Japanese conformist behavior most familiar to foreigners is the package tour. The Japanese are quite taken with the notion of tourism, and the trip to Europe or America is a sign of wealth that has itself become a boom. Increasing numbers of brave Japanese tourists set out on their own for foreign lands, but many still seek the security of a group.

The group is desirable for three reasons. First, the Japanese are so acutely conscious of cultural, racial, and linguistic differences that they are nonplussed at the thought of bearding the *gaijin* in his lair unassisted. Second, many Japanese tour groups are made up not of strangers but of work colleagues, association members, and other people who already make up a group of some kind. The tour is a reaffirmation of an established group. Finally, most Japanese go overseas not for a unique experience but rather to reproduce the experience all other Japanese tourists have had. The best group tour is one which, down to its particulars, is a copy of the tour one's neighbor took the year before. The only way in which it need differ is that it cost a little more and be a bit more luxurious.

There is not much debate over where to go and what to see. The grand tour of the United States must include Disneyland, the Grand Canyon, Niagara Falls, and the Empire State Building. As more people go to these places, yet more will go. The accepted pattern solidifies.

Americans are hardly immune to the mass-market package tour; in fact, we snapped it up as soon as the British invented it. But Americans are attracted by tours that at least claim to be different from everybody else's, whereas most Japanese like to reproduce the safe, standard experience.

As for the photo madness of Japanese tourists, I am familiar with only one theory that suggests an explanation. According to a Japanese scholar who lives in America, it has to do with how ill at ease the Japanese feel in foreign lands. Of tourists to America he writes, "Photography is the means to cope with the alien American space: while they are unable to put themselves verbally and intellectually into America, within the pictures they take, they do stand *in* the place."[17] This theory has a plausible ring to it, but Japanese do not take pictures only in alien space; they take plenty of pictures in Japan as well. Photography is to hobbies what golf is to sports: so popular as to be virtually obligatory.

Nevertheless, when the Japanese travel, they try to take along a familiar group environment, and they seek out the bits of Japan that have been transplanted overseas. They are most comfortable staying in hotels with Japanese management and are relieved to find so many Japanese restaurants away from home.

Japanese eating habits must be among the most inflexible in the world. Even Japanese who have lived overseas for many years have told me that unless they have rice with a meal, they do not feel as though they have eaten properly. In a nation that feeds rice even to cats and dogs, this should perhaps be no surprise. Many Japanese are perfectly happy to travel around the world and eat only in Japanese restaurants. Some take along a supply of instant ramen for fear that once they leave Japan, they may find nothing edible.

Another characteristic of the Japanese group tour is that every minute is accounted for. The group is always on the run, with little time for individual activities or even for rest. Exhausted Americans on Japanese-style group tours soon find themselves longing for a peaceful half hour away from the group. The tour organizers seem to feel that their charges will worry if they aren't told how to spend every spare moment.

Even Japanese who are posted abroad on business cannot entirely free themselves from the list of must-see attractions and the frantic pace of the group tour. Thus, if they simply pile into the car for a family drive, they are not likely to go on an unplanned ramble. They will dash from place to place just like a group tour, seeing the standard sights.

A friend who grew up in Japan and later worked with Japanese tourists for Hawaiian Airlines once told me about the money that could be wrung from obedient tour groups.

"I knew a guy who had the perfect racket," he says. "He would check with Japan Air Lines to find out when a tourist group was supposed to show up in Honolulu and would meet them just as they got off the plane. He would line them up right there on the tarmac for a quick group photo. Then he would actually assign some member of the group to collect money from all the rest and would have the prints ready for the group when they came to catch their flight home. The crazy thing was, he almost always got away with it. Nobody would quibble over the price of the picture, and everybody would buy."

The photographer was not alone in exploiting the Japanese willingness to be told how to spend money. "You could get an entire group to buy the same Hawaiian shirt, or you could convince every one of them to buy leis. Store owners who arranged to have the tour buses stop in front of their shop had it made. The Japanese were very, very predictable."

When Japanese travel alone, they often cut slightly pathetic figures because they are used to so much conformity and predictable behavior back home. They are not prepared for a nation like America, where people come in all varieties and where not all play by the same rules. Americans are used to making up their own minds and are tempted to take advantage of anyone who is willing to be told what to do.

Shysters of all kinds grow fat on the Japanese. A year or two ago New York police finally cracked down on unscrupulous taxi drivers who were charging outrageous fares for rides into town from the airport. One cabby, who, of course, claimed to be innocent of the practice, told me he had heard that Japanese made the best victims for this swindle because they never complained. I have also known plenty of Japanese who were shamelessly cheated in some of Manhattan's better-known clip joints.

Japanese submit to this kind of treatment as much because they are too timid to assert their rights as because they don't know the correct price. They are also intimidated by America's well-advertised reputation for violence and may submit to petty injustices out of fear for their lives.

Japanese are, in fact, perfect targets for muggers because they often carry large amounts of cash, are small, and rarely fight back. In 1981 a Japanese woman vacationing in Rome had her purse snatched. The purse contained more than $900,000 in cash and jewels. When asked why she was lugging around so many valuables, the woman explained that she didn't want foreigners to think she didn't have money.[18]

In Japan almost everyone can be expected to stick to the rules, and differences with strangers can usually be ironed out without so much as a raised voice. In the rough-and-tumble of America or Southern Europe, behavioral norms may be vague or entirely absent, and the Japanese have trouble shifting for themselves. All Japanese are now aware that they should keep up their guard overseas, but many who travel alone still get pushed around. Once he has safely returned, the traveler slips happily back into the comfort of Japanese predictability.

Japan is a dependable place, where the predictability of society at large is reflected in the uniformity of its smaller units. Once again, the university system is a good example. Before the war, Japan had a dozen well-known imperial universities and a handful of excellent private colleges. After the war many regional universities were founded, all modeled on the famous prewar institutions. They each built up a large number of departments and tried to compete in all disciplines, with the result that in no field could they surpass or even equal the older universities. If the new schools had not stuck so slavishly to the same model, they might have won distinction as specialized institutions. As it is, they all try to do the same thing, but with varying degrees of success.

This makes Japanese universities easy to rank and compare: Kyoto University is better in nearly all respects than Nagoya University. Things are more complicated in America. Every so often Japanese ask me whether Harvard is a better school than MIT or if Yale outranks Stanford. I have to tell them there is no simple answer; it all depends on what you want to study. Universities are a little like diamonds: They may fall into broad categories, but each must be examined for its unique qualities.

Japanese companies are as easy to rank as universities, and for the same reasons. In electronics, trading, heavy industries, or steel-making, all the leading firms do basically the same thing. The "personality" of a pulp and paper company, for example, is well defined in Japan, and managers are not likely to dilute that personality by venturing into unrelated lines of business.

In America many large companies are so diversified that there is no handy name for what they do, which is why they are called conglomerates. In 1974 Gulf Oil nearly bought out the Ringling Brothers and Barnum and Bailey Circus. This was a flight of fancy even by American standards, but the very idea left Japanese businessmen in drop-jawed amazement.

In the service industry as well, Japanese managers keep a wary eye on the competition to make sure they haven't fallen behind. If a bar or nightclub comes up with a new service gimmick—say, escorting customers out to their taxis—soon every equivalent establishment is doing the same thing. When one luxury hotel in Tokyo started playing different Muzak to match the season and time of day, every hotel of a certain class had to follow suit. There is firm agreement on standards for hotels, bars, or restaurants, and excellence is achieved by sticking to them as closely as possible. Decor, for example, must meet clear standards. Only establishments that cater to Westerners or that mean to affect a foreign look will try out something original.

Japan's major papers are famous for their timidity and uniformity of views. A well-known Japanese media personality, who has spent time overseas, explains how easy it is to stand out in Japan. "Japanese newspapers . . . all say exactly the same thing," he says. "If there were eight newspapers in Japan and each developed its own ideas, I would have to come up with a ninth new idea. But as they all say the same thing, all I have to do is come up with a second idea, and it is unique."[19] There are sensationalist weeklies in Japan that believe in racy copy and investigative reporting, but all the respectable papers are well behaved and speak with the same voice.

Japanese radio stations are equally uniform. None has a personality distinct from any other, and all try to program something for all tastes. Japanese are envious of the rich variety of jazz, rock, top forty, country, and classical stations they find in America.

Regional capitals also seem doggedly determined to resemble each other as much as possible. In any one of fifty Japanese cities a visitor arriving by train could be excused for thinking he had not left home. Train stations are invariably on a square in the center of town, surrounded by identical-looking banks, department stores, bars, and coffee shops. At least one elevated pedestrian crossing is visible from the station. To one side is the main city bus depot; to the other, a covered shopping street bustles with activity. And from north to south the people look, dress, and act the same.

"Japan is a homogeneous place, distinguished by its lack of distinctions,"[20] writes one foreign observer. It is just this lack of distinction that feeds the Japanese mania for hierarchy. Units that all are trying to meet the same standards are easy to compare and rank.

If society and its institutions sometimes give the individual short shrift, it is in the *nakama* group that the demands of conformity are strongest. It is in this context—the family, the village, the work group—that thoughtful Japanese bewail their lack of individuality.

In all societies each person's desires are in conflict with the rules of the group. For the Japanese, this battle is of such absorbing interest that they have a pair of familiar words that neatly define the opposing forces: *tatemae* and *honne*. *Tatemae* are principles and expectations. They need not necessarily be hypocritical, but they are often seen as conflicting with *honne*, or one's true desires or intentions.

As one *interi* puts it, "It is generally said that the Japanese behave according to *tatemae*. This is because they consistently submit to the logic of the group and suppress *honne*—that is, the logic of the individual. Japan's heroes are those who smother their individuality in order to serve the group."[21] For most Japanese, it is still very much a virtue to submit quietly to the authority of the group.

Japanese young people, for example, are much more likely than Westerners to break off an engagement if their parents disapprove. Likewise, an eldest son is expected to follow in his father's profession, whether or not he has any talent or interest in the business.

Nonfamily groups can be just as demanding, and the *nakama* that form around the workplace are the tightest of all. A member who is reluctant to share some of the group's interests, or who does not make himself as available as the group would like, runs the risk of losing his status or even being excluded. Groups thrive on regular doses of *otsukiai* ("fellowship"), and someone who does not gather for drinks often enough gets the unpleasant label "Poor at *otsukiai*."

Groups like PTA mothers can form a kind of *nakama*. Mrs. Yamashita, a woman who has lived for some time in America with her businessman husband, once told me a story about the last time she returned from an overseas assignment. "My daughter's grade-school teacher asked everyone in the class to raise his hand if he was going to cram school or taking private lessons of some kind. Everyone in the room except my daughter put up his hand. The story got around the PTA, and one day the mother of a classmate came up to me and said, 'It must take great courage to be the mother of the only child who isn't taking private lessons.'

"It didn't take any courage," says Mrs. Yamashita. "It was pure ignorance. I didn't know every single child was going to lessons after school. But the other mothers felt so pressured about it they thought I was being brave."

Conformity comes most easily in a society that values agreement for its own sake, and the urge to agree lies at the heart of *nakama* behavior. Earlier we noted Yamamoto's theory that Japanese groups cannot function until they begin to act like a group of virtual blood-kin relations. Whatever the group's official functions are supposed to be, one of the things the virtual blood kin are seeking is *wa*, or harmony.

Wa represents the absence of conflict. It is love of consensus and dislike of individuality. *Wa* is so important in group undertakings that a tremendous amount of effort goes into discussing alternatives so that everyone in the group will agree. Except for a few traditionally authoritarian settings like the classroom or army barracks, Japanese leaders begin to lead only after they have found out where their followers want to go. Agreement can be more important than what has been agreed to. The best solution is one that all can support even if a somewhat divisive one might have yielded better results. Many Japanese executives decorate their offices with a hanging scroll with one character on it: *wa*.

Language tells us a great deal about the importance of *wa*. As an adjectival prefix *wa* means nothing less than "Japanese." Thus *washoku* ("harmony food") means "Japanese food." *Wafū* ("harmony style") means "Japanese style." The *wa* of *wakon yōsai* ("Japanese spirit, Western learning") is, of course, the same *wa*. Japan is referred to poetically (and accurately) as the Land of *Wa*. When the *wa* ideogram follows the one for "large," the combination is read *Yamato*. This is an old, emotion-laden name for the nation of Japan, and means "great harmony." It was also the name of Japan's most powerful battleship during the Second World War. "Great harmony" among the Japanese could be dangerous for the rest of the world.

Wa is so important that not even the hardball world of politics can do without it. When Prime Minister Masayoshi Ohira died in office in 1980, his party, the Liberal Democrats, had to choose a successor. What was expected in the West to be a power struggle among the strongest faction leaders in the party turned out to be a gentlemanly agreement on a man with no power base but whom everyone could accept: Zenkō Suzuki.

When Suzuki resigned in the fall of 1982 rather than seek reelection, he explained his decision by saying, "I want harmony and unity in the party."[22] He had lost the support of party chieftains and decided to bow out gracefully rather than fight for survival.

This kind of compromise is not unheard of outside Japan. Western politicians can sometimes swallow their personal ambitions if the stakes are small. But when they have a good shot at the top job, they come out of their corners swinging. If the Italians, for example, were more interested in *wa*, they wouldn't have to form a new government every eleven months or so, as they have since 1945.

One foreign observer has coined the term "wamocracy" to describe Japan's political system. He writes that European democracies work on the principle of majority rule, whereas Japan works on the principle of majority rule *plus wa*.[23]

Harmony is, of course, possible only among people who conform to the same standards; it can't be achieved when people think and behave in different ways. In America harmony would be too much to expect, so business contracts usually end with a clause outlining arbitration procedures or specifying which jurisdiction's laws will apply if a dispute goes to court. The equivalent clause in a Japanese contract states that if any disagreement should arise, the parties to the contract will sit down together and discuss the problem. They don't expect to have recourse to the law but to settle disputes themselves. This is possible because businessmen share a huge fund of common values and can count on goodwill and cooperation from each other. This is conformity at its most useful.

An American businessman writes, "One recalls Aristotle's prophetic comment in the *Ethics:* 'If all men were friends justice would not be necessary.' In Japan, if all men are not necessarily friends, they are almost all of them relatives."[24] It is no coincidence that there are twenty times as many lawyers per capita in America as in Japan; the Japanese almost never sue each other. American law firms have recently been complaining to the State Department about how hard it is for their attorneys to get working visas for Japan. Some reports have suggested that the Japanese are deliberately trying to keep them, and their litigious habits, out of the country.[25] Too many lawyers filing too many lawsuits would disturb Japan's *wa*.

Everywhere the Japanese seem to be searching for agreement. On television talk shows, no one goes any further than the politest suggestion of disagreement. What are billed as debates are really contests in accommodation, love feasts of harmony and consensus. In the United States panelists will stoutly defend differing points of view, and on French or Italian TV they will heap abuse on each other.

Japan's constant yearning for agreement can have an odd effect on Westerners. Recently I met an American woman who had been back in the United States for six months after seven or eight years in an almost exclusively Japanese context. She told me that after such a lengthy period of total immersion she was afraid she had lost the capacity for argument. "I no longer enjoy disagreement or a spirited intellectual exchange," she told me. "If I'm watching a discussion on American TV and the people start arguing emotionally, I change the channel. I don't want to watch.

"But it goes further than that. I recently visited my family, who have, of course, known me all my life. At one point we were planning either to go sailing or go to a movie, and my sister asked me which I would prefer to do. I told her I didn't care. She finally blew up and turned on me, saying, 'Why can't you tell us what you want? You've *got* to have an opinion!' But you know, it really didn't matter to me. I was sure we would have fun either way, and I really *didn't have an opinion*. Sometimes I worry about this change in my personality."

In Japan harmony is at work in the oddest places. It is instructive to watch a group of businessmen order a meal in a restaurant. Often the junior members of the group will take their cue from the senior member and order exactly what he does. Or, if they are in a Western-style restaurant, where the menu is a little unfamiliar, there may be a brief discussion to establish a consensus on what seems to be the most promising dish, and everyone will order it. The Japanese will eat the same food with a comfortable feeling of solidarity, whereas an American would find it boring and a little childish if everyone ordered the same thing.

One summer day in Tokyo, as I watched an entire table of business associates happily drinking corn soup together, it occurred to me that running Japan must be a little like ordering a meal. Once the country has talked things over and decided to go with the pot roast, nearly everyone will cheerfully eat beef. In America someone would hold out to the very end for fried chicken. In Japan consensus is actually possible and often genuine. Charles de Gaulle once remarked that is was impossible to govern a country that produes 350 different kinds of cheese. In Japan everybody eats rice.

This is, of course, an oversimplification. Japan has opposition movements, factions, and disagreements of all kinds. Nevertheless, the very process of disagreement takes on a formal structure with rules of its own. Management and labor make ugly faces at each other, and the union may even call a fifteen-minute strike; but both sides know that they will reach a reasonable agreement in the end. In government, politicians of the same conservative stripe have been in power since 1948. Communists, Socialists, and everybody else have been in opposition so long that they have become irresponsible and obstructionist, but that doesn't matter. National policy is arrived at through stylized forms of opposition between different factions within the ruling Liberal Democratic party. The factions have arrived at a steady state of constructive antagonism that has kept the country on an even keel since the end of the war.

In Japan the very act of opposition can come from submission to a new group as much as from intellectual disagreement. A Chinese observer writes about the bands of student demonstrators who, in the sixties and early seventies, used to throng the streets of Japan, waving placards and chanting slogans: "If you pulled just one person out of the group and asked him if he agreed with what was written on the placard he was waving, he would probably say, 'Well, this was something we all got together and came up with. I don't really feel strongly about it one way or another.'"[26] A demonstrator who has abandoned the national consensus is still bound by group consensus.

At all levels of society, no matter how shrill the voices of opposition may sound, there is a vast fund of agreement on which all Japanese draw. The cracks in society are only so deep, and the gaps that separate antagonists are only so wide. Special interest groups scatter the energies of society far less than in America or Europe.

A Japanese economics professor once said to me, "Japanese Catholics have more in common with Japanese *Communists* than they do with foreign Catholics." This is surely an exaggeration, but a tempting one when talking about Japan.

"Look at it this way," says a Japanese whom I have known since high school and who now lives in America. "Say you took half the population of the U.S. and shoved it into the state of California. Then you stripped California of all its natural resources, chopped it off from the mainland, and set it adrift in the Pacific. What do you think you would get? You'd either get Japan or Bangladesh. The Japanese have got *no choice*. Either they work together or they starve."

The Japanese have chosen to work together. They have built an extraordinarily powerful economy and a smooth-running society. But they have paid a price. Consensus can be built only on the backs of individuals. It leaves little room for the autonomy and independence prized in the West. Until recently most Japanese have been happy to be a part of the crowd and were only dimly aware of how much they were the prisoners of consensus. Where Americans would feel invaded, smothered, and shackled, they have felt fulfilled.

Lately, however, the authors of *Nihonjin-ron* have become increasingly worried about the pervasive sameness of their society. One *interi* complains: "Should the individual try to express his self ever so slightly, the merciless severity of the group will crush him. His budding individuality will be defeated by the power of the group, and he will be forced back into the mold of conformity."[27] Recent *Nihonjin-ron* is full of such despairing statements.

The Japanese have long been fascinated by the firm, Western sense of the individual. Many are clearly envious of it and have racked their brains to figure out where it comes from. Some have searched for its roots in religion. Christianity and Judaism, they point out, put each believer on a one-to-one footing with God. Every man stands naked before his Creator and is personally answerable to Him. Western man is blessed like Peter or cursed like Job, as an individual.

Japanese Shinto, on the other hand, has many minor deities, which are often worshiped by the group as a whole. Village festivals may celebrate any number of nature gods at the same time, and their blessings are sought in the name of the collectivity. The Nirvana of Japan's other major religion, Buddhism, literally means the extinction of self. Salvation is the complete obliteration of the individual, whose drop of self-consciousness is lost in an ocean of universal consciousness.

This kind of thinking lies behind the old *ichi-oku* expressions. *Ichi-oku* means "100 million," which was approximately the population of the prewar Japanese empire. *Ichi-oku isshin* means "100 million [Japanese] and one heart" or perhaps "100 million hearts beating as one"— a poetic expression for national unanimity. More disturbing was the wartime expression *ichioku-gyokusai* ("100 million crushed gems"). This meant *Götterdämmerung* in the Pacific, or 100 million glorious deaths.

Japanese have also pointed out that during the war their soldiers were taught to die shouting, "*Banzai*" (["May the emperor live] ten thousand years"). The small were to die so that the great might live forever. One scholar contrasts this with Jesus' death on the cross. The Son of God accepted the sins of the world so that each man, no matter how humble, might hope for eternal life. In the West the great sometimes sacrifice themselves for the small.[28]

The Japanese also cite their language as either a symptom or a cause of their weak sense of the individual. As we noted earlier, the Japanese use several different versions of the pronoun, "I," depending on whom they are talking to. The word that denotes the self is constantly changing to suit the circumstances. With such an unsteady "I," ask the Japanese, how can we ever develop a firm sense of ourselves?

Japanese think of Westerners as endowed with an indomitable sense of self, impervious to outside forces. They see this quality as the touchstone of Western civilization.

Sometimes, of course, they overrate us. Recently I had a Japanese houseguest for several days. He was a college professor and had been overseas before but not to the United States. One day he was hanging up some of his clothes in my closet and discovered a half dozen pinstriped suits left over from my businessman days.

"What's this, Taylor-san?" he wanted to know. "Why do you have all these conservative suits?"

"I used to wear them to work."

"Every day?"

"Yes," I said, "every day."

"Why was that?" he wanted to know.

"Because that's just the way you dress when you do business in New York," I said, a little surprised.

"So no matter how good you were at your job, you had no choice about what you could wear?"

"Nope. Had to wear a suit."

"That's just like conformist Japan," he said. "I thought America was a place where ability counted, not appearance. I didn't realize Americans could be so conventional." Americans certainly can be conventional, and it might ease the pain for a few breast-beating Japanese intellectuals if someone would tell them so.

An increasing number of Japanese are less willing to see submission to the group as an unqualified virtue. Young people can often afford to travel and study abroad, and many are fascinated by the freedom and diversity of expression that they find in other cultures.

Even older Japanese—and not just the *interi*—have begun to wonder if conformity doesn't stifle originality.

Several generations of Japanese have had to live with a reputation as skillful imitators with no real creativity of their own. A few still claim not to be bothered by it. "Isn't it just as remarkable," writes one, "for a society to mass-produce top-quality industrial products as it is to write good novels or do brilliant scientific research?"[29] No doubt it is. But more and more Japanese want to do both, and the nation will not rest until it can.

Already the Japanese have no peer in bringing "state-of-the-art" technology to the shop floor. In no other country can production engineers so quickly take the very latest technological breakthroughs and build them into inexpensive consumer products. No one can seriously compete with Japanese manufacturers of quartz watches, electronic cameras, stereos, video equipment, or pocket calculators. Although the basic technology for all those products came from the West, in some other areas Japanese technicians are already nipping at our heels.

Americans were the first to make 16k computer memory chips, but Japanese companies took the lead in 64k chips and could easily be the first to mass-market a 256k chip. This is the kind of race in which they excel, for it is one in which the goal is clear. It takes no conceptual breakthrough to realize that 256k chips have four times the capacity of 64k chips. Constant incremental improvement and superb production technology will win the day.

What is true of computer hardware is not true of software or programming, which is more art than effort. The best programs are written by talented individuals, not by production teams. This, explains one American programming consultant who has worked with the Japanese, is why the United States still has a substantial lead in the field. "But it may not last," he adds. "The Japanese are spending millions of dollars trying to find the hidden patterns in all good programming. They are trying to reduce it from an art to a process. And once they do, they'll be the best."

Pure science is a field where there is always room for geniuses. But geniuses do not fit standard molds, and Japan has not been a congenial place for them. It was a proud moment for the Japanese when Leo Ezaki won the Nobel Prize in physics in 1973. It was a disappointment for them to learn that he had left Japan in 1960 to go to work for IBM. When Ezaki went back to Japan in 1974, to what was nevertheless a hero's welcome, he said bluntly that he thought Japanese society was not conducive to originality.[30] Now he writes a regular column for the *Yomiuri* newspaper in which he regularly roasts the Japanese for their conformity.[31]

Nobel Prizes are awarded for creative breakthroughs, not for production engineering or plant layout. Japan has won a total of six Nobel Prizes. Denmark, with less than one-twentieth of Japan's population, has won nine.

In the liberal arts hardly anything that is new comes out of Japan. Its universities devour the latest from the West but contribute next to nothing of their own. Even Western specialists would be hard pressed to name a Japanese economist, psychologist, philosopher, historian, or critic.

In the fine arts Japan's oppressive uniformity is an obstacle to creativity. "Japanese culture tells us all to be the same," says a Tokyo video artist. ". . . society makes it very difficult for an artist to create something that is entirely new or threatening to what already exists."[32]

A few Japanese have always managed to defy society. Literature has a long tradition in Japan, and the author Yasunari Kawabata won the Nobel Prize for his work in 1968. Nevertheless, since the war only one Japanese writer—Yukio Mishima—managed to establish a real international reputation. A few Japanese film directors have attracted a following in the West, but the industry does not have the youthful vigor that it does in Italy, France, and now Germany.

For a country of such size and energy, Japan cuts a poor figure in the arts. Try as it may, it offers the world no great sculptors, playwrights, choreographers, painters, composers, or even rock and roll bands. Artists and performers who show real promise leave Japan for Europe or America, in search of an environment more conducive to creativity.

The standout in this drab scene is classical music. Japanese string players are excellent, and some are world-class. This, however, is not so surprising. Of all the Western arts, classical music is most like traditional Japanese arts in its veneration of the masters and its preservation of tradition. Few other arts revolve around the repetition of works that may be centuries old. Semipermanent standards of excellence deeply appeal to the Japanese appreciation of form. Also, classical music is an art that requires flawless technique, something that comes only with hours of practice. Japanese musicians work out with their instruments as if they were in training for the Olympics. Technique is amenable to discipline—of which the Japanese have plenty—but creativity is not.

In only a few fields have Japanese drawn on both the Western and Eastern aesthetic to create dramatic new forms. Designers such as Issey Miyake and Kansai Yamamoto have left a distinctive mark on women's fashions, and Japanese autos and electronic products owe their clean, pleasing lines in part to Japan's long-established genius for packaging. Nevertheless, the union of two formidable artistic traditions has not produced the torrent of originality one might have expected.

I think that for some time Japan will continue to follow rather than lead in science and the arts. All creative geniuses are nails that protrude. A nation that takes such pains to pound them down values conformity over creation. No matter how much the *interi* scream about the evils of group pressure, I don't think Japan is ready to reverse its priorities and give up the comforts of conformity.

Nevertheless, Japan is changing. In science and technology, at any rate, it has made a firm commitment to innovation. The government has decided that high technology will be the secret to success for the rest of the century, and money and encouragement are flowing into electronics, fiber optics, genetic engineering, robotics, and soon aerospace. Japan has decided, cautiously, to become creative.

Many would pooh-pooh the notion of creativity by fiat. Some might argue that in order to raise a handful of geniuses, Japan must bargain away its social harmony in return for a riven society, that only in the flux of conflict can new ideas be born. However, if any society can square the circle, it is Japan. After all, it has been brilliantly successful in teaching its citizens to mind the rules. What is to prevent it from teaching them just as successfully to break a few? A "homogeneous people on an island nation" might just be taught to bubble with creativity without boiling over.

At least one Westerner has complained that "the very idea of a consensus to be creative is a contradiction in terms."[33] No doubt it is, to a writer for the *Economist*. For the Japanese, perhaps not.

CHAPTER FIVE

REASON, FEELING, AND RELIGION

Japan is a nation where feelings, attitude, intuition, and emotion often take precedence over mere reason. Some years ago I was out for a drive with an American friend named Mark when we were pulled over by a policeman. Mark, who was at the wheel, was new to Japan and understood very little Japanese. Our three-way conversation with the policeman, in which I was interpreter, went something like this:

Policeman: "Does the gentleman realize that by driving fifty in a thirty-five-kilometer-per-hour zone he was endangering the lives of many people?"

I: "Mark, you were speeding."

Mark: "Damn. Is he going to give me a ticket?"

I (to policeman): "He apologizes very sincerely for breaking the law."

Policeman: "Tell him that this should be a lesson for him and that in the future he should observe the speed limit more carefully."

I (to Mark): "I think he's going to let you off."

Mark: "Great. Let's get out of here. The movie starts in ten minutes."

I (to policeman): "He promises to be more careful in the future and regrets his reckless behavior."

Policeman: "Very good. Please follow me to the police station, where the foreign gentleman will write a *hansei-sho*."

I (to Mark): "Follow the police car, Mark. We're going down to the station."

Mark: "What? I thought you said he was letting me off."

He was let off, but not before he had written a *hansei-sho* ("document of reflection"), expressing his remorse at breaking the law and promising to drive more safely in the future. The key sentence in his "reflections," which Mark wrote in English, was "I'm sorry I was caught," but with emphasis on the "I'm sorry" I convinced the authorities that Mark was contrite. In Japan a minor offender is often let off with a *hansei-sho* instead of a fine if the authorities think he has shown proper feelings of remorse.

It is not only at the police station that human feelings get a more sympathetic hearing than they might in the West. In all areas of daily life Japanese resist any appeal to cold reason that ignores human relations. Many Japanese distrust eloquence and pure logic because they may not take proper account of feelings. Although routine departures from logic sometimes shade into what Westerners would call plain superstition, they are at the core of what the Japanese feel makes them different from other people. Attitude, intuition, and implicit communication are important parts of Japan's mythology and are the sources of its religions. They are so much a part of daily life that one scholar suggests that simply being Japanese may be a kind of religion.

Logic-chopping *gaijin* often overlook the importance of nonrational considerations. They seldom take their *hansei-sho* seriously because they do not understand that a Japanese policeman pays careful attention to an offender's attitude. A sincere apology, which amounts to a humble request to be let back into the community of law-abiding citizens, can make the difference between a stiff fine and a friendly warning.

Attitude is so important in Japanese courts that it can be worthwhile to fake the right one. If two cars collide and one driver goes to the hospital, the other had better send flowers and visit the wounded if he wants to be absolutely safe. Expressions of regret and concern will have a substantial bearing on how a judge handles the case if it goes to court. The victim himself is likely to be asked by the authorities if he thinks the other driver behaved decently [1]

In Japan a wrong is not righted simply by paying damages. Fines strike the Japanese as a cold, unfeeling way to settle a difference. The victim and society at large expect a criminal to show remorse and to reflect sorrowfully on his crime. Americans are much less interested in being visited at the hospital or in hearing heartfelt apologies. So long as the offender pays up or goes to jail, justice has been served. Japanese react to crime as if a family member has turned against them and do not consider the case closed until a sincere apology has restored good relations.

One Japanese writer suggests that a legal system that pays so much attention to attitude and feeling must seem dangerously unstable to Westerners. He explains that in a society where there is fundamental agreement on how people should behave, the law does not require the aloof majesty it takes on in the West. In a nation of diverse values like the United States the law must be consistent, even inflexible, or society will fly apart. It cannot afford to make room for such intangibles as attitude.[2] Japanese society requires the law to ponder intangibles, and it permits it to do so through a social consensus that will not be shaken by selective lenience.

Westerners, who think of the Japanese as no-nonsense operators, are surprised at the way intuition, emotion, and respect for the feelings of others can crowd out logic. The Japanese word *rikutsu* means "logic" or "reason." It has all the positive connotations that "logic" does in English, but it also has distasteful connotations of coldness, hairsplitting, and pointless dispute. The word *rikutsuppoi* ("too reasonable") is used to criticize thinking that does not take human relations into account. The expression "to speak reason" means "to argue" or "find fault." Logic is useful, but it can be thrust aside when straightforward reasoning might bruise feelings.

The Japanese have taken to using the English words "dry" and "wet" to distinguish between "logical" and "emotional" behavior. They think of Westerners who leave jobs, drop customers, change wives, or switch political parties as disconcertingly "dry." A willingness to sacrifice human relations for tangible gain strikes the Japanese as self-centered and callous. They think of their own society as dripping "wet"; its web of personal ties can be constricting, but it is also humane and emotionally supportive.

A Japanese woman once told me about her first day at a new job. "They introduced me to the president, and we went into his office for a little chat. One of the first things he asked me was whether I was married. When I told him I wasn't, he wanted to know if I had any good prospects or if I would like for him to introduce me to people."

This woman has since moved to America, where she learned that things were different. "In America I found that the boss is interested in whether I am married only if he wants to make a pass at me. But in Japan, even from the first day, the president of the company was concerned about my private life and wanted to help if he could. At the time I thought that atmosphere of concern was oppressive. Now I sometimes miss it. Americans can be so businesslike they seem cold."

Many of my Japanese customers used to offer their services as a matchmaker when they learned that I was a bachelor. This is partly because many marriages are still arranged in Japan but also because of the close ties that Japanese like to build with their regular business partners. These ties are part of the right "feeling" that must be established before they are ready to do business with new clients.

A businessman writes that one of the first experiences of culture shock for Japanese moving to America is the straightforward, unadorned way that people treat each other. "However," he adds, "after six months or a year we learn not to presume upon people or worry about their feelings so much and begin to feel at ease with human relations that are simpler and less involved than they would be in Japan."[3]

Japanese often establish personal relations when Americans might stay more distant. Superfluous workers may be kept on in recognition of past service and because firing them would ruin personal relations. A shopkeeper may give regular customers a discount for "feeling." Elaborate steps are taken to conceal disagreement or soften its impact.

Perhaps a good symbol of Japan's concern with feelings is the *tamamushi*, a small beetle native to Japan. Its wings and back are the same shimmering color as a patch of oil floating in the ocean—blue, purple, or gold, depending on the angle. The Japanese find the *tamamushi*'s iridescence very attractive, and in the past the insect's wings were used as a costly decorative veneer.

Today the importance of *tamamushi* color is more psychological than aesthetic, for it is the color of compromise. In spite of their love of consensus, Japanese sometimes find that all the discussion in the world is not enough to reconcile conflicting views. In such cases they may arrive at what is called a *tamamushi*-colored conclusion, one that reflects a different color depending on the angle of view. This is a deliberately ambiguous decision that warring factions can interpret to suit themselves and that preserves the appearance of harmony.

Obviously a beetle-colored decision isn't really a decision at all but a face-saving gesture that prevents irreconcilable interests from colliding too spectacularly. It is just one example of the measures Japanese take to preserve a feeling of agreement. A decision which is objectively wrong, but which fosters harmony, can be preferable to one that is correct but results in divisive bitterness.

Too much of this kind of face-saving only postpones the day of reckoning. The Mitsui industrial group's $500 million Iranian refinery project is a good example. The plans were drawn up back in 1968 for a massive industrial complex that was to cement ties between Japan and the shah. In spite of the attention the project's misfortunes have received from the press, Mitsui has not made the hard decision to cut losses and get out—nor has it convincingly committed itself to hang on to the end.

"That," says a man who works for a rival industrial group, "is a perfect setting for one beetle-colored decision after another. The situation is so complex and so controversial that any decision will humiliate somebody. But now they've dithered for so long the whole Mitsui group is losing face."

Curiously, some Japanese seem to confuse the "logic" of firing unnecessary workers with the "logic" of rational thought. They seem to think that because they back down from harsh solutions so as to spare feelings, or make legal decisions on the basis of attitude, their emotions somehow get in the way of clear thinking. Many Japanese actually have the bizarre notion that as a people they are intellectually handicapped by their feelings. They think of themselves as impressionistic and emotional, compared to rational Westerners, and that too much agreement dulls their minds.

In a passage that is typical of what Japanese say about themselves, a specialist in Greek philosophy writes, "[Japanese] do not rigorously examine new theories and lack the intellectual thoroughness that flushes out new truths."[4] The Japanese president of Arthur D. Little, Inc., in Japan says, "The Japanese fundamentally cannot absorb the methodology of analytical, scientific reasoning per se."[5]

What are we to make of this kind of talk? It is true that Japan is not a nation that encourages originality, and there are social barriers to a freewheeling willingness to think the unthinkable. Brilliant creativity is rare. Moreover, Japanese tend to circumvent disagreement rather than go after each other with hammer and tongs the way Westerners often do. They get less practice at beating down each other's arguments. "Ideas are built up . . . through argument," writes one *interi*. "Unfortunately, Japan is a nation where there have been few opportunities for argument."[6]

None of this, of course, means that there is anything wrong with how the Japanese think. We can only admire the logical precision with which they have set out to build the most productive factories in the world and make their 120-miles-per-hour trains run on time. When the objectives are clear and the group is in agreement, the Japanese proceed with sparkling efficiency and relentless logic.

I believe that when Japanese complain about not being able to think straight, they are confusing incoherent thought with sensitivity to feelings and bad logic with an unwillingness to challenge accepted truths. A Japanese manager who has "every reason" to fire excess workers but keeps them on because of their past loyalty is perfectly aware of what he is doing. He is following a logic of human relations rather than the strict logic of profits. The Japanese are just as rational as anyone else when they want to be, but sometimes they set reason aside for more human considerations.

It may be that there is one kind of deep, intellectual probing that Japanese avoid. An American who knows Japan well once said to me, "The question 'Why?' doesn't have the same significance for the Japanese that it does for us. They never seem to ask themselves, 'Why am I here? Why do I exist?'" College sophomores might at least be expected to ask such questions, but perhaps radical skepticism poses too great a challenge to social consensus. A Japanese professor once told me, "You Westerners take care of those problems for us. We're too busy making cameras and motorcycles." In Japan there is no such thing as philosophy in the Western sense. Meaning, morality, and existence are not real issues for the Japanese. The debate on these questions is closed, and any attempt to reopen it would be abstract, irrelevant, and *rikutsuppoi*.

Hazy Japanese thinking is supposed to be related to Japan's emphasis on nonverbal communication. In Japan's "wet" atmosphere it is very important to be able to dope out the feelings and sense the emotions of a situation. Japanese work harder at this than Americans and, in fact, share so many values and expectations that they can often pack a lot of meaning into a voice inflection or a gesture. Sometimes they seem to communicate with the same subtlety and economy of means as old married couples who know each other inside out—or at least they think they can.

Japanese believe that the ultimate form of communication is silence, the wordless exchange of pure feeling. One Japanese writes about his country: "It might be said that the culture is primarily visual, not verbal, in orientation, and social decorum provides that silence, not eloquence, is rewarded."[7] The Japanese commonly think that they can communicate among themselves by a kind of telepathy.

One scholar thinks that Japanese expect too much from implicit understanding and that their habits among themselves lead to serious misunderstandings with foreigners. "The Japanese must learn to love words, must train themselves in rhetoric and the love of argument," he writes. "This is all the more necessary for the Japanese because these qualities are so foreign to their nature."[8]

At least one Western writer thinks that all this talk about how the Japanese don't talk to each other is pure nonsense.[9] I think it is probably true that Japanese see silent communication as yet more evidence of their uniqueness and tend to exaggerate their telepathic abilities. Nevertheless, even if only because they believe in it so strongly themselves, the emphasis on feelings and disdain for speech are important elements in their behavior.

Eloquence, for the Japanese, is a suspect quality, for it is too often the handmaiden of cold logic. They can jabber endlessly about trivia, but when serious issues must be resolved, they try to catch the feeling of a situation and will often justify a decision by how they read the mood. Fast talk, no matter how rational, can sometimes prejudice a case.

In Japan the belly, or *hara*, is the seat of true emotions. The word *haragei* ("belly arts") means an actor's ability to express his feelings directly to his audience without saying or doing anything. It also means a person's ability to transcend logic and solve problems with intuition or spirit. In both cases it is a process that circumvents speech and deals directly with feelings. To read a man's belly is to read his mind, and conspirators hatch a plot by putting their bellies together. Japanese are convinced that strong emotion can spring from belly to belly without taking the form of speech.

Japanese drama is full of scenes in which powerful feelings or terrible news are communicated wordlessly in circumstances in which Americans might be screaming at each other. The movieland samurai, with his purity and wisdom, is the perfect strong, silent type. With a grunt or a nod he can say it all.

Tora-san is the name of the hero of a popular Japanese movie series about a typical blue-collar Tokyo family. In a recent episode an American blunders into Tora-san's life and at one point makes a pass at a happily married woman. In the discussion that follows between Tora-san and his friends, the American is not so much condemned for desiring the woman as ridiculed for being thick; he actually had to be told no. A real man, Tora-san points out, would get the message long before it was verbal and then suavely withdraw. For the Japanese, it is rude to insist that something be spelled out when it should have been understood implicitly.

"Those of us who grew up in the 1930s were raised on the principle of action before words," writes a Japanese businessman who was recently assigned to America. "'No unnecessary talk,' we were told. 'Just do what you are expected to do; don't look for excuses; if you have done your best, it will show.' This doesn't seem to be the way Americans think."[10]

The reason they don't is that implicit communication works only among people who have a great deal in common. Americans take it for granted that they will not be understood by strangers unless they make themselves clear. They are used to saying, "I think this," or, "I want that," and if they have done their best, they may very well brag about it. Americans are a diverse lot, and only among close friends can they expect a subtle hint to be understood.

This difference is at the heart of Oriental "inscrutability." The Japanese do not say yes when they really mean no. As far as they are concerned, they may have communicated a perfectly clear no, but in a formula that Westerners might interpret as a maybe. The classic misunderstanding occurs when a Japanese turns down a business deal.

For example, a senior American colleague named Joe and I are making a serious pitch, in English, to a prospective customer. Suzuki-san brings up some objections, which we hash over for a while, and then Joe moves to close the deal: "What do you say, Suzuki-san? Are we ready to draw up the contract?"

"It is a little difficult," says Suzuki, giving us a faintly pained look.

Joe doesn't realize that we have just been told no. It takes another fifteen minutes, which are increasingly uncomfortable for Suzuki and me, before he gets the message and I can drag him away. In Japanese, *chotto muzukashii* ("a little difficult") really means "No thank you, gentlemen." After that point, we were wasting our words.

Sometimes Japanese seem so convinced of the futility of speech that they will not even try to put their feelings into words. One evening I was having dinner with a man who works in the finance department of a Japanese company when, to my surprise, he began to complain about his boss. It is unusual for Japanese businessmen to grumble about their superiors to outsiders, but Arai-san, as we will call him, had had several drinks and had sworn me to secrecy.

"He knows I hate accounting," he said. "He knows that the two years I spent doing it were the worst years of my life. I was perfectly happy doing investments, but three weeks ago he put me back on accounting. I can't understand it."

"Did the business suddenly require more bookkeeping?" I asked.

"No. And Kondo-san, who was doing it, likes that kind of work."

"Have you told the boss how you feel?"

"Are you kidding? If he doesn't understand the situation by now, do you think talking about it would do any good?"

This was a very Japanese reply. Arai-san was convinced that by now the boss should know how he felt about accounting but had given him the new assignment anyway. Complaining would only bring hard feelings into the open and make matters worse. On the other hand, if the boss were actually so insensitive as to be unaware of how Arai-san felt about the new assignment, then what sympathy could he expect if he grumbled about it now?

Misunderstandings with foreigners seem even more intractable to the Japanese. Time and again I have heard men who work for American companies finish a complaint about management with the remark "And there's no way they'd even understand what we're talking about." With foreigners, Japanese rarely get that "feeling" that permits real understanding. Americans are not used to having to ferret out people's feelings all the time. They expect people to talk rather than sulk.

Westerners who spend time in Japan begin to learn the importance of wordless belly reading. In Tokyo I knew three Americans who worked for the Japanese subsidiary of a major U.S. corporation. They all had spent some years in Japan and had made a serious effort to learn the language and understand the culture. Whenever they had a bone to pick with their boss, they would march into his office and do a silent "belly" dance around his desk. Gyrating and grimacing, they would wordlessly invite him to read what was on their mind. This was, of course, a comic travesty of *haragei* that only a *gaijin* would think of, but it reflected their understanding of the importance of implicit communication and their frustration with its difficulties.

The masters of traditional Japanese disciplines are almost explicit about the importance of implicit communication. In the most ancient schools of pottery, for example, there is no real teaching. Apprentices are expected to absorb the spirit of the clay through direct communion with it rather than learn specific techniques from the master. Robert, whom we met earlier, was apprenticed to one of Japan's oldest and most prestigious families of potters.

"In the beginning," says Robert, "they wouldn't even let me touch the clay. My job was to sweep out the studio, haul wood for the kiln, and run errands. It was a big day when I finally started making pots."

However, Robert discovered that there was no such thing as instruction. "I would ask the master how to do something, and he would just laugh at me. Like all Americans, I wanted to hear reasons, principles, theories. It was frustrating." Over the years Robert persevered and eventually became a respected journeyman potter. I asked him how he would go about training an apprentice, how he would teach the techniques he had learned.

"There are no techniques to be taught," he replied. "Either you develop a relationship with the clay or you don't. I would tell an apprentice to sweep the floor, haul wood, and just keep at it." Robert has clearly been won over to the traditional view.

Attitude and intuition are the foundation of what is probably Japan's greatest contribution to man's spirit and intellect: Zen Buddhism. Enlightenment cannot be learned; it can only be experienced. Zen masters do not give real Zen lessons; like the master potter, they create an environment where their disciples must learn for themselves. Zen is a world of feelings, of flashes of insight that transcend the limitations of speech and reason.

Sports are another area in which attitude and feeling are considered more important than they might be in the West. In the martial arts, enlightenment and spiritual superiority were thought to be key factors in a man's prowess. This thinking has spilled over into the way the Japanese play Western sports. An American, writing about what he calls "baseball samurai style," reports that ". . . training goes beyond the physical level, for masters of the martial arts taught that with sufficient powers of concentration the mind can make the body do almost anything. Consequently, a player's mental health is regarded [as] just as important as his physical shape."[11] The author goes on to describe the meditation, practice drills, and discipline used to develop "fighting spirit," the most admired quality in a baseball player.

The Japanese have an almost mystical faith in what can be accomplished with the right attitude. On the playing field, in the office, at home, in the artist's studio, attitude is almost as important as ability. Fortified with fighting spirit, the Japanese throw themselves into the contest.

Americans may be tempted to hold back a bit rather than go all out. They may think a half effort is all that is needed, or they may want to give themselves an excuse in case of failure. Japanese are generally not at all shy about trying their very hardest; fighting spirit requires a total commitment. In competitive endeavors Japanese admire an ostentatious show of determination. It is a sign of proper attitude and is meant to intimidate the opposition. Americans, by contrast, sometimes like to make it look as though they had won without even trying.

The Japanese have gotten in trouble on account of their belief that the right attitude could move mountains. During the Second World War the immense power of the United States was not supposed to matter; Japan would win because of its spiritual purity and unshakable resolve.

Fighting spirit is only the active, outward manifestation of the old Japanese virtue of *gaman*. This is patience, perseverance, self-control, the ability to endure quietly. The word has an instructive etymology. The characters used to write it literally mean "pride," and its original meaning was "self-importance" or "lack of consideration for others." That such a word should evolve to mean "uncomplaining, even heroic submission to adversity" is part of a peculiarly Japanese idea of virtue. To submit stoically, even to injustice, is a high calling, and the man who endures is morally superior to his tormentor. In this sense, what might seem humiliating to Westerners can be a source of pride.

Gaman is still highly praised in Japan. Whiners and quitters are admonished with a stern *"Gaman shiro!"* ("Perform *gaman!*"). The common Japanese proverb "Three years on a rock" is in praise of *gaman*. Even a cold, hard rock will warm up and feel comfortable if you sit on it for three years. *Gaman* is exactly what the Japanese finance man we met earlier was prepared to do—he hated his accounting assignment but was going to tough it out. *Gaman* is yet another nonverbal quality; the strong, "proud" man keeps his suffering to himself.

As a child I was introduced to a different kind of *gaman*. On the playground at school a boy's reputation depended on how well he could fight. There were always wimps who never fought at all, but if a boy was to have any real status, he had to duke it out with some tough guy every so often. Usually a girl (no boy would interfere with these manly rites) would run to get a teacher to put a stop to things before we did each other much damage. However, when we actually got past the squaring-off stage, the worst, most humiliating way to lose was to cry. It was more honorable to run away than to give proof of suffering.

Recently a French market researcher did a study of how pain was perceived in a number of countries. Not surprisingly, in the United States he found that pain is just plain bad. Americans knock it out with painkillers just the way John Wayne shoots a bad Indian.[12] In Japan, however, he found that shrugging off pain is part of being Japanese. Children endure pain to show how grown-up they are.

The Japanese, of course, want relief from pain just like everybody else, but it would never do to scream about it. The Frenchman explains:

> . . . the doctor will not insult the patient by giving him a pain-killer, even though, of course, the patient would be glad to have it. . . . [The patient] will never ask for it because it would make him lose face. . . . [You] can still sell pain-killers in Japan, but, in that case, you should never call them pain-killers. You can say that it is a product to rebalance the body or to put you in harmony with your surroundings, with your family. But you can never say directly that it's a pain-killer because in Japan, a pain-killer is a culture-killer.[13]

One Japanese I have known for many years thinks that *gaman* is the secret to Japan's modern success. "You figure out where the Japanese get their *gaman* and you've got Japan figured out," he says.

If *gaman* represents the stern, joyless side of the nonrational, Shinto festivals represent its merrymaking side. Shinto, which is Japan's major indigenous religion, is more a part of daily life than Buddhism. It is unconcerned with reason.

As missionaries to Japan sometimes point out, the world view of Shinto is in many respects opposed to the rational monotheistic world view of the West. Shinto is the worship of ancestors and countless nature gods, whose number is traditionally put at 800 myriad. These gods do not live detached from human beings but inhabit the same world people do. They can be whimsical, eccentric fellows whose powers are limited, and different gods are sometimes in conflict with each other. Shinto gods seem to be happiest when people are prosperous and enjoying themselves. Shinto is, therefore, a religion of festivals in which the Japanese eat, drink, and make merry, thank the gods for all good things, and ask for more. It is also a religion of charms and magic, but not one in which sin or evil plays an important part.

By contrast, the Western God is a single, all-powerful Creator, who establishes universal justice and order. He may move in mysterious ways, but His first principles follow a kind of holy logic. No single god of Shinto's confused jumble of minor deities demands exclusive loyalty or lays down rigid rules of behavior. A great many Japanese describe themselves as both Shinto and Buddhist; neither religion claims the exclusive universality that Christianity, Judaism, or Islam does.

In this environment of tolerance and relativism the distinction between gods and men can blur. The emperor, for example, is said to be a direct descendant of the sun goddess Amaterasu. After the Second World War the Americans ordered him to renounce his divinity. They felt that a living god was too tempting a focus for fanatical nationalism. In some respects, however, this renunciation was meaningless for the Japanese. The emperor had never claimed anything like the omnipotence that Americans associated with divinity.

In fact, the emperor has retained his vital role as the chief priest of Shinto. Every year one of his jobs is to plant some rice seedlings in the spring and reap a few ripe ears in the fall. This harks back to prehistoric times, when the tribal leader was thought to have a special ability to gain favors from the gods of fertility and harvest. Even in modern industrial Japan the leader of the Japanese tribe guarantees the success of the rice harvest.

The emperor is not the only person who can be thought of as a god. Any powerful or accomplished individual may be referred to as *kami-sama*, or god. Recently, when former Prime Minister Tanaka was attacked on charges of corruption, one of his admirers defended him simply by saying that he was *kami-sama*.[14] In Japan anyone who is indisputably at the top of his field may occasionally achieve the status of minor deity. The novelist Naoya Shiga (1883–1971) was known as *shōsetsu no kami-sama* ("the god of the novel"). At the extremes, divinity and humanity can merge.

At a more popular level this laxness of distinctions between god and human, rational and irrational, can shade into what appears to Westerners as just plain superstition. Shinto charms and amulets, for example, are big business. Wives who want to get pregnant wear them, mothers buy them for their children at exam time, and people about to go into the hospital take them along for speedy recovery. Practically every vehicle in Japan has hanging from the rearview mirror a small, embroidered pouch which contains a special charm to prevent traffic accidents.

Drivers who want further protection can always take their cars for a special blessing at the Nishiarai Daishi Temple in Tokyo. In a quaint ceremony that is held half a dozen times a day, drivers park their cars in a neat row and stand respectfully beside them while a Buddhist priest conducts a short service. Afterward the priest gives each vehicle an individual blessing to ward off accidents.[15]

Names can have occult powers. There is a brisk trade in books that explains how the characters used to write a person's name affect his health, career, and love life. Parents about to have a baby often buy a numerology book that explains the significance of the number of brushstrokes in a child's name. They are careful to choose a name that will not bring bad luck.

Another important consideration for some parents is the conjunction of zodiac signs at the time of the child's birth. The Japanese use two different Chinese calendars for identifying the years. One system gives each year the name of one of a dozen animals—mouse, cow, tiger, rabbit, etc.—in a cycle that repeats itself every twelve years. According to the other calendar, each year is named after an element—wood, fire, earth, etc.—in a similar cycle that repeats itself every decade. Each year, therefore, is identified with both an animal and an element, and each of the sixty possible combinations is thought to be freighted with significance.

One of the worst conjunctions is that of fire and horse, which is a year of conflagrations and a dreadful time to have baby daughters. Women born in such a year are believed to be ill-fated shrews who are likely to murder their husbands. The last time that combination came around was in 1966; the Japanese birthrate dropped by 19 percent from the previous year and then rebounded by 28 percent the next year. Some parents who had a horse-fire daughter have tried to falsify the child's birth certificate.

A common way to solicit the mysterious forces is to buy a small wooden tablet at a local shrine, write a wish on it, and tie it onto a special rack built to hold the hundreds of wishes that soon accumulate. The wish collection hangs in a public area of the shrine, so an amusing way to get an idea of what is on people's minds is to read through a batch of them.

Most fit a straightforwardly selfish pattern: Men want to do well on exams and get good jobs; women want to get married and have babies, although increasingly, they, too, want to do well on exams. Occasionally wishes take a tone that seems inappropriate for suppliants. I once ran across a tablet written by a woman who wanted to make her debut as a professional singer *within the next six months*. Virtually all the tablets conclude unselfconsciously with the wishers' names and addresses, and I sometimes wish I had written the singer to ask about her debut.

Commenting on these widespread superstitions, an American missionary who has spent thirty years in Japan says, "It's tempting to assume that because of their industry and technology, the Japanese are pretty much secularized. That's a big mistake. A great frustration for missionaries in this country is the continued existence in modern Japan of what Westerners think of as a 'primitive,' preindustrial religious mentality."

Even mainstream Buddhism has a vast subculture devoted to magic, divination, and get-rich-quick schemes. Just like some American preachers who urge the flock to parlay Christianity into worldly riches, a number of Buddhist authorities are pushing quick-fix religion. The author of a raft of Buddhist bestsellers explains why you should read his books:

Far too many people have run into disaster and bad luck because they ignored the spirits. . . . The only way to make it through the tough 1980s is to work hard and improve your luck. If you treat the ancestral spirits right, your whole family will be healthy and prosperous.

The spirits of your ancestors can be your guardian spirits, and whether or not your family has guardian spirits makes a world of difference. The spirits will ward off misfortune and arrange success in studies, work, business, family problems—anything at all.[16]

For a religion that was originally meant to help people transcend the material world, this all sounds remarkably down-to-earth.

Keeping the spirits happy can be expensive. A Buddhist equipment store I know of sent around full-color glossy flyers in the local papers to advertise a big sale on spirit cabinets. These are elaborate pieces of furniture that stand as tall as a man and provide a suitable home for friendly spirits. The cabinets in the flyer ran from a bargain-basement $1,000 model all the way up to a lacquer and gold-leaf extravaganza for $11,000. The store even offered vacation trips to northern Japan and a motorscooter sweepstakes for whoever bought a cabinet during the sale.

In recent decades Japan has been fertile soil for new religions. An estimated 20 percent of the Japanese population is involved with these new cults, most of which have sprung up since 1945.[17] These religions tend to be eclectic and simpleminded, promising earthly rewards in exchange for a few simple techniques or a little mumbo jumbo.

One of the best known is Sōka Gakkai, which was founded in 1930 but did not really catch on until 1956. It is an offshot of Nichiren Buddhism and teaches that simply by chanting the sutra *Nammyō hō rengekyō* over and over, the believer will get whatever he wants. This religion has launched a major political party, claims 11 million members, and has done extensive missionary work in the United States.

Many of the new cults borrow elements from major religions and blend them together. They add a new twist to the Japanese love of harmony by teaching that all religions are good and true. In the main worship hall of one such cult there is a Buddhist image in front, a

Christian cross on the left, and a star of David to the right.[18] Other religions appeal to the credulous by promising outright shamanism: miracle cures, magic, and divination.

However, the most important contribution these religions make is not their lightweight doctrine or success in life. They provide a tightly knit supporting group for those Japanese who do not have one. Lonely Japanese come to prayer meetings and stay to talk over their troubles. They are welcomed into the camp of the faithful, where they find the context of concern and involvement that Japanese so appreciate. Many of the new religions offer the equivalent of group therapy.

Compared to Westerners, Japanese tend to be frankly expedient about religion. It is not a lofty, high-minded realm of doctrine and duty. It is another angle on how to get that promotion or a little extra protection against traffic accidents. It is such a part of worldly concerns that the line between the religious and the secular is easily blurred.

A veteran missionary who has lived for years in rural Japan tells of being approached by a representative of the village for a contribution to help maintain a local Shinto shrine. "I told him that I was a Christian," she says, "and that I couldn't in good conscience contribute to the fund. The man looked at me in surprise and said, 'But everybody contributes. It doesn't have anything to do with religion.'"

A similarly hazy notion of what is or is not religion seems to be part of the present controversy over government support for Japan's Shinto memorial for its war dead, the Yasukuni Shrine. Nearly 2.5 million spirits have been deified and enshrined at Yasukuni, which sits on twenty-four pleasantly wooded acres in downtown Tokyo. Although Japan's Constitution strictly separates state and religion, high government officials have taken to making public appearances at the shrine on government time, at government expense. Many Japanese see no constitutional obstacle to government support for the shrine and argue that looking after the spirits of the war dead is simple patriotism. Others are calling for an amendment to the Constitution that would permit state support and lay the question to rest once and for all.

Yasukuni has also been involved in a bizarre instance of involuntary deification. In 1973 Takefumi Nakaya, a member of the Japanese

Self-Defense Force, was killed in an auto accident. As a professional soldier he was qualified for enshrinement and was duly deified. However, Nakaya and his wife were Christians. His wife sued the government for this affront to her husband's faith, pointing out that his spirit was deified without her knowledge or permission. Finally, in 1982, after years of legal proceedings and an unsuccessful appeal by the government to higher courts, Mrs. Nakaya succeeded in getting a final court order to have her husband's spirit desanctified. During her years of struggle Mrs. Nakaya received reams of poison-pen letters accusing her of "un-Japanese" behavior.

For many of her detractors, ritual deification was not primarily a question of religious conscience. There is something about Shinto that is to them far more *Japanese* than religious. They saw Mrs. Nakaya's refusal to accept "pagan" rites for her husband's soul as some form of political treachery rather than as an act of religious conviction. The missionary's refusal to contribute to the village shrine was likewise an offense against village unity rather than a religious statement. Modes of thought and behavior that seem clearly religious to Westerners are tradition, culture, or folklore to the Japanese. Westerners are amused by the very idea of touching a Christian missionary for a Shinto donation; that it should happen at all shows how unselfconsciously the Japanese practice their religion.

According to the very earliest Shinto creation myths, the home islands were born from the physical union of two creator gods, and the Japanese people sprang from this sacred soil. As one scholar writes, "Probably the number of Japanese who believe [these] myths . . . is very small nowadays. But I think that some of these ideas still have a strong influence on the world view of Japanese and their ways of thinking."[19] At some level Shinto is so natural to the Japanese that to call it a religion is to make more of it than it deserves.

Before the Second World War the Japanese government capitalized on this mystical undercurrent by promoting a form of State Shinto, which revolved around patriotism and veneration of the emperor. The government claimed that church and state were still separate because State Shinto had nothing to do with religion—it was merely part of being Japanese.

Today very few Japanese consider themselves strongly religious. However, virtually all observe the midsummer festival of Obon, which honors the spirits of departed ancestors, and funerals are almost without exception conducted according to Buddhist rites.

The Buddhist flavor of death does not exclude numerous Shinto observances during life. Groundbreaking for a new building must wait until a Shinto priest in full regalia has made a pass over the area to alert the local gods to the coming construction. Ships cannot be launched without a similar ceremony to win the favor of the sea gods. Most Japanese would agree that Buddhist funerals are genuinely religious but might argue that a Shinto groundbreaking has no more religious significance than a turkey dinner on "Thanksgiving" Day does for most Americans.

The pseudonymous author of the Japanese best seller *The Japanese and the Jews* has an interesting perspective on religion in Japan. In his view, all Japanese, no matter how secular they may seem, are members of a religion he calls Japanism. He maintains that there is something faintly religious about being born Japanese and that in Japan Christianity, Buddhism, and all other religions are nothing more than subcults of Japanism.[20] This theory is all the more intriguing to Japanese because the man who is now known to be the book's author is a Japanese Catholic.

Missionaries have been baffled by what appears to be hard evidence for Japanism. I know one young American Christian who spent several years in Japan and discovered the kind of resistance many Japanese have to Christianity. "One woman told me quite plainly that she had a great deal of respect for the teachings of Christ," he recalls, "but she said she could never become a Christian because she was Japanese. For her, Christianity was too alien. It might work for Americans, but it was incompatible with being Japanese."

This attitude is related to the tendency to operate according to group and context, rather than universal principle. Missionaries arrive in Japan preaching a doctrine they believe to be true for all circumstances. The Japanese think that Christianity is too universal, too abstract, and not concerned enough about the specifics of human relations. In short, it is *rikutsuppoi*.

Put differently, the reason why Japanese balk at Christianity is that it demands exclusive loyalty. If the demands of the community are in conflict with the demands of God, Christianity teaches men to follow God. This takes great courage in any society but is part of the Western mythology about individual autonomy. For the Japanese, it is well-nigh unthinkable to forsake the group for a principle or belief, no matter how deeply felt.

Christianity seems to be one of the few forces from the West that actually threaten the Japanese identity. Japanese have absorbed everything else—from Jean-Paul Sartre to roll-on deodorant—but in spite of intensive missionary efforts both before and since the war, fewer than 1 percent of all Japanese are Christians. This is one of the lowest figures in the world and puts Japan at the same level as Kampuchea, Mauritania, or mainland China. Korea, by contrast, is 10 percent Christian, and the church there has considerable authority.

It may be that what has made modern Japan impregnable to Christianity is at the heart of its porousness to other Western influences. Japanese do not live by abstract codes and instinctively reject them. They prefer the warmth of human relations to the cold elegance of abstract systems. At the same time, a culture that never built up rational systems based on universal principles also never erected philosophical barriers to the entry of new ideas and techniques.

Not many nations are able to accept huge doses of alien thought and culture without upheaval. Iran, which had strict, universal values of its own, gagged so violently on Westernization that recovery is still not in sight. China, Burma, Saudi Arabia, and all the East European countries tightly ration alien influences.

Since the war Japan has had no choice but to throw open its doors to an onslaught of foreign forces. It has not fallen apart, become a dictatorship, or ceased to be Japanese. It has flourished. This is in part because there are no exclusive ideologies native to Japan. Absorption has thrived on the Japanese love of harmony and knack for reconciling the irreconcilable.

I also suspect that Japan's emphasis on feeling, emotion, and attitude has meant that the Japanese identity has not been bound up with the style that people adopt or even what they profess to think. At a much deeper level what defines the Japanese in their own eyes is how they feel. Being and feeling Japanese is a state of grace into which all Japanese—but only the Japanese—are born. It is this powerful sense of exclusion and uniqueness, this profound identity with the nation and its people that allow them to absorb all kinds of non-Japanese art and science without much fear of losing their grip on what it is that makes them Japanese.

Japan's exclusiveness is made not of ideas but of blood and emotions. It is the conviction that the Japanese are unique. Science, technology, art, ideas—none of these threatens that uniqueness, and all are welcome.

The last thirty years have seen their share of confusion and bad choices. Also, the Japanese probably spend more time agonizing over their national identity than any other people on earth. This is not because they are afraid they haven't got one; it is because it is so strong and obtrusive that it constantly demands explanation and definition. No matter how much Japan takes from the West, the Japanese have not for a moment ceased to *feel* Japanese.

PART

2

CHAPTER SIX

❊

THE
CORPORATION

Every morning, before work, the 400 employees line up in neat rows on the company grounds to hear a brief peptalk from the plant manager. Usually his theme is the company philosophy: "service, quality, and profits." All the workers are dressed in company uniforms—pink, blue, or yellow, according to seniority. After the day's message the employees do calisthenics in unison, while the plant manager counts out the beat. Then it's off to work for the company that its employees praise for its no-layoffs policy and family atmosphere.

Is this Yokohama? Hiroshima? No, this is San Diego, California, and the 400 uniformed employees are Americans. They work for the Kyoto Ceramic Company, which has had a California assembly plant since 1971.[1] Has Japanese-style management come to America? It has certainly come to San Diego, and some say it should spread out across the nation.

In recent years the corporation, as the driving force behind Japan's economic miracle, has caught the imagination of Western scholars and businessmen alike. As Japan continues to flood the world with exports, its hard-pressed trade rivals have begun to wonder if they shouldn't drop their own management strategies and imitate the Japanese. Because of close postwar ties with Japan, Americans have been among the first to take Japanese management seriously. More than ten U.S. business schools now offer courses on Japanese business strategy and the Japanese economy, and New York University recently announced plans to set up a brand-new center for Japanese business studies.[2]

Other countries are not far behind. For the new socialist France of President François Mitterrand, Japan—not the United States—is now the standard by which managers and government planners are judged. For many developing countries, the Japanese model seems more promising than any in the West. The Ivory Coast, for example, styles itself the Japan of West Africa.

Scholars and management specialists of all nations have traveled to Japan to plumb the secrets of success. Once there they found a lot to write about. Some Japanese management practices are nothing more than successful applications of Western techniques, but others are unique to Japan. The structure of the economy itself encourages distinctive business strategies.

Students of Japan have now come home to report their findings. They have broadly publicized Japan's close business-government relations and such typical practices as bottom-up management, lifetime employment, enterprise unions, quality control circles, and management by generalists. With a flourish they have announced that Japanese-style management is the secret of Japan's success and that Western executives have important lessons to learn from the Japanese.

Several of the techniques that have won such admiration are excellent, and I will examine them at some length. Also, since they are part of the same system, I will take a close look at some unattractive methods that Japan's admirers have chosen not to publicize.

Nevertheless, I should make it clear from the start that I think the entire issue of management is a red herring. Japan's success is not due to management tricks that any ambitious executive can learn. It is built on the national characteristics outlined in previous chapters, on a powerful combination of diligence, loyalty, and devotion to the group that makes Japanese workers unique. It is the Japanese worker, not the executive, who has made Japan great. In my view, management's main achievement is to have channeled and directed the qualities that workers bring to the job in the first place.

In any discussion of Japanese business practices, two things should be borne in mind. The first is that in Japan business is very much a man's world. What is true of male employees is often not true of women.

The second is that the Japanese economy is divided into two tiers. The top tier consists of the large, successful companies and the government departments that work closely with them. Although this group employs only about one-third of the Japanese work force, it is the overwhelming power center of the economy and is the focus of almost all foreign attention. It is here that some would find lessons for the West.

The second tier includes family businesses and other small operations, which often have close ties with first-tier companies. There is no clear demarcation of tiers; between the topflight companies that are household words and the mass of struggling small fry, there is a hazy middle ground of expanding companies with first-tier aspirations.

The two tiers are worlds apart in pay, prestige, and working conditions. I have seen many second-tier shop floors that were greasy, rag-littered places with mobs of workers struggling over old, wheezing machines. First-tier shops are as clean as a hospital, with a few well-groomed workers to tend the gleaming machinery. It's no trick to tell the tiers apart—that is, for anyone who has seen both. The Japanese, of course, prefer to take visitors through their showpiece factories. Plenty of Americans, therefore, end up seeing so much supermodern technology in Japan they come home wondering if the United States isn't an underdeveloped country. All they have seen is the first tier.

Of all the top-tier practices to gain notice in the West, lifetime employment is probably the most important. Big companies hire only at the entry level and are committed to complete job security. New recruits, just out of school, match that commitment with a determination to stay with the company until retirement. This system has advantages for both sides. The company can lavish training on its men with the assurance that they will never quit and go work for a competitor. Management also knows it will never be left in the lurch by the sudden defection of key personnel. In return, the employee is confident that come hell or high water, he will never be laid off. Management and labor develop a warm sense of cooperation and shared interests.

On the other hand, once a man has thrown in his lot with one top-tier company, he is stuck. A Sony employee who discovers that he can't stand electronics cannot pick up and go work for a bank. Like Sony, the other big names hire only young, entry-level graduates. A former Sony man is too old to rehire and is tainted by the Sony experience. Unless he is willing to drop down to some unglamorous second-tier company that will hire secondhand labor, he will be with his company for thirty-odd years. His fortunes are tied to Sony's until retirement.

Sometimes, just for fun, I needle my Japanese friends about lifetime employment. "Aren't you the slightest bit bored after twenty years with Yamaguchi Electric?" I ask.

The Yamaguchi man looks at me as if I were crazy. "After all these years with Yamaguchi how could I possibly work anywhere else? What a silly idea!" The longer he stays, the more loyal he feels. Changing jobs would be an unthinkable betrayal.

Another common personnel practice in top-tier companies is the rotation of employees through different corporate divisions. In America a finance man is likely to change companies but may stay in finance all his life. In Japan new employees are often put through an initial tour of the entire company and may then go on to work four or five years at a time in several different departments. This means that by the time Japanese managers reach the top they are familiar with all aspects of the company's business.

Bottom-up management and consensus decision making are two processes that complement each other. In Japanese companies there is a tendency for initiatives to come, or appear to come, from below. A new position paper will slowly circulate up through the layers of management with repeated trips back to the bottom for change and clarification. Everyone remotely involved in the proposal has a chance to see the paper and stamp it in red with his personal chop. A paper that has made the rounds can end up looking like the Treaty of Versailles.

The final decision comes out of numerous meetings in which every point of view is aired and the all-important consensus is finally reached. Great care is taken to reconcile differences and reach a decision that everyone can live with.

Japanese top management, of course, does not sit on its hands. However, when it takes the initiative, the decision-making process is much the same. A junior employee is assigned to write the position paper and shepherd its passage through the company. Other low-level employees have a chance to read the proposal and add their comments. When the order finally comes down, everyone knows what considerations went into it and can act upon it with confidence.

An obvious flaw in this sytem is that decision making takes longer than in the West. An American educator I know named Johnson has been working in Japan for more than thirty years. Early in his career he used to come home, fuming, after faculty meetings where every possible option was hashed and rehashed late into the night. "I couldn't understand why the president wouldn't just decide one way or the other," he says.

Recently Johnson was elected president of the college, but faculty meetings still stretch late into the night. "It may be crazy," he admits, "but that's the way it has to be done. If I were to let everybody say his piece and then announce, 'OK, the English department gets two floors of the new building,' it would poison the air for weeks. The dean would come up to me and say, 'Now, Johnson-san, you know better than to do that. Professor Tanaka felt very strongly that the physics department needed one of those floors. The discussion was not finished.'" Johnson has discovered that the power of his position is mostly theoretical. The group decides.

Japanese managers are impressed by the way Americans issue crisp, well-defined orders from the top. They are also surprised at how much authority a negotiator for a Western company may have to adjust his company's position. Their system requires that each new proposal be looked over by many different people, so negotiators keep running back to head office for more consensus.

One result of group decision making is that responsibility is diffused throughout the whole hierarchy. This is fine when the decision was the right one; everyone thinks of it as partly his own and fully supports it. But if the decision turns out to be wrong, it has such a head of steam behind it that it may be very difficult to correct. In American companies decisions are more closely linked to individual executives. This makes it tough on the handful of decision makers, on whom failure can be clearly pinned. They may find themselves out of a job, but the entire organization is less likely to keep charging on in what is clearly the wrong direction.

This process highlights an important difference between Japanese and American executives. Americans associate high position with authority, decision making, and personal responsibility. Managers are admired for innovative ideas and the ability to mobilize subordinates to execute those ideas. In Japan business executives are like all group leaders in that the quality that counts most is the ability to manage consensus and steer the group toward harmony. Thus American top executives tend to be sharp, forceful men, while their Japanese counterparts are less colorful but may be wizards at managing personalities.

Another striking aspect of Japanese companies is their international perspective. Even the managers of small firms think of all Asia as a potential market and source of low-cost materials. The great trading houses, which handle half of Japan's foreign commerce, have played a key role in alerting their domestic customers to overseas opportunities. In America, on the other hand, the same trading companies are likely to run into a brick wall when they try to persuade a small firm to export.

"You Americans make plenty of things we Japanese would like to buy." A trading company man is giving me a lesson over Bloody Marys. "We even have a guy whose job is to go to Safeway and Woolworth's to look for things he thinks would sell in Japan. But chances are, when he contacts the manufacturer, the Americans aren't willing to meet us halfway. They won't downsize the product to meet Japanese requirements or even package it properly for overseas shipping. They won't take the basic first steps to open up a new market."

Some large U.S. companies are just as stubborn. Japanese automakers sell Americans more than 1.5 million cars every year. They have been so successful that we have had to negotiate quotas on imports to protect our tottering domestic manufacturers, who can sell only 4,000 or 5,000 cars a year in Japan.

U.S. automakers have a familiar refrain of excuses to explain the imbalance: Japanese import duties; nontariff barriers; administrative delays; different emission standards. These complaints may have been valid in the past, but are no longer. The main problem is that American manufacturers never bothered to wonder what kind of car the Japanese would like to buy. They have tried to push off on the Japanese the same huge cars built for the American market. No one in Detroit even seems to realize that the Japanese drive on the left. We keep trying to sell them cars that have the steering wheel on the wrong side! No Japanese manufacturer would ever dream of trying to export such an ill-suited product.

At least American automakers have not entirely ignored export markets. Most U.S. companies never even take a look overseas. They should. "Did you know," a Japanese friend once asked me, "that there are certain brands of American hi-fi equipment that are better than anything made in Japan?"

"JBL," he continued, "makes speakers that put the Japanese to shame. But Japanese hi-fi nuts have to come all the way to America to buy them—they're not even sold in Japan. Now, if I were running that company, I would give it a brand-new marketing strategy."

He is not the only Japanese who would. One admiring *gaijin* has written, "If you rounded up a bunch of Japanese grade school kids and asked them, 'How can Japan survive with no natural resources?' one hundred out of one hundred would probably reply: 'Exports!'"[3]

Quality control (QC) circles, which have become famous in Japan, were actually invented in America. They are work teams of up to fifteen people who are responsible for one aspect of the production process. They meet regularly to figure out ways to do the job better. QC circles encourage greater employee identification with the company and the product and put this identification to work, cutting costs and eliminating defects. They may be pitted against each other to see which can come up with the most money-saving suggestions and bring the defect rate closest to zero. The most successful circle may be recognized at an annual QC banquet. QC circles develop team spirit and pride in workmanship.

Whole companies can be run like one big QC circle. Since 1951 Japan's top firms have competed for the annual Deming Prize, awarded for outstanding achievement in productivity and quality control. Quality and productivity are such important concerns in Japan that the hoopla of the awards ceremony is broadcast on nationwide television. W. Edwards Deming, whom the Japanese venerate as the high priest of productivity, is an eighty-year-old professor who is little-known in his native land: the United States.[4] Although Deming's ideas were first formulated to help American business, it is in Japan that they have been best received.

A second group of Japanese business practices is directly related to the structure of the economy and might be difficult to imitate elsewhere. For example, Japan does not have trade unions. It has enterprise unions that function within a single company. In the United States teamsters, auto workers, and machinists band together by trade *across* company lines.

In Japan a single union represents all the employees of one company. All but the top executives are members, and the union concentrates on conditions in its own company rather than in the entire industry. Strikes are therefore a double-edged sword. If one enterprise union votes to strike, it cannot expect sympathy strikes from union members in other companies. It will be the only company in the entire industry that comes to a halt. Its competitors can swoop in on its customers, leaving the struck company permanently weakened. Only the wildest unions would dare run such a risk. American unions cannot always strike an entire industry, but by organizing horizontally, they have built a much broader power base.

American unions do not hesitate to use their power. In 1979 the United States lost 33 million man-days to strikes. Japan, with about half America's population, lost less than 1 million man-days. In second-tier companies, labor-management confrontations can be bitter and sometimes even violent, but in the first tier, strikes—when they occur—are often nothing more than *pro forma* expressions of union resolve.

The ritual of confrontation has been formalized in the *shuntō*, or spring labor offensive. Unions plaster the walls with their demands, and workers march around the streets, chanting and waving signs. The *shuntō* is often more bark then bite; in 1982 the spring offensive did not result in a single lost workday.

"Sure, we talk about strikes," says a chemical company man who used to be active in his union. "We even had one a couple of years ago—a fifteen-minute strike. It was all part of the game; we knew management was going to be reasonable. It's only the government unions in monopoly industries that really go on strike. National railway workers walk off their jobs all the time, and look at the mess they've made: the railroad loses money hand over fist."

Private Japanese unions thus take a cooperative stance toward management and endorse its long-range goals. It is not unusual for the chief executive of a company to have spent part of his career as head of the company union, something unthinkable in America or Europe. According to one survey, two-thirds of the directors of major Japanese companies were at one time labor leaders.[5]

Japanese management style is also colored by friendly relations between government and business, an intimacy that has attracted a lot of foreign attention. Some observers have seen such a close and unholy alliance between the two that they have coined the name Japan Inc. There is no question that Japan's Ministry of International Trade and Industry (MITI) and the Ministry of Finance keep jealous watch over their domains. MITI is the direct descendant of the wartime Munitions Ministry, an institution so feared and respected that the very mention of its name is said to have been enough to hush a crying child.[6] Today MITI is credited with a major role in running the economy, and its bureaucrats have come to take wry pleasure in their overseas reputation as master manipulators. "My name is Yoshida," a MITI man once announced to me in perfect English. "I am from the notorious MITI."

MITI is actually a little like the league officials who police professional sports in America. They create optimum playing conditions for the teams, without telling the coaches who to put in the lineup.[7] MITI tries to create optimum economic conditions by encouraging efforts in promising industries, seeing that the right technology is imported, urging mergers when necessary, and generally keeping an eye on the needs of the economy as a whole.

When times are bad, MITI organizes "antidepression cartels" so that competing companies share a shrinking market equitably rather than fight each other. MITI has little statutory authority, but its "administrative guidance" comes from the top of the national hierarchy and is generally respected by the consensus-seeking Japanese.

Clearly MITI's functions go beyond those of American regulatory agencies. Some of MITI's objectives are more like those of the French Ministry of Planning, which plays a similar role in governing the overall direction of the economy.

Tax laws reflect the priorities of a society and influence the flow of resources. In the United States all interest payments a person makes are tax-deductible, whereas interest income is fully taxed. This encourages Americans to borrow, not save, and stimulates the building industry by easing the pain of mortgage payments. In Japan these priorities are reversed. Individuals get no tax break on interest payments but get generous exemptions on interest received. Households save rather than borrow, and the money they put in the bank is passed along at low rates to corporate borrowers. As a result, the Japanese live in cramped housing but work in handsome, up-to-date factories.

The structure of the Japanese economy also encourages companies to emphasize growth and market share at the expense of current profits. Several factors allow this. One, of course, is the lifetime employment system, which means that a company's managers are in for the long haul. They needn't be in a hurry to show quick profits because they will still be around when the returns on long-term investment begin to come in.

In American companies success is much more closely linked to personal executive talent, so top managers are eager to see profits *now*. Unlike the Japanese, they may also have profit-sharing and stock option plans. These encourage executives to pursue quick profits rather than design long-term projects that may not bear fruit until after they have moved on.

Another stimulus to capture market share is the remarkable resemblance most companies have to their competitors. As we noted earlier, Japanese companies tend to concentrate in´one field rather than branch out like American conglomerates. This means they are directly comparable with each other. In the prestige rankings for companies, size, which is directly related to market share, is just as important as profits.

Japanese financing patterns also permit a more relaxed attitude toward immediate profits. Japanese companies have much higher ratios of debt to equity than their Western counterparts, so debtholders often have a greater say in operations than stockholders do. Debtholder control is further consolidated by large stockholdings; a company's lead bank is often its largest stockholder.*

---

*Banks and other institutions like to control Japanese companies without the inconvenience of answering to small, private shareholders. Their distaste for shareholder democracy has given rise to a profession that is perhaps unique to Japan: the *sōkaiya*.

Sōkaiya started out as small-time thugs who would buy a few shares of a company's stock and then come to the annual meeting just to make trouble. Many executives were willing to pay them just to keep quiet, but gradually the *sōkaiya* assumed a new duty: policing the annual meeting and bouncing anyone *else* who asks awkward questions. Japanese chief executives have thus been spared public interrogation on questionable practices, unexplained losses, or investments in South Africa and are often able to polish off an annual meeting in less than ten minutes. Recent changes in the law are expected to make it harder for them to operate, but as late as 1979, 58 percent of the companies listed on the Tokyo Stock Exchange admitted to police that they hired *sōkaiya*.[8]

Since the bank's loans to the company dwarf its equity holdings, fat interest payments are more important to it than dividends. It favors expansion and the capacity to take on more debt. Therefore, company executives don't have to worry so much about high dividend rates to raise their stock price. Instead, they can concentrate on the long-term measures that will make their company a good risk for long-term lenders.

Finally, in Japan, there is a strong Confucian ideal of the gentleman merchant who runs his business with an eye to serving society. I have heard plenty of bigwig speeches about the higher calling of business. "Profits are necessary," runs the argument, "only in order for our company to reach its nobler goals. Of course, we must think of the welfare of our employees and the satisfaction of our customers, but the real goal of Takenaka Cement is to build a brighter, happier Japan. . . ." Most of the time I think they mean it.

So far we have seen some of the distinctive features of Japanese companies that have attracted the interest and even the admiration of their competitors. Let us now look at a few that have not.

One surprising phenomenon that no one suggests as a model for the West is industrywide imitation. Japanese companies within the same industry not only look alike but act alike. Booms hit Japanese business just the way they hit Japanese society. No country's businessmen are immune to fashion, but Japanese managers have a peculiar weakness for it.

Recently Japanese trading companies went on a spree of buying grain elevators in the United States. As soon as one or two big names moved into the field, the half dozen other companies felt they had to follow suit. Their men posted in America were ordered against their better judgment to go out and hunt for grain elevators. At the time several disappointed trading-company men told me that anyone who wanted to get into the American elevator business should wait five years. By then, they added, the Japanese companies will have realized they made a mistake and will decide, once again all together, to unload their loss-making elevators at bargain prices.

In a similar move not long ago the major Japanese steelmakers upgraded their small U.S. representative offices and incorporated them as full subsidiaries. There had been no change in their activities that would require incorporation, so I decided to take a steelman to lunch and get the inside story. After I had expressed polite skepticism at several flabby reasons that didn't ring true, he finally explained: "All right, I think the main reason is that everybody else is doing it. It wouldn't look good to be the only company without a full subsidiary." The Japanese manager of a U.S. consulting firm's Tokyo office writes, "A me-tooism mind-set is common in Japanese companies, the notion that 'whatever the competition does, we *must* do.'"[9]

Japanese businessmen readily admit that decision making by imitation is sometimes silly but explain that companies feel better when they all are running in the same pack. It is just as unusual for companies to make brilliantly original moves as it is for their employees to break out and start companies of their own. Japanese businessmen seem to be happiest when they all are doing the same thing.

A recent fad has been the revival of an old business technique that went out of fashion during the heady days of double-digit GNP growth. More and more Japanese managers are turning for help to Inari, the Shinto fox god that is in charge of business prosperity. As times get tougher, Japanese companies try to outfox the competition by building private Inari shrines on corporate property.

This is big business for the Fushimi Inari Shrine in Kyoto, the headquarters of the Inari cult. For a new branch shrine to take effect, the builders have to buy a dollop of divinity from Fushimi as a kind of starter culture. The priests at Fushimi report a big jump to about twenty requests a day for shares of the holy spirit, which can run anywhere from $20 to $400 apiece.

Rooftops are the best place to build shrines because there is usually plenty of space and the fox god likes fresh air. The New Miyako Hotal in Kyoto recently spent more than $25,000 on a splendid rooftop shrine. In Osaka securities executives meet every month to pray for good markets at the Inari shrine on the roof of the Osaka Securities Exchange.[10]

Shinto magic turns up in surprising places. In 1981 I toured one of the Tokyo Electric Power Company's nuclear generators. In the control room I noticed a large Shinto charm fastened to the central console to ward off breakdowns. Just below the charm, in large letters, was the name of the console's manufacturer: General Electric. "Does that thing really work on GE equipment?" I asked.

"Yes," was the answer, "and we have smaller charms on all our IBM computers, too."

The fox god must be on the job in America as well. Recently I have started seeing miniature Inari shrines in the New York offices of Japanese companies.

One aspect of Japanese corporate behavior that has never gone out of fashion is hierarchy. As in most hierarchies, seniority determines rank. Each batch of new employees enters the company together during the annual hiring season immediately after school graduation. They all are paid the same salary and form a peer group, or class, that moves up through the ranks together. For the first six or eight years the entire class is promoted simultaneously, strictly according to length of service. These lads do not scramble up the corporate ladder at their own pace; instead the swiftest and dullest rise together in what has often been likened to an escalator ride. Each class gets on at the bottom and rides up together. Naturally some assignments of equal rank are more desirable than others, and competence is subtly rewarded. Pay differentials may even begin to appear, but they are often no more than a few dollars a week.

"It's kind of clever, when you think about it," says a young employee of a major Japanese bank. "The only people you are in direct competition with are your classmates, and none of them really gets that far ahead of you. Everyone feels as though he is hot on the heels of the leaders, so no one ever gives up and just coasts. For the first fifteen years we all think we're still in the running for the top job."

Even blue-collar workers who have little hope of gaining increased responsibility are nevertheless constantly building up seniority. A British student of Japanese labor practices puts it this way: "Men are paid for being older, even though there is no clear evidence that the experience they accumulate in any way improves their work performance; they are paid for being loyal and cooperative, even though there is no obvious difference in the quality of a loyally produced gasket and a disloyally produced gasket. . . ."[11]

In large companies, executives follow the rigid, time-in-grade promotion patterns that Americans associate with inefficient bureaucracies. However, for the Japanese, the system works well. Men who have cleared all the hurdles to get into a top-tier company are usually bright, and it is rare to find a real dummy in a high position.

Also, Japanese rank structure may be very rigid, but actual work assignments are not. A mediocre supervisor can turn over lots of responsibility to a talented subordinate while maintaining all the advantages and prestige of his own position. He can even afford to give the younger man credit for his work because in a rigid seniority system the manager need not fear that his subordinate might be promoted over his head.

It is only nearer the top, where jobs get scarce, that the less capable employees are held back. The worst fate is that of the *madogiwa-zoku* ("window-seat tribe"). They are the recognized incompetents that an American company would fire. They are given desks by the windows, the daily newspapers, and no responsibilities. In hardworking Japan they must be among the unhappiest of men.

In Japanese companies there is also a clear difference among regular employees, temporary employees, and subcontractors. It is only the regular employees, who may actually be a minority, who enjoy total job security and automatic promotions. "Temporary" employees, who may work for the company for years, are women, retirees, and anyone else the company feels it can let go in hard times. They may be an important part of the functional group, but they are not part of the virtual blood-kin group.

Once I was visiting one of the Sumitomo companies and noticed four or five men cleaning up a nasty oil spill. I was just thinking how unpleasant that job must be when I noticed that they were wearing not Sumitomo blue but some other uniform. I asked who they were. "Oh, they're with a subcontractor we bring in to do the cleaning" was the answer. "They have to bid for that job, you know. There are plenty of little companies that would be glad to do that work for us." No Sumitomo man need dirty has hands taking out garbage or work up a sweat on the loading docks.

Subcontractors are second-tier companies that take care of the unpleasant, dangerous work. Their employees are often poorly trained, and their safety records are not up to first-tier standards. An investigation into a recent accident at a nuclear power station found that negligent subcontractors were at fault.

Major Japanese companies are openly elitist about their regular employees. They would laugh at the idea of being made to hire a certain quota of women, minorities, or handicapped workers. Such a plan would violate the sanctity of hierarchy and dilute group solidarity.

A formal call on a Japanese corporation is a charming exercise in hierarchy. Today Saito-san, a senior man in our company, has arranged a meeting with a major shipbuilder we would like to do business with. A uniformed receptionist meets us at the elevator and leads us to a conference room. Since we are visiting prospective customers on their territory, we are "guests." We sit down side by side in the place of honor, facing the door. Saito is my senior, so he sits farther from the door than I do.

Our three contacts arrive. We hop up and apologize for disturbing their busy schedule. They apologize for not coming to see us. This is a first meeting, so we exchange business cards. They have brought along an older man, so I assume he has a very senior position. I make a point of taking his card with both hands and make a deep bow over it as he hands it to me. After expressing our enchantment at this meeting, we all take a little time to read each other's cards. The information on the cards gives us clues to what level of speech to use with each other.

We take our seats on opposite sides of the coffee table, as our hosts instinctively arrange themselves according to rank: senior man farthest from the door, junior man closest to it. The receptionist brings us each a cup of green tea. Naturally she serves us in rank order. Protocol requires that Saito and their senior man do most of the talking. We probably won't hear a single word from their most junior man, and my comments should be brief. However, I am our side's performing flea—an American who speaks Japanese. We bend the rules, and I join in the conversation.

We talk about the weather, the economy, exchange rates, the price of bunker fuel—anything but business. It wouldn't do to launch into a sales pitch on the first meeting. Saito makes a few sly remarks about hoping to see them again very soon, and it's time to leave. Once again we apologize for interrupting their busy schedule, and they apologize for making us do the traveling. Our good-byes are punctuated by a little dance of stiff bows from the waist. We carefully match the depth of our bows to the rank of our partner. Our hosts see us to the elevator, where there are more bows. Then we are off.

In business it's always clear who is subordinate to whom. Speech and forms of address are finely tuned to match the hierarchy. Japanese who deal with Americans complain that they can't always tell who is the boss. Younger men may supervise older men, and everyone uses first names. Americans are certainly aware of each other's rank but do little of the bowing and scraping so common in Japan.

Recently a Japanese friend who works for the Tokyo subsidiary of an American company was sent on his first trip to the head office in New York. "I thought I knew all the people at headquarters who handle Japanese business," he told me, "but they kept talking about someone named Jack. I was a little shy about asking who Jack was, but in a day or two it dawned on me that they meant Mr. Gilbert, the senior vice-president! I still have a hard time thinking of an SVP as Jack."

In Japan rank on the the job makes demands on private life; out of the office, businessmen observe the same protocol. Even their wives are part of the pecking order and defer to each other according to their *husband's* rank. I have heard plenty of stories about the boss's wife "inviting" a flunky's wife over to the house to help with moving, wedding preparations, or other big chores.

The wife of a Japanese diplomat once told me a few of her duties. "When my husband and I are assigned to a new post," she said, "the very day we arrive, I am duty-bound to pay my respects to the Japanese ambassador's wife. It would make no difference if I were tottering from jet lag or if all my children were sick. The first thing you do in a new country is report to the boss's wife. And this is no casual chat. You wear *white gloves*."

She also explained that wives of subordinates must never dress better or wear more jewelry than the wives of senior diplomats. "That must be an implicit understanding," I said. "No one would actually tell you you were wearing too many diamonds, would they?"

"Implicit nothing. I would hear about it right away."

Not all Japanese are happy about the intrusion of corporate rank into private life. A few outspoken wives have told me that they avoid other company wives because they hate the artificial ranking they must submit to. However, these women see themselves as mild misfits and complain that most wives accept the system without question.

When they are assigned overseas, the families of Japanese businessmen spend a lot of time together, but language and behavior always reflect the hierarchy. I was once visiting the home of a U.S.-based businessman when the wife of a slightly senior colleague arrived unexpectedly. As the husband went to answer the door, the wife hurriedly reminded the children that the woman was a "superior" and had to be addressed in honorific language.

Westerners are often surprised that in spite of Japan's acute sensitivity to hierarchy, top executives do not indulge themselves in the symbols and benefits of office so dear to Americans. Company expense accounts can be enormous, but salary differentials are not nearly so great as in America, and private offices are few and often Spartan. Even a vice-president with an office of his own is likely to keep a working desk in the bull pen with his men. That is where executives can usually be found, pitching in with their sleeves rolled up. Private offices are nothing more than rooms for receiving guests.

Few companies have special dining rooms for executives; even the president eats with the plebes in the company cafeteria. In manufacturing, blue-collar workers wear company-issue smocks to keep the grease off their own clothes. High executives, who don't touch a tool all day, often sport the company work jacket. This is good for company morale. The troops like to see the general in combat gear. At the same time, in Japan the sense of hierarchy is so thoroughly hammered into the corporate mind that Japanese executives don't need ostentatious signs of success. Even if they posed as gods from Olympus, they would inspire no more awe than they do now, dressed in work clothes, eating a bowl of noodles in the company cafeteria.

In America a whiz kid may be promoted over the heads of elders and find that he needs a big desk and two secretaries in order to gain their respect. Hierarchies in America are much more fluid than in Japan, and material reminders of their existence are necessary to counter the spirit of rebelliousness and democracy. These are much less a threat in Japan. The hierarchy can be enforced without the same power symbols.

Rank in an American company is an artificial, corporate creation. Off the job, and man to man, the assistant foreman and the company president can dust it up as equals. In Japan company rank is founded on the entire society's concern for hierarchy. It is personal, as much as corporate, and just as real out of the office as in it.

What Japanese top executives forgo in material benefits they recoup in deference and personal services. I once worked for a company that had offices in the Tokyo headquarters of one of Japan's largest banks. It was always a treat to watch the bank president go home for the day. A uniformed receptionist would carry his briefcase for him and hold the door as he got into his limousine. Then as the limo pulled out of the driveway, she would take a deep bow . . . and not come up until the car had disappeared around the first corner. Paradoxically, that man probably had no more real, independent power in his bank than my friend Johnson has at his college.

In the corporate hierarchy a special place is reserved for women: the bottom. They are inducted into the company in the same manner as men, in an annual lot once a year. However, they are hired for different jobs that are reserved for women. These are invariably low-paying, dead-end slots. Very occasionally a determined woman may be able after many years to move into a job that would normally be filled by a young man, but even the first-level supervisory ranks are firmly closed to women. To make matters worse, companies that long ago got rid of uniforms for male office workers retain them for women. By their dress as well as their gender, women are labeled as low-level drudges.

Japan is also one of those rare nations, along with Korea and Indonesia, that allow menstrual leave for women. In most companies women are allowed one or two days off every month, although in 1976 it was leave without pay in 40 percent of all Japanese companies.[12] Menstrual leave is an ambiguous benefit. Many women are too embarrassed to ask for it, and if they do, it only confirms them as fragile creatures who cannot be expected to do a man's work.

Many pretty women serve as a kind of decorative corporate fauna. Once I made a call on a company based in a provincial capital. I was met at the door by the usual uniformed receptionist, but she did not usher me to the conference room herself. She handed me off, like the Olympic flame, to a series of five or six receptionists, who each got to escort me down no more than twenty-five feet of corridor. That was sybaritic luxury even by Japanese standards, but all companies seem to have a flock of young ladies on hand to serve tea, give directions, and run errands.

There is an old-fashioned logic to keeping women on the bottom. All female employees are expected to be looking for a husband and to resign once they have found one. After a few years on the job this is exactly what most of them do. Work in a major corporation is not a career but a chance to meet a young man who is on the escalator to success. Once a Japanese woman has married, she leaves her job to prepare for the children who will inevitably follow.

Companies thus have no incentive to treat men and women equally. Men can be trusted to stay until retirement, whereas women will be married and gone in a few years. When a major corporation hires a woman, it is not hiring a worker. It is hiring a potential wife. The company expects to squeeze a lot of quality work from its brides-to-be, but beauty and culture are important hiring criteria. Many companies are quite open about the qualities they are looking for. Some, for example, will not hire a woman unless she lives at home with her parents. There is no telling what manner of mischief an unsupervised woman might be up to, and a woman with a past does not make a fit wife for a future executive.

The corporation finds this arrangement entirely satisfatory. Many women come into the company with the same qualifications as men and are quick, capable workers. Some are wasted as tea servers or hostesses, but the rest provide Japanese business with a level of clerical efficiency unmatched in America. Furthermore, this pool of carefully selected women offers vital romantic possibilities within the company to young men whose lives tend to revolve around the workplace. Marriage within the firm is very common. Once a man is safely married, the company can be confident that the wife, as a former loyal employee, is prepared to accept the heavy demands on her husband's time she knows it will make.

The top Japanese companies, therefore, do not offer women real careers. Ambitious woman find that their talents are more readily recognized by American or European companies working in Japan. For men, a job with a foreign company offers little prestige; foreign companies are near the bottom of the corporate hierarchy. Capable women, on the other hand, are delighted to find employers that do not have such patronizing rules about what jobs women are allowed to do.

American companies, in particular, have a reputation for giving women responsibility. One mid-level executive I know who works for a Japanese oil refiner told me that when he telephones another company and a woman picks up the phone, he always asks to speak to a man. Only if he is calling an American company will he agree to talk to a woman. "Women who take a real interest in business," he adds, "turn into old war-horses."

This view is typical. Japanese businessmen have the greatest difficulty taking a professional woman seriously. They will grudgingly do business with a foreign woman representing a foreign company because they know that practices are different in the West. However, much of Japanese after-hours business, both with colleagues and customers, takes place in a raucous male environment of bars, heavy drinking, and loose talk. The evening is often enlivened by bar girls and professional hostesses. The presence of a woman executive would deaden this locker-room atmosphere almost as surely as if someone had brought his wife.

Many American companies have been reluctant to send women to Japan for fear that they may not be taken seriously. Recently I spoke with a woman who had just returned from Tokyo, where her company had assigned her for several years to test the waters. She had strong feelings about her experiences. "Would you send a black to do business in South Africa," she asks, "or a Jew to work in Saudi Arabia? They would actually be better off than a woman in Japan because everyone knows what they would be up against. Head office has no idea what a woman faces in Japan. If a company sends a woman to Tokyo, it is setting her up for failure and frustration."

Not all American women would agree. "I think a smart *gaijin* woman can do very well in Japan," says one. "You can always bow out of the bar scene early, and how many American *men* are willing to go drinking with customers until all hours every night? Besides, I think women are better at establishing the kind of personal relations with customers that the Japanese think is so important." The debate continues.

In the low-prestige second tier, opportunities for women are greater than in the top tier. If they are not afraid of being thought of as old war-horses, strong-willed women can carve out positions of power in small service companies. In manufacturing, even on a small scale, women are extremely rare anywhere but on the assembly line.

Just as women are subordinate to men, Japan's second tier is subordinate to the first. It is also a source of the first tier's strength and flexibility. The big names in industry are powerful enough to regiment their suppliers and subcontractors entirely as they see fit. Some have a huge number of suppliers. Fully 70 percent of the production cost of a Nissan automobile comes from work done by subcontractors. In some industries that figure can be as high as 90 percent.[13] Riding herd on subcontractors is therefore a crucial part of a top-tier company's business.

A small-scale subcontractor for, say, low-technology car parts can very well be drawn into the orbit of a major automaker and lose all autonomy. Its products and production runs are tailored to the needs of the larger company, which may be its only customer. This is fine during boom times, when the big company can take the little company under its wing. However, during a slump it is the suppliers and subcontractors that feel the pinch. If the demand for cars drops, the automaker can take work back from subcontractors to occupy its own workers, who might otherwise be idle. Since the subcontractor is so closely tied to one company, it cannot quickly establish relations with another. It must lay off its workers or go out of business.

It is in the second tier that recession takes its toll. First-tier companies use the second tier for the unglamorous, low value-added segments of their business and view it as a buffer against recession. The second tier is not the place to look for prestige, high pay, or lifetime employment. Its workers get little training or job security and must sometimes move from job to job.

Retirement benefits are another area in which even the Japan advocates find nothing to admire. Except for directors and other top executives, who may work on into their eighties, the usual mandatory retirement age is fifty-five to fifty-seven. Workers are sent on their way with a bow and a lump sum; the Japanese labor standards law does not require companies to set up pension plans. Some workers contribute to a government-run pension program but benefits are far too meager to live on.

One Japanese writer explains that there are two different Japanese words that are translated as "retirement" in English: *teinen* and *intai*. *Teinen* literally means "age limit," or the age at which a man must leave his company, while *intai* is the end of his working life. The writer points out that in the West there is no difference between the two; the worker leaves his company with the expectation that he can stop working and still live decently. For the Japanese, *teinen* is nothing more than the age at which a man is booted from the company he has worked for all his life. His future is not secure, and he must scrounge up another job.[14]

Some companies agree to keep their men on after *teinen* as "temporary" workers at reduced wages and benefits. This is often the most satisfactory solution for the worker but is not something he can count on. Whether he stays or goes is up to the company. The top tier has developed a retirement scheme informally known by some as the 7-5-3 system. Their older workers are routinely farmed out to important subsidiaries or subcontractors at perhaps 70 percent of their pre-

"retirement" pay. After a few years they are then moved down to a lesser subcontractor at, say, 50 percent of their peak salary. This way a man who started out in a top company can keep on working into old age but in gradually less prestigious companies and for decreasing pay.

Once in Tokyo I found I was having trouble getting through to a senior Japanese who had been quite accessible to me when we had done business in New York. I finally cornered him in his office late one evening.

"What," I asked, "is keeping Mr. Division Head so busy that he can't see his old friends?"

"I am preparing for my retirement, Taylor-san," he said sadly.

"What do you mean?"

"I have been visiting the companies in our group to see which ones might take me." Kishi-san had not been slotted for a top job. He was getting ready for his first step down the 7-5-3 ladder.

Still, he was better off than most men his age. For workers in second-tier companies, the fifty-fifth birthday is an ominous one. If their company does not agree to keep them on at reduced wages, they are on their own. They must hustle for any job they can get. A recent survey conducted on behalf of the Japanese Ministry of Labor found that "only 33 percent of those soon to retire said they were assured of a comfortable old age either through promised reemployment or through sufficient savings, while 41.6 percent expressed strong anxiety about their future."[15] In 1980 nearly half of all Japanese men over age sixty-five were working, and many of the rest were looking for a job. In America only a fifth of the men that age were still at work.

As one Japanese writer laments, retired workers immediately lose their status. Since many have no income and poor prospects, they cannot borrow from banks, buy property, or enter into long-term leases. "In Japan," he complains, "retired people are treated almost like the lumpenproletariat."[16] The government is urging companies to push back retirement age and to convert to pension plans, but at present many older Japanese have no choice but to live off their children.

We have now covered most of the important differences between Japanese and Western management practices. It is difficult to evaluate the cumulative effect of all of them, but so far none seems decisive. Mainly we have seen differences in emphasis; only guaranteed job security, enterprise unions, and lump-sum separations rather than pensions are unique to Japan. In fact, so many of the same methods are found on both sides of the Pacific that one best-selling book on management has argued that the most successful American companies have been practicing "Japanese" techniques all along.[17]

Quality control was originally an American science, but we seem to have forgotten its importance. Our competitors—not only the Japanese but also the Europeans—have reminded us how vital it is, and American managers are once more demanding high standards on the assembly line. The Ford Motor Company has even based a major ad campaign on its renewed commitment to quality.

Western executives have experimented with job rotation within the company and participatory decision making for years. These methods have always raised the questions of specialization versus broad experience and efficiency versus consensus. That the Japanese should tend to favor broader experience and greater consensus means only that those approaches seem to work better for them. There are no clear answers that work for every country or every company.

Japanese are certainly better attuned to the potential of overseas markets than Americans are. We are now in an age in which the entire world is one huge market, but Americans have for too long been content with success in the U.S. market alone. It is not just the Japanese who have grasped today's economic realities more quickly than Americans. Holland and Germany export even more of their GNP than Japan does. Here, once again, we must learn from both the Japanese and the Europeans.

The effects of structural differences between economies are more difficult to evaluate. Close government-industry relations, for example, have undoubtedly been good for Japan, especially during the period of postwar reconstruction. More recently some American businessmen have complained that MITI and other government support give Japanese industry an unfair advantage.

These critics don't seem to realize that MITI does not hand out money. It is a superregulatory agency that often urges companies to do things against their will. The French, the Austrians, and the Scandinavians are like the Japanese in giving government considerable authority over business. There is a lively debate in all these countries over the actual benefits of close government involvement in the economy. The same Americans who complain about MITI probably complain about excess government regulation in America. Nevertheless,

Japanese willingness to cooperate with the public sector is surely better for the country than the mistrust that American business feels for government.

A tax structure that encourages capital formation rather than consumption has helped give Japan some of the most vigorous industries in the world. In America subsidized borrowing has been the government's way of helping citizens buy their own homes. Perhaps it is time we rethought a system that benefits only the relatively well-off and that drains funds away from industrial investment. Americans save only 5 or 6 percent of their disposable income, while the Japanese save 25 to 30 percent. Household savings are the primary source of business borrowing, and an ample supply keeps interest costs down.

Another structural ingredient of Japan's success has been the cooperative attitude of its enterprise unions. The British must certainly be envious of Japan's labor relations. Some wags have suggested that the best way for Britain to ease its trade deficit with Japan would be to export its workers. Japanese unions have trusted management to keep all regular employees at work no matter what happens. Thus, they have not opposed the introduction of laborsaving machinery that Western trade unions might have fought to keep out.

It is probably no coincidence that the American industries suffering most visibly from foreign competition—steel and automobiles—are those that are the most heavily unionized. An industry with trade unions is at a definite disadvantage compared to one in which they have no real power. This, of course, is not news to Western managers. Many would be delighted to see trade unions disappear from the face of the earth.

Nevertheless, adversarial relations between labor and management are to no one's benefit. American industry has been scarred by years of antagonism; a company may have to skirt disaster before the two sides can recognize their common interests. With Chrysler suffering enormous losses and on the verge of collapse, the United Auto Workers were willing to give up benefits to help it survive. However, as soon as the company turned in two barely profitable quarters and began to look as though it might squeak by, 9,500 Canadian auto workers walked off the job, demanding more pay. Four thousand six hundred American workers had to be laid off because their jobs depended on the steady flow of parts produced in Canada. This kind of systematic union militancy leads to the British disease. The Japanese have sensibly avoided it; so should we.

The comparative benefits of long-term planning are difficult to assess, especially because many wisely run American companies are just as serious as the Japanese about preparing for the future. U.S. auto companies have not distinguished themselves in this respect, but IBM, Exxon, Procter & Gamble, and a host of small, dynamic firms have consistently been able to stay ahead of the field. It is probably easier in Japan to sacrifice today's profits for tomorrow's growth, and this has certainly helped the Japanese. Still, I doubt that anyone would suggest that it has given them a critical advantage.

The same can be said for the differences between Japanese and Western retirement systems. In strictly financial terms, a company may be better off if it does not have to make payments to a pension fund. However, in most of the industrialized world society requires that employers support their retired workers, and that requirement is not likely to change.

Individually none of the management techniques we have seen is of earthshaking importance. Even taken together and under the assumption that they all work in Japan's favor, they still do not account for the incredible advances that Japanese industry has made since the war. What, then, is the secret of Japan's climb to the top?

Deceptively simple as it may sound, *the single most important ingredient in Japan's success is the Japanese attitude toward work*. The Japanese have succeeded because they have worked harder. It should be clear from the subjects of the previous chapters—conformity, submission to hierarchy, group loyalty, a sense of national uniqueness—that the individual worker brings to his job a set of attitudes and expectations that make him the perfect company man. Although increased affluence is bringing changes to Japan, the nation as a whole still has a unique propensity for loyalty and hard work.

The clichés about the Japanese as workaholics and economic animals have caught on for a reason. The Japanese probably love their companies more, and work harder at their jobs, than any other people on earth. From the chief executive to the grease monkey the Japanese employee can identify with the company and make its values his own.

Let us take just two examples. In 1981 the Toyota Motor Company's 48,000 employees came up with 1.3 million formal suggestions to improve quality or lower costs. That was 27 suggestions per employee! *Ninety percent* were accepted by management for an estimated savings that year of $45 million.[18]

At the Zama factory of Toyota's competitor, the Nissan Motor Company, there were only 17 suggestions per employee in 1979. The factory manager thinks that's not bad. After all, he points out, the Zama factory is the most highly automated car assembly plant in the world and is already so efficient that there are no more improvements a single employee is likely to think of. His men got together in groups after work to think up their 17 suggestions each.[19]

Americans do not have that kind of relationship with their employers. Chrysler workers do not spend their free time thinking up new money-saving suggestions every two weeks the way Toyota men do. For Americans, such faithful devotion to an employer is difficult even to imagine, but it is common in Japan.

The vaunted secrets of Japanese management are mainly techniques to channel and encourage the potential for loyalty, dedication, and enthusiasm that Japanese workers bring to their jobs in the first place. Let us now look at some of these methods.

The main technique Japan's top companies use to make their hardworking employees work even harder is simply to make the company the most important thing in a worker's life. The first step in that process is to be sure to hire people who have the potential for the right kind of devotion. As we have seen, the rigid Japanese school system cooperates by supplying the top corporations with a steady steam of bright young men with uniform backgrounds. Because these companies hire only entry-level graduates, a period of travel and experimentation after college or even a year or two of graduate school is out of the question. The mildest degree of adventurousness makes a man too old and too odd to fit the company mold. Joining the company is thus the main event in a life which has up to then been single-minded preparation.

The induction ceremony is a significant and solemn occasion. All the men hired that year are brought into the company as a group. The president and other top executives welcome the newcomers and formally invest them with their new responsibilities as productive members of society. The most common theme is vintage John Kennedy: "Ask not what the company can do for you but what you can do for the company." Parents of new employees are often invited to the ceremony; their presence marks the transfer of their child's primary loyalty from the family to the corporation.

After induction many companies put their men through loyalty training. This may involve sending the new class on a retreat together, for an intensive series of peptalks, physical conditioning, and meditation on what it means to be a new employee. I have even heard of companies that sent their new recruits through army boot camp together to give them a sense of camaraderie and a firm respect for authority.

Others, including Hitachi Shipbuilding and Sumitomo Metal, send their new hirees for a dose of old-fashioned Shinto training at the Grand Shrine of Ise. The shrine bills its four-day sessions as "a drastic human education through love and sweat," designed to instill respect for rules by disciplining the mind. The training involves meditation, expressions of respect for authority, and mortification of the flesh through cold baths. The training must work. One satisfied company spokesman is reported to have said on recovering his recruits, "Closing the school's training this spring, the entering youth unanimously voiced their determination to never leave the company."[20]

Employment is the beginning of an association that will last until retirement. When the doors of a company close on a new man, he must be prepared to go the distance. There is no running away from enemies and not much room for eccentricity or wave making. However, there is every reason for devotion. The new employee has become a member of a family that will stick together through thick and thin.

The corporation deliberately fosters a family atmosphere by embracing every aspect of an employee's life. Single men are offered housing in cut-rate company dorms. A loyalty-building stint in the dorm is often obligatory even for men who have their own lodgings. Married workers may get subsidized housing in company subdivisions, where company buses come to pick them up every morning. To fill the off hours, the company provides sports and recreation clubs of all kinds and organizes outings and weekend trips. Employees can do their shopping at company commissaries. The company maintains club houses, beach cottages, or ski chalets, where workers can relax together. There are even company marriage services to see that the corporate family is a happy one, free of lonely hearts.

Every possible technique is used to make the employees identify with the firm and with each other. Virtually all companies issue uniforms to their blue-collar workers. A decade ago many required their white-collar employees to wear identical suits. Now they give them company lapel pins, which are worn with great pride. Many firms start the day with all workers booming out the company song in unison. This is one of the verses that the halls of Matsushita reverberate to every morning:

> *We trust our strength together in harmony*
> *Finding happiness.*
> *Matsushita Electric!*
> *Animating joy everywhere,*
> *A world of dedication.*[21]

Kōnosuke Matsushita, founder of the company and one of the most respected men in Japan, has said, "Matsushita is a place where we build people. We also build electronic equipment."

As we saw earlier, not even union membership dilutes a worker's loyalty to the firm by giving him an affiliation that extends beyond it. An American union man's primary loyalty is to his trade, to his function as an individual. For the Japanese, loyalty to the union is a different version of loyalty to the company.

Even in a private capacity the lowliest Mitsubishi or Mitsui man represents his company wherever he goes. One evening I was congratulating a Japanese manager who had just been promoted. This was Yamada-san's first step into the heights beyond automatic promotion, and he was clearly pleased.

"This job does have one big disadvantage," he told me. "If any of the men working for me get in trouble with the police or cause a scandal of some kind, I'm the one who's got to go make the formal apology. You can imagine what a pain that's going to be." His company will not normally pay damages, but Yamada-san has to apologize in person to the authorities or the injured party. He takes symbolic responsibility for the misdeeds of a "family" member.

Just as the worker is brought in as a member of the corporate family, the Japanese supervisor becomes an honorary elder in the worker's family. He is the feted guest at employee weddings which he may well have arranged in the first place. He gives fatherly advice on how to raise a family and may be invited to attend children's graduation ceremonies. His involvement in the personal lives of his subordinates is so great that the line between his authority at work and his influence at home is easily blurred. As one Japanese business writer puts it approvingly, "The company manages the worker's entire personality."[22]

When Japanese are assigned overseas, to an out-of-the-way place with no Japanese community, the supervisor plays his "father" role to the hilt. A Japanese woman recently told me about her brother-in-law, who is stationed with two bachelor subordinates in a small town in Texas. "Those two are over at his house for dinner two or three times a week," she said. "He really looks after them as if they were his sons. I once asked his wife if she didn't get tired of having them around all the time. 'Oh, no,' she said, 'there aren't any Japanese restaurants in town, so where else can they go to eat?'"

This is the kind of relationship that develops in a system designed to blend the employee's whole life into the corporation. In Japan a worker can easily spend every waking hour in a company context. The company quickly becomes the primary focus of loyalty, the pivot around which his whole life turns. The Japanese call this system *marugakae* ("total embrace"). It is an embrace that offers meaning and security in a society that looks to the group to fulfill those needs.

But if the company gives a lot, it also asks a lot. The Japanese Ministry of Labor estimates that in 1978 the average Japanese outworked the average American by 212 hours, or twenty-seven 8-hour days. I suspect this is an understatement; the government is trying to downplay the workaholic image. I have seen Japanese put in astonishing hours. Twelve-hour workdays are not unusual for low-level office workers, and if need be, they will cheerfully work around the clock. Saturdays and Sundays belong to the company when business is heavy.

Many Japanese are too absorbed in their work to take vacations. One man I know has been with his company for twenty years and is theoretically entitled to forty days of vacation each year. Until he was posted to the United States, he had never taken more than two days in a single year. While in America, he decided to go native and actually took a full week off. Rather than tear off on a frantic round of tourism like most Japanese, he hired a beach house for the family for a week—and nearly died of boredom. This mans knows plenty of people in his company who are proud to say they have never taken a day of vacation in their lives.

In early May several national holidays fall together to give Japan a four- or five-day weekend called Golden Week. The economy shuts down for Golden Week, so not even the most fanatical workers can go to the office. For men who take no vacation, this may be the only chance all year to visit the relatives or take to the hills. The nation mobilizes with a frenzy that makes Labor Day weekend look sedate. One commentator calls this madness "Golden Weakness," a condition, he adds, for which there is no known cure.[23]

Toil on the job is only part of the workday. Many off-hours are devoted to *otsukiai*. Men who work together may go out with their supervisor several times a week to fraternize over drinks. A certain amount of after-hours chatter is obligatory; it is very bad form not to appear eager for *otsukiai*. Work may not even be discussed, but a boisterous time together in a local bar is good for the group spirit. Evening *otsukiai* is liberally doused with alcohol and can go on until near midnight, or whenever the last train leaves for the suburbs. It takes physical stamina just to meet its demands, but *otsukiai* forges close bonds. A man's social life is an extension of his work life.

All these methods work beautifully for the Japanese. Hung-over or not, Japanese workers have the lowest rate of absenteeism in the world and apply themselves to their jobs with touching enthusiasm. Tokyo garbage men scour and shine their trucks every morning before they start work.[24] QC circles celebrate their success by throwing up their arms together to shouts of *"Banzai!"* Factory floors are crisscrossed with white lines showing the shortest route to the toilet. The afternoon "coffee break" in some factories is ten minutes of calisthenics. Workers stand right by their machines, bobbing and bending in unison to piped-in music. After that it's back to work.

When I visit Japan, I don't even have to set foot inside a factory or office to know why the nation has been so successful. The service industry is just as enthusiastic and hardworking as manufacturing. In fancy restaurants the maître d' not only holds my chair as I sit down but comes rushing to pull it back out as soon as I make a move to rise. The waiter pours my first glassful of beer and dashes back every couple of swallows to make sure the glass stays full. As a final punctilio, he sets the bottle down every time with the label facing me.

In Tokyo's best French restaurants my salad dressing may be prepared at a little table at my side. When the dressing is ready, a tiny lettuce leaf is dipped in it and served alone on a small plate. I take an exploratory taste, just as I would from a newly uncorked bottle of wine. Nightclubs are staffed with effeminate men in tuxedos whose only job is to run out for cigarettes, help people in and out of their coats, and hover deferentially.

The Japanese eagerness to please can get out of hand. On every form of public transportation the conductor gets on the PA system before each stop and reminds the passengers not to forget their belongings and to watch their step getting off. Before every single subway or bus stop, this ritual incantation is unnecessary noise. However, only foreigners feel they are being treated like morons. For the Japanese, this is a sign of concern and good service. Some retailers are thinking of designing automatic vending machines to squawk out a recorded word of thanks after every sale. More service!

Until a few years ago Japanese department stores posted women at the foot of each escalator to welcome customers with a bow and warn them to watch their step getting onto the escalator. Apparently that got too silly even for the Japanese, but the women who operate elevators still warn all customers to watch their step getting off. Customers rarely have to stand in line to make a purchase; they can hardly wander around the store without being politely pestered by attendants. In Tokyo's fanciest hotels guests don't even have to push elevator buttons. A uniformed flunky zips into the car, presses the right button, and zips out before the door closes.

In Japan the customer is king. He goes straight to the top of the hierarchy and gets the same treatment as the company president. As one writer puts it, "In Japanese business, you say '*hai*' ('yes, *sir*') to the client and '*hai*' to the boss and run like hell."[25]

What does how a department store treats its customers have to do with Japan's dominance in so many international markets? This almost obsessive attention to customer service is only the public manifestation of the same spirit that drives all Japanese workers. Behind the closed doors of its offices and factories all Japan is working just as hard to please the customer, please the boss, and make the company a success.

Even the smaller companies that cannot afford to wrap their employees in benefits still profit from Japan's diligent, loyal work force. A worker and his employer, no matter how humble, form a group with strong ties. Work is a Confucian virtue. Even for the many sec ond-tier workers who do not devote their lives to the company, obedi ence to superiors and snappy execution of orders are part of the fabric of society. As a Japanese executive once said to me, Japanese children are taught to say "*hai*" the way American children are taught to say "please" and "thank you."

Second-tier companies do the best they can to match the benefits of the first tier. As soon as they can afford it, they buy a company vacation home, even if it's only a shack. A family atmosphere of total embrace is the ideal that both workers and employers dream of.

In the top tier, company housing, sports teams, clubs, vacation homes, marriage bureaus, and the company song all fortify the group framework. If the mix is right, the company becomes the group that gives life its meaning. The company is not an antagonist or merely a contractual partner from whom one expects certain rewards for cer tain services. It is a family, a club, a church, all in one. A worker who corrects a flaw in the production process takes personal joy in serving that great organization of which he is a part. The company takes on a holy aura; it is the altar on which he will sacrifice nearly everything.

A generation ago Japanese went to their death in battle shouting, "Glory to the emperor!" "Now," writes one commentator, "men have appeared who could meet death proclaiming 'glory to the com pany.'"[26] It has already happened. Nisshō-Iwai, a major trading house, was one of the companies swept up in the Lockheed bribery scandal. A director of the company took responsibility for the scandal by leaping to his death from the top of the corporate headquarters. He ended his suicide note with the words "Long live Nisshō-Iwai."

To recapitulate, I believe that Japanese firms have been successful because their employees work harder. They do this for a number of reasons that are unique to Japan. One is their acute consciousness of the vulnerability of their rocky island home. They feel the threat of natural disaster, they have suffered the horror of nuclear war, and they live in fear of trade war. This sense of fragility imparts a special energy to their efforts to subdue all problems not beyond human con trol.

Another reason is their sense of uniqueness, of isolation in an alien world. All peoples feel a greater sense of solidarity in the face of an outside threat. The sensitivity of the Japanese to what distinguishes them from other people makes them quick to see a threat where others might see friendly competition. Even in times of peace they can feel something of the solidarity of war.

Finally, the Japanese work harder because they take the company's larger interests as their own. They do this because Japan is a nation where the individual learns to subordinate his interests to those of the group, to conform to its desires, to seek harmony, and to find meaning and identification in service to the group. The corporation has brilliantly harnessed these national characteristics to its own ends. It becomes the primary focus for loyalty and offers meaning and significance that transcend individual concerns.

This is a very special combination of factors. Those who would have us imitate the Japanese would do well to bear this in mind. There may be other societies where Japanese management would be effective, but what works in Japan may fail in America.

Japanese corporations have not always been so paternalistic. Before the Second World War managers treated their men with ruthless expediency; it was during wartime labor shortages that they first began to entice workers with job security and automatic promotions. Only in the last thirty-five years has "total embrace" become synonymous with Japanese management. Does this mean it could be made to work in America, too?

Some people think so. Writing about the transcendent quality of corporate loyalty in Japan, a recent best seller on Japanese management insists that "what is needed in the West is a nondeified, nonreligious 'spirituality' that enables a firm's superordinate goals to respond truly to the inner meanings that many people seek . . ."[27] The authors are saying that if Western firms are to match the Japanese, they must play the same, overarching "spiritual" role in their employees' lives. Only then will they acquire a holy aura and inspire the love and enthusiasm of their workers.

This may be what American managers would like, but is it what the American people want? Do Americans really seek "inner meanings" at the workplace? Do they really want to wear the company uniform and sacrifice their private lives to the group? At the mythic level America is a nation of rugged individualists, not organization men. It is a nation of diversity, not a nation of conformity. Its heroes speak out for what they believe in, whatever the group may think. They are individuals who cheerfully cooperate with other individuals but who never lose their sense of self. Individualism exacts a high price in loneliness and dissension, but it is one of America's most cherished values.

Nevertheless, things are changing in America. It no longer has a frontier, and some would argue that the personality that won the West will wreck the organization. Yesterday's gunslinger heroes may be today's stickup men. As more and more Americans go to work for large corporations, it may be that indivdualism will become a troublesome anachronism. Perhaps America needs new heroes who are paragons of obedience, who sacrifice their own interests for the harmony of the group.

It is more than thirty years since David Riesman wrote *The Lonely Crowd*. He wrote of the decline of the rugged individualist and the rise of the floundering, rudderless man who looks to the group for constant clues to proper behavior. Some Americans would gladly lose themselves in the enveloping security of the Japanese company. It may be that the greatest happiness for the greatest number can be found in a society like Japan's, where the centrifugal forces of individualism are muted by the centripetal forces of harmony and subservience.

Has individualism outlived its time in America? Do Americans no longer want to act for themselves? Corporate executives may be tempted to think so, especially if by giving their employees "inner meanings," they think they can drive them to loyal, blissful exhaustion.

I think that is a mistaken and dangerous approach. The success of Japanese companies is largely due to their employees' willingness to submerge their interests in those of the company, to find happiness not as individuals but as a group. I think any serious attempt to pattern American companies on a Japanese model will founder on diversity and individualism. America needs more individualism, not less, though it must be individualism that is built on a firm sense of responsibility. There is certainly room in America for more pride in workmanship, for greater efficiency, for honest work for honest wages. But these are our own values, from our own sturdy past. They grew out of individual responsibility and self-respect, not subservience and self-denial. America's greatness was built on values that are American. Dissipating the nation's energy on models that do not suit our national temperament may only leave us weakened and confused.

I think Americans would feel like fools singing the company song. They would feel smothered by attempts to clasp them to the bosom of the corporate family and violated by a boss who tried to "manage their entire personality." They lead lives of multiple loyalties, and work is only one of them. At the end of the day they are happy to leave it behind to pursue other interests, to fraternize with people of all sorts. The American idea of a great vacation is not a week at a company beach house full of other company employees. Americans draw a clear line between their corporate lives and private lives. Americans do not merge their personalities with that of the company.

Or do they? As we saw at the beginning of this chapter, Japanese companies have already started managing Western workers. They have set up electronics and auto assembly plants in the United States and television factories in Britain, using local labor. They have tried to keep their paternalistic management and in some cases have achieved higher productivity rates than at similar factories run by Americans or Britons.

These good results are not entirely due to management style. One of the first things that Japanese companies do in Britain or America is hire the sharpest labor lawyers that money can buy. They have been remarkably successful in keeping the unions out. Brand-new equipment, the enthusiasm of start-up, and a younger work force than at established competitors—all have helped productivity. Still, better worker-management relations and greater employee identification with the firm have no doubt helped.

On the other hand, Japanese managers have had to modify their methods and make no secret of their preference for the docile, loyal workers back home. The manager of the Kyoto Ceramic factory in San Diego we saw earlier put it this way to a Japanese reporter: "The only way to give Americans a sense of loyalty and belonging is through endless education. Over and over, we educate them through morning meetings, work groups, lectures and brain-storming sessions. However, all our efforts only give these employees a veneer of group consciousness. We do our best to keep that veneer as thick as possible, but if the Japanese staff were to leave, it wouldn't be long before the veneer wore off and they were just the way they used to be."[28] This Japanese manager probably has an easier time than most in getting his American workers to adopt a Japanese style. Almost all are women, and most are recent immigrants from Mexico, who may be delighted to find an employer that can give them a family. Even for them, Japanese-style devotion hardly comes naturally.

When the Japanese are engaged in manufacturing overseas, they have no choice but to hire local people. In any other business they load their overseas subsidiaries with Japanese and hire locals only for the lowliest jobs. For example, a U.S. bank operating a branch in Tokyo will have only a handful of American staff in key positions, and everyone else at the branch will be Japanese. By contrast, the New York branches of Japanese banks are staffed with Japanese right down to the first-level supervisors.

This is partly because Japanese are more comfortable working with each other and think Americans are not likely to understand the subtleties of Japanese business. But it is mainly because they are under no illusions that they could get the same devotion to the job from locals that they will get from Japanese. One reason the Japanese car companies have hesitated to build factories in the United States is that they are afraid they can't teach Americans to work as hard as Japanese. Whenever possible, if they want the job done right, the Japanese do it themselves.

The policy of sending over droves of junior Japanese to work in American subsidiaries has been so blatant that the U.S. State Department has started refusing to grant work visas. The department says that these jobs can be done by Americans and that Japan has no right to export labor.

Americans working for Japanese companies agree. In 1977 twelve women filed suit against the Sumitomo Corporation of America for discrimination against Americans and women. Early in 1982 the Supreme Court ruled that the U.S. subsidiary was an American company and thus subject to U.S. equal opportunity laws. However, it sidestepped the issue of whether Sumitomo had violated those laws, and the case was returned to lower courts for a ruling on this key issue. Japanese managers are anxiously following this case. They wince as the thought of having to dilute their Japanese solidarity with American women.

In fact, most Japanese managers doubt that their techniques could ever work in America. Recently a New York-based Japanese executive was complaining to me about his American secretary, who goes home every day promptly at 5:00 P.M.

"Try a little Japanese voodoo on her," I suggested. "Teach her the company song."

"Taylor-san knows as well as I do," he said with a smile, "that there is no sense in using Japanese management techniques on anybody but the Japanese."

This man's view is typical. Why is it, after all, that all the books about Japanese management are written by foreigners? Why is it that the only translation of a *Japanese* book that claims to reveal the secrets of Japanese management is a mumbo jumbo pamphlet by a seventeenth-century sword fighter, entitled *A Book of Five Rings*? Japanese authors will eventually be persuaded to tout their methods to the West, but if they were convinced these methods were universally applicable, they would have done so long ago.

Ironically, just as foreign businessmen have begun to show interest in how Japanese companies win the devotion of their employees, the Japanese have begun to wonder if epidemic workaholism is such a good thing after all. In the spring of 1979 an internal Common Market document about trade friction with Japan was leaked to the press. It claimed that the Japanese were willing to work like fiends and live in rabbit hutches if that was what it took to conquer world markets.

The incident was quickly forgotten in the West, but it rocked the Japanese. They were not angered so much as chastened. Gallons of ink were spilled on editorials about Japan's national priorities. A business magazine even published a reader's haiku about how demoralizing it was to work so hard and still live in a rabbit hutch. Three years later my Japanese friends were still inviting me for dinner to their "rabbit hutches." The phrase is now part of the debate on social policy.

The Japanese have begun to realize that single-minded devotion to work results in a deformed life-style. Several have told me that their work is a vicious circle. They work so hard they have no time to cultivate other interests and soon become restless if they are kept from their jobs. One man told me he suspects he deliberately works long hours and keeps up with *otsukiai* so as not to be burdened with free time.

In response to this dawning consciousness, and to pressure from trade partners, the government has done something that perhaps no other government in the world has ever done before: it has started urging the Japanese to work shorter hours and take more vacation. There are unmistakable signs that the pace is slowing.

Still, it is not the Japanese government but the Japanese corporation that must be convinced. Even a Japanese company is in business to make money, and the harder its employees work the more money it will make. It would take a wrenching change of heart for today's executives, who may never have taken a day's vacation in their lives, to urge their men to relax and take it easy.

Part of the problem is that in many areas the only competitors the Japanese really fear are each other. If Honda slacks off, it's not afraid that Harley-Davidson will take over the motorcycle market. It is Yamaha and Suzuki that are threats.

Nevertheless, younger Japanese may need no encouragement to relax. There are sacrifices that even the most loving total embrace can no longer wring from them; they can be as startled as Americans by the crazed behavior of the elders.

"Recently we got orders from top management to cut entertainment spending," says a young banker, "but did that stop my branch manager? No way. He started dipping into his *own pocket*, so he wouldn't have to cut corners with the customers. I knew he was a solid company man, but that's just too much. You'd never catch me doing that."

Many young Japanese have begun to discover that there is life outside the company universe. A new word has crept into the Japanese business vocabulary: "my-homeism." Older Japanese complain that younger men actually want to go right home after work and spend time with their families. The postwar generation has seen too much affluence ever to match the fanaticism of its elders. If Japanese companies ease the pace, it will be due to creeping individualism and a growing satisfaction with what has already been achieved.

For now, however, the pace is still hot, and the Japanese still throw themselves into their work with a zeal all their own. On a recent trip to Japan I called on a company that had the following message, in English, on the back of its business cards:

COMPANY RULES

1. *For self*
Are you carrying out your mission?

2. *For society*
Are you rendering service to society?

3. *For the world*
Are you acting without shame as an
international businessman?

This company does not build nuclear reactors or supertankers. It makes gloves.

CHAPTER SEVEN

❀

SEX
AND
SEX ROLES

Probably one of the most persistent myths about Japan is that its women have an almost tantric obsession with sex. Buried somewhere in the minds of many Western men is an image of pliant raven-haired beauties, all trained in even the most contortionist ways to please a man. Although their numbers are mercifully dwindling, there are still some American men who only want to hear about "geesha girls" when they learn that I have lived in Japan.

The men of all countries seem to have exaggerated ideas about the sexual habits of foreign women. Furthermore, the Japanese have had certain attitudes and institutions that lend themselves to misinterpretation. Thus it is a shock for many Westerners to discover that in terms of sexual latitude, Japan lies far closer to Spain and Portugal than to Sweden.

Confucian teachings are probably still the single most powerful influence on how Japanese men and women relate to each other. Confucius taught that women were inferior to men and that sex was for making babies. These two principles remain at the heart of sexual behavior in Japan.

Even the most Confucian prudery was never entirely able to curb male appetites. During the Tokugawa period, which came to an end after Perry's arrival, Japanese cities had pleasure quarters where men could seek the company of professional entertainers. The most polished of these were the geisha, a word which means "artistic person." Though they might strike private deals with regular customers, these women were by no means for sale to all comers. As their name suggests, they were highly trained in music, dance, impromptu poetry, and sprightly conversation. Most men were perfectly content to spend an evening in their dazzling company and sleep elsewhere. More straightforward services were available from less accomplished ladies. What was recreation for men was strictly business for women. The country lass or city shop girl who ope'd her chaste treasure to passing samurai soon found herself in the pleasure quarters.

Modern Japan, until after the Second World War, kept an even tighter rein on sexual expression. Japan was going through an ascetic period of nation building, and the increasingly powerful military frowned on frivolous dissipation of energy. Prostitutes were available to the middle class, as were geisha to the rich, and a kept woman was part of the paraphernalia of power. Nevertheless, such irregular activities were a kind of shady business deal transacted with a special class of woman who lived outside the normal bounds of shame. Respectable women were closely supervised until marriage and were expected to be completely faithful thereafter.

During the first half of the twentieth century Japan was thus by no means sexually liberated. Sex had its place: in marriage and, occasionally, with a mistress or in the bordello. Just as the pleasure quarters had been clearly marked off from surrounding neighborhoods, sex was shoved safely into a corner of most people's lives.

In Japan prudery went hand in hand with a very casual attitude toward nakedness. Even today professional sumo wrestlers still practice their sport in G-strings, and though tournaments are televised, no one takes offense at the wrestlers' near nakedness. On more than one goodwill tour of America sumo wrestlers have been asked to wear boxer shorts under their G-strings.

Public baths are still common in Japan, and until perhaps twenty years ago a great many did not separate the sexes. Men and women bathed together with no sense of indecency. Nowadays there are still a few places where both sexes are ostensibly welcome, but no young women would make the mistake of wandering into one.

Traditionally the Japanese have not taken much erotic interest in women's breasts. Until well after the war female sponge divers wore only loincloths, and mothers thought nothing of breast-feeding their children in public. In the early sixties I remember seeing older women walking about bare-breasted on hot summer days. Thanks to Western influence, the Japanese breast has now been fully eroticized, and today any grandmother would be insane to walk the streets topless.

Visitors to Japan of a generation or two ago confused casual nakedness with licentiousness. They did not understand that the Japanese could be so free with their bodies precisely because eroticism was under such strict control.

Until recently Japanese were equally free about their bodily functions. During the fifties and sixties grown men and women relieved themselves by the side of the road with no effort at concealment. Even today older public buildings do not have separate rest rooms for men and women. The sexes share the same facilities without confusion.

Women have pretty much given up relieving themselves in public, but men still urinate most anywhere with great nonchalance. For drunks especially, any tree or wall is fair game. A recent visitor from Japan complained to me about American strictness. "In a city like New York," he said, "where there aren't that many public rest rooms anyway, it's a real inconvenience."

Nevertheless, this traditional male prerogative is seriously threatened. In the summer of 1982 a Japanese state minister, Ichirō Nakagawa, was photographed urinating onto a gingko tree in the garden of the Diet, or legislative assembly. The opposition Socialists made a big fuss and demanded an "explanation" for what the Japanese press dubbed "the urination incident."[1] Before too long the casual pee will have gone the way of bare breasts in the summertime, one more vestige of traditional innocence to be swept aside by Western prurience.

Japan today is perhaps one of the most sexually charged, sexually confused places in the world. The invasion of sex and sexual imagery into all areas of life is probably the most disorienting of all the influences from the West. Japan's traditional Confucian prudery has taken on a tensely erotic overlay.

Sexual imagery is everywhere. If anything, it pervades advertising to an even greater extent than in America. Young female bodies bump and grind out the virtues of anything from instant ramen to sports cars. Every city has a liberal quota of strip joints, porno theaters, and

"Turkish" baths. But Japan has not been content merely to copy the ways the West sells sex; it has added a few wrinkles of its own.

When I was a child, I was an avid fan of a pulp comic series for boys. In those days it was all solid macho stuff: doughty Japanese fighter pilots shooting down Hellcats and Corsairs over the Pacific or gritty twelve-year-olds making the junior high baseball team. The only women who ever appeared in the strip were anxious mothers who made their gritty twelve-year-olds stop practicing their curveballs just long enough to eat a meal. Little girls were the enemy.

On a recent trip to Japan I was seized by a fit of nostalgia and picked up the latest issue at a newsstand. I was shocked to find a picture of a *girl* on the cover. I was shocked again by four glossy color pages featuring a doe-eyed preteen lass prancing in a playground. My childhood heroes, the fighter pilots, seem to have polished off the war in the Pacific and have been retired from the comic books, but the twelve-year-olds still play baseball. They also blow-dry their hair, daydream about their pretty homeroom teachers, and get to date the class sweetheart after they win the big game.

For adult readers, serious business magazines have taken to throwing in a few pages of naked women for the amusement of their mostly male readership. It is as if *Boys' Life* did features on little girls' fashions and *Business Week* ran a centerfold.

Another Japanese innovation is the sex comic book. These are on sale everywhere and are the print equivalent of film pornography. If they are any indication of the fantasy life of the Japanese male—and I think they are—Japanese society has some rocky times ahead. Voyeurism, sex for money, rape, scatology, and mutilation are frequent themes. A typical episode might begin with an unshaven samurai striding through the woods. He spies a lone maiden mincing through the pine needles. He coolly strips and rapes the maiden—she is inevitably endowed with practically Caucasian curves—and for good measure carves off her breasts with his samurai sword. He resumes his stroll through the woods.

This sort of twisted pornography no doubt exists in the West but is not nearly so popular as in Japan. Americans with a taste for rape fantasy seem to enjoy it in private. In Japan sex comics are sold and read everywhere. They can be bought from vending machines, but this is more for twenty-four-hour convenience than to protect shy customers. Men happily read the most hair-raising stuff on trains and in other public places. Many *gaijin* visitors first get wind of these delight-ful periodicals when they idly pick up a magazine that someone left behind on a train seat.

Another Japanese invention is the "no-pants" coffee shop, a craze that swept the country in 1981. It started in Osaka, which, as any Japanese will explain, is always the first test market for kinky new ideas. As customers linger over their $10 cups of coffee, they ogle waitresses dressed in short skirts and no underwear.

Even the venerable striptease has conquered new heights. At one Tokyo club the performers reportedly auction off their underwear to the highest bidders, who then "drape their trophies over their faces."[2]

Television has become an important purveyor of prurient sex. Practically every night of the week at least one channel offers late-night smut. These shows follow a distinct TV talk-show format and are not reruns of movie pornography. Several years ago I saw a show that opened with a group of male show biz personalities sitting around a table, wondering what it would be like if a naked woman were suddenly to appear. Sure enough, the creature of their dreams, dressed only in a bikini bottom, walked into the studio and stretched out on the table in front of them. They spent the next half hour discussing her anatomy and telling each other how much fun it all was. The woman never spoke. Another show I saw started with some shots of a nude woman cavorting in a bedroom and then running naked through a forest. The same woman then appeared fully clothed before a panel of tittering middle-aged men who interviewed her about her sex life.

Television can take astonishing liberties in shows that are not even supposed to be about sex. Recently I saw another middle-aged man interviewing a high school girl who had just won a nationwide singing contest. He made a pointed remark about her large breasts and asked if they ran in the family. The poor girl dissolved into a puddle of giggles. In Japan there is no pay TV or cable; all shows are beamed into every home.

Japanese women seem to put up no resistance to this portrait of themselves that varies only in degree of undress and availability. They studiously ignore the titillation that surrounds them and do not seem inclined to retaliate in kind: Japan has no equivalent of *Playgirl* magazine.

In spite of this constant barrage of sexual stimuli, Japan is still wrapped in its old Confucian prudery. Many boys and girls keep their social lives within the group and may feel shy if left together face-to-face as couples. They indulge in less free-lance recreational sex than Americans or Europeans and are more confused about it. Cohabitation is a scandalous thing, and premarital sex is often just that: experimental lovemaking for engaged couples. Men still prefer to marry virgins, and many can still find one.

Even the scholars have taken official notice of Japan's straitlaced attitudes. A recent issue of the *Journal of Psychology* found that compared to British students, "Japanese students were much less permissive and advanced in their attitudes, showing an almost Victorian reticence."[3] Sex in Japan is perhaps what it was like in America a generation or two ago, except that tensions are much closer to the surface because of the strident sexuality of the media.

Tight control of the pill helps keep Japanese women Victorian. Abortions are legal and inexpensive, but health authorities are unswerving in their insistence that the pill is hazardous to health. I suspect they are also afraid it may be hazardous to public morality, though rumor has it that vigorous lobbying by the abortion interests has helped keep the pill off the market. The diaphragm is legal, but has had poor sales, perhaps, as one writer speculates, because Japanese women are not comfortable handling their genitals.[4]

The most popular form of birth control is thus the condom. It is used by fully 76 percent of all Japanese couples who practice some form of birth control, a figure far greater than in any other industrialized country. Condom companies go to great lengths to make it easier for the "Victorian" Japanese to buy their products. Condoms are packaged in quantities that can be priced at a nice round sum. The embarrassed customer can drop a single bill on the counter and make off with his purchase without having to wait for change. Most manufacturers include a mail-order form in each package, so that customers can send in for refills rather than face the pharmacist again.

In the mid-sixties an enterprising businessman hit upon a new way to deliver the goods to shy consumers. Struck by how uncomfortable people were about buying condoms in his brother's drugstore, he hired a troupe of saleswomen to make door-to-door calls on housewives during the day. His $17 million business, encouragingly named The Every Day Trading Company, has had many successful imitators, and discreet, door-to-door sales now account for 30 to 45 percent of the Japanese condom market.[5]

In this curious context of shame, prudery, and prurience, many Japanese still choke on the idea that women might enjoy sex. Women who play the field are soiled creatures whose prospects for marriage may be seriously compromised. Singles bars do not exist in Japan, though many young Japanese men who come to America have heard of them. Nevertheless, I have known several who, even after having visited one, thought they were places men went to meet prostitutes. It didn't occur to them that women, just like men, might be cruising for a good time.

Japan is thus probably unique. Sexual imagery is just as pervasive as in the most permissive Western societies, yet behavior lags far behind. Men are constantly bombarded with sexual imagery but find few partners outside marriage.

Prostitution is the standard safety valve in many repressive societies, as it is to some extent in Japan, but even the oldest profession has a distinctly Japanese flavor. Technically prostitution has been illegal since 1956, and there is virtually no public solicitation. However, there is no doubt about what goes on in the "Turkish" baths. These are garish places, decked with neon, made out to look like castles or tropical paradises. Inside, customers choose from a menu of exotic services performed by a dependable core of skillful operators who keep the myths of Japanese sensuousness from dying.

Many Turkish baths have almost a theme park atmosphere, where customers can live out specific fantasies. I know of one in a Tokyo suburb that sports a giant red cross over the entrance. Inside, all the women are dressed like nurses. Men who fancy an airline stewardess, or even a schoolgirl, can find a *Toruko* that specializes in creating the right illusion. A favorite spot for sportsmen is called Hole in One; it has a miniature putting green in the lobby.

The baths, however, do not appear to do the mass business one might expect. For one thing, they are expensive, and their clientele seems more married and middle-aged than young and single. Another reason is that many Japanese use the same method to deal with sexual frustration that they use for other frustrations: *gaman*. Especially outside the big cities, young men may hold out until marriage. There is still a flicker of life in the old samurai notion of manliness—that women are a trifling distraction and that abstinence is a source of strength.

The primary sexual focus for many young Japanese men seems to be skin magazines and sex comic books. These have two distinct themes that quickly strike Westerners. The first is voyeurism. Whether or not Japan is a primarily visual culture, as some Japanese argue, sex comic plots and other pornography often suggest seeing rather than doing. Even more explicit are voyeurs' handbooks that describe the best techniques for spying on women and photographing them unawares. Bookstores sell collections of photos by voyeurs, amateur and professional, of women changing clothes at the beach, getting ready for bed, or peeing in the woods.

The latest attraction for voyeurs is the peeping room. These are individual cubicles, built around a circular bedroom, where young girls pretend to behave as they might in private. One of the pioneer establishments in this new growth industry is called Akai Ana, or The Red Hole. At $8 for twenty minutes, the men of Tokyo can peep in privacy from cubicles thoughtfully furnished with a stool and a box of tissue paper.

Perhaps voyeurism is so popular because it seems to account for a good part of the sex life of many young Japanese. Unfortunately for them, Japan has strict censorship laws that reflect the nation's underlying prudishness. Women in strip shows or in peeping rooms must never remove their drawers. In film or print there is a complete ban on the depiction of pubic hair or genitalia. This means that bouncing black balls follow the actors around during bedroom scenes in Western movies, and sex comic characters are drawn with curious anatomical deficiencies. *Playboy* magazine can be bought in Japan but with the offending portions crudely blacked over. There is rumored to be a large warehouse somewhere in Yokohama, where little old ladies with Magic Markers bowdlerize foreign magazines before they go on the newsstands. Businessmen returning from abroad gleefully smuggle in the hard stuff.

In the big cities, racier fare can be had in the legal twilight of private clubs and "pink cabarets." Here, young men and women perform together onstage in ways that might divert the most hardened aficionado. The vice squad keeps these amusements from flourishing openly but doesn't bother to stamp them out completely.

The other striking twist to commercial sex in Japan is the frequent association of sex with violence. I think this murky trend must stem from Japan's persistent contempt for women. In Japanese society the traditional role of the woman is to serve a man. The saturation of

Japanese media with sexual imagery encourages men to think of women as sexual servants as well but by no means encourages women to assume that role. Women have the power of bestowal or refusal. That these second-class citizens should have such a hold on the male imagination is a source of bitterness for Japanese men. I suspect that it is frustration at the manifest powers of an inferior that makes Japan receptive to violent pornography. Abusing women is sweet revenge; it forces women back into their role as servants.

Many Japanese porn films thus have themes of sadism and humiliation. A typical movie poster advertises a naked woman tightly bound in ropes and chains, while a fully dressed man threatens her with a samurai sword. I have clearly failed in my research for this book by not attending one of these shows, but the words of a noted world traveler have the ring of truth:

> The man was behind the woman now and it took very little imagination to conclude that he was resolutely sodomizing her as he worked at her breast like a man squeezing lemons. . . . The man in the film hopped into the missionary position and at the moment of orgasm—a wince its only warning—drew a glittering sword from beneath the mat and cut his lover's throat. There was a close shot of the fatal laceration, of blood running between the dead woman's breasts (this seemed a popular climax), and I moved to the lobby for a breath of fresh air.[6]

Fortunately an occasional feast of the imagination is enough for most Japanese men; Japan has a low incidence of rape. Nevertheless, crowded trains and subways are favorite haunts for maulers and gropers. They are an established big-city phenomenon; one was the protagonist of a recent movie, called *Jun*, that was even—unsuccessfully—released in America. It is not clear whether *gaijin* women are especially likely to be pawed or whether they just complain about it more. In any case, many who live in Japan are shocked by the experience.

I was shocked just *hearing* about what happened to one American woman. She is tall, with long brown hair that hangs nearly to her waist. "I was in one of those subway trains that are so packed you can't move," she said, "when I began to feel a gentle tugging at the back of my neck. I was able to turn my head just enough to realize that the man behind me had stuffed *all my hair into his mouth* and was having a climactic experience right there in the subway. I yelled for help and was saved by a tall, wordless man, who threw the creep out at the next stop."

An American man once told me of his surprise at hearing a Japanese acquaintance confess his love of subways. "He told me that when he gets on a crowded train, he always makes a point of picking out a pretty girl and rubbing up against her. He had just moved from one suburb of Kobe to another a little farther out and was really looking forward to that extra fifteen minutes on the train every morning."

"The subways are something you never get used to," says a British woman who lives in Tokyo. "It probably makes me angrier than anything else about living in Japan." She is also frustrated by the stoic attitude of Japanese women. "My friends tell me they never resist or make a stink. They just get off at the next stop." Again the solution is *gaman*.

I recently read an article in a Japanese women's magazine that described ways to block the groping hands of subway maulers. It included color illustrations of how to position oneself in a crowd and how to protect vital organs with a handbag or rolled-up overcoat. Not once did it suggest that a woman should scream or fight back.

Offenses against women have reached the point where a number of lonely pedestrian underpasses in Tokyo have posted signs reading, "Watch out for gropers." Such assaults are, of course, a far cry from being buggered and butchered or from what might happen to an unwary woman in Chicago or New York. Offenders rarely want more than a quick feel, and Tokyo is still astonishingly safe for men and women alike. Nevertheless, these acts are clearly part of the growing frustration and anger of men who are urged to desire women in a society where a woman's reputation is still very important. The unavailability of women would probably not be so maddening if Japanese society did not hold them in such low regard.

Marriage is the respectable solution to these problems, and one of Japanese society's strictest unwritten rules is that everyone must marry. Once married, a couple must have children. There is a well-defined marrying age of about twenty to twenty-six for women and twenty-four to twenty-nine for men. A few men manage to stay single into their thirties, but most women get desperate for a husband once they are twenty-five or so.

Japanese are unabashedly curious about single adults and childless couples. Many of my business contacts were surprised to learn that I was in my thirties and still unmarried. To this day I don't know what kind of answer they expected, but many would ask me with genuine concern why I didn't take a wife.

I used to work with an American who was younger than I but safely married. Our Japanese customers approved of his fine example but were taken aback to learn that five years of marriage had produced no children. It did not occur to them that a couple might be childless by choice.

In part this is because one of the most important reasons for marriage in Japan is to produce sons who will carry on the family name. "It is an offense to the ancestors," a Japanese once explained to me, "to let the name die out." Satisfying the ancestors can be tricky when all the children in a family are daughters. The usual solution is for at least one daughter to marry a man who agrees to be adopted by her family and assume her name. The family may even forbid a daughter to marry a man who is not willing to be adopted. In this respect, marriage is very much a group undertaking; the desires of the individual count for far less than they would in the West. It is this concern for the family line that makes marriage to a Korean or *burakumin*—or *gaijin*—so distasteful for many Japanese.

Ingenious solutions can be found for carrying on the family name. A Japanese college professor once described the curious case of one of his students: "Both the boy and the girl were single children," he recalled. "The girl's family insisted on adopting the boy and giving him their name because otherwise their name would die out. The boy's family, of course, refused. The boy was also a single child, and that would mean the end of *their* name. It looked like a dead stymie."

"What happened?" I asked. "Did they break off the marriage?"

"No," said the professor. "The couple was too much in love. The families compromised. The girl married the boy and took his name. However, both houses agreed that the bride's family would adopt the first grandchild and give it their name. This way, so long as the couple had at least two children—preferably sons—both family names had a chance of surviving." To Americans, elaborate contortions to carry on the family name smack of medieval aristocracy. These were middle-class folks in contemporary Japan.

About half of all Japanese marriages are "love marriages"—that is to say, the partners found each other on their own initiative. The rest are arranged. In the past the go-between, or *nakōdo*, was usually a friend of the family who would arrange a formal meeting with a likely mate. Now there are many professional *nakōdo*, and the marriage business means big money. Many of these pros are also insurance salesmen. This is because Japanese men usually buy life insurance when they marry, and who could refuse a policy from the man who found him a wife?

Young people work up a kind of marriage résumé which describes their background and interests and includes a photograph. Copies are delivered to the *nakōdo*, who in turn passes them around to people he thinks would make a good match. When both parties have had a chance to study the other's qualifications and agree to meet, an introduction, or *omiai*, is arranged. This is a stiff, well-dressed affair, often held in a swank restaurant or hotel lobby, with parents and *nakōdo* in attendance. At the end of the formal session the couple may have a chance to spend some time together alone.

If the young people like each other, they inform the *nakōdo*, and then can arrange to see each other on their own. If either party is disenchanted, the word is diplomatically passed along by the *nakōdo*. Usually a decision to go on seeing each other is a decision to marry. The good news is announced perhaps a month, and just a few dates, after the *omiai*. Japanese decide to get married at what for Americans would be the drop of a hat. Rarely do they explore each other's personalities with anything like the thoroughness common in the West.

Not long ago I attended a party for a woman who had just announced her engagement. She told me that she had looked through hundreds of marriage résumés and gone to twenty or thirty *omiai* before she met the right man. On the fourth date they decided to get married. "By that time," she told me sweetly, "I knew what I wanted." Perhaps she did. An American is five times as likely to get a divorce as she is.

Marriage is grievously expensive in Japan. It used to be said that marrying off three daughters was enough to bankrupt a man. It still is. Unlike some other societies, where the groom pays the wife's family a substantial bride price, the bride is traditionally sent along with a huge, expensive trousseau. In effect, her family pays the young man to take her off their hands.

Nowadays, when the engagement is formally agreed on, the groom's family hands over a substantial sum of money—say, $5,000—

to the bride's family to help get the trousseau together. However, her family is expected to spend several times that amount, buying furniture, clothes, appliances, and perhaps a small automobile. By this time the prospective bride has probably quit her job, if she had one, and equipping the new home is full-time work.

"What," I once asked a Japanese friend, "prevents the bride's family from spending only the money they got from the groom's family and none of their own? Who's going to check up on what everything in the trousseau cost?"

"Don't be silly," he said. "Anybody can tell the difference between a trousseau that cost five thousand dollars and one that cost twenty thousand dollars. The face of the bride's family is very much at stake. The groom's family might never forgive her if she skimped on the trousseau.

"Besides," he added, "if there are any other unmarried daughters in the family, it could affect their chances of finding a husband. That's just the sort of thing someone might check up on."

The marriage ceremony itself is a gala, costly affair. People used to be married in private homes or on the grounds of a Shinto shrine, but as the celebration has grown in scale, "marriage palaces" have sprouted all over the country to handle the trade. These are substantial profit-making enterprises with banquet halls, catering services, changing rooms, and photo studios.

Just as American funeral homes often talk their customers into paying for fancier service than they really wanted, wedding palace operators are past masters at persuading a young couple to keep up with the Tanakas. They are always thinking up new gimmicks to enchant their customers and bring in more money. "One of the latest tricks," says a college professor who is invited to many student weddings, "is to rig the wedding cake so it will let fly a big cloud of smoke as soon as the couple cuts into it."

The same man also told me of another optional feature that is on its way to becoming standard. This is the preceremony slide show for the couple, their family, and their closest friends. It is put on by a professional employee of the marriage palace, who has collected pictures in advance from both families. During the show, which covers the lives of the bride and groom, he gives a sentimental commentary on the couple as children and how their parents cherished them. He describes their school days, tells how they met, and ends with a rapturous description of the happiness in store for them. "The show is not considered a success," says the professor, "unless everyone is in tears at the end." Many marriage palaces are apparently building special darkened rooms just for the slide show.

It is now customary for the ceremony to have both Japanese and Western elements, and the bride, especially, is kept busy leaping in and out of different outfits. She will often appear first in a magnificent wedding kimono, complete with elaborate ceremonial headgear. Later she may change into a different kimono and then into a Western wedding dress. Just before the ceremony ends and the couple dash off on their honeymoon, both bride and groom change into fancy Western-style street clothes.

Hundreds of guests may be invited to the wedding. They bring money, rather than presents, but this is not the windfall it could be. The couple's parents must give the *guests* costly presents to take home. Often the expense of the ceremony itself is split between the families, but even so, a solid middle-class wedding can easily cost the bride's family $40,000 or $50,000. The children of important or well-known people may have to go through several different receptions on different days in order to fit in all the guests. Costs can easily become astronomical.

Parents often save conscientiously for their children's weddings, but many still go into debt. The Japanese complain all the time about the killing expense of marriage, but it is a problem, like examination hell, that is not likely to go away. Weddings are a direct expression of the wealth and prestige of a family, and few Japanese are willing to cut corners. "The whole thing," explains a Japanese friend, "is geared to the families, not to the couple. It's not two individuals who are marrying. It's the union of two houses, and a shabby wedding means loss of face. The couple, as a matter of fact, are the least important part of the whole affair."

In marriage, sex roles seem to harden permanently. It is the final crackdown on any feminist tendencies. As college students men and women may enjoy a brief period of near equality, but the first step into the corporate world is a big step backward. The male supremacy that lurks in the background on campus is a sacred institution at the office, and women soon learn their place. Thus schoolmates who were on an equal footing in the classroom easily slip into a more hierarchical relationship as the men move into positions of responsibility and the women get jobs as clerks.

By the time they marry most Japanese seem to be ready for their traditional roles. For the man, marriage is a convenient institution that gives him a base of operations for devoting himself to what is really important: his job. The home supplies him with a steady stream of clean shirts and hot meals so that he can work twelve-hour days without petty distractions. As one author put it recently, on the women's page of a major Japanese daily, "A man doesn't get married with any high-minded ideas about making a woman happy. What he wants is her devotion—such as it is—and her young body. He wants to squeeze a lot of free labor out of her as well, and marriage is the best arrangement for all this. Men want sex without having to pay for it and free maid service, and they figure they can't get it unless they offer marriage in return."[7]

Most women leave their jobs when they marry and become full-time housewives. It can be a bit of a surprise to see a once-lively college lass fold herself into the traditional role of homemaker. Her husband is probably working long hours, keeping up with after-hours *ostukiai*, and taking very little vacation. He probably spends most of his weekends playing golf or Mah-Jongg with the boys. Our home-maker would not have much to do were it not for the inevitable children, and soon she is caught up in looking after the brood that will carry on the family name. A wife devotes herself entirely to the service of her husband and his progeny. When the children start going to school, one of the mother's main jobs is to make them study for the all-important examinations. This mode of motherhood is so important it has been consecrated with the term *kyōiku mama* ("education mom").

Women basically manage the home and rear the children single-handedly. Sex roles tend to be very rigid, and anything that goes on inside the house is women's work and beneath the dignity of a real man. As one conservative says about the young devotees of my-home-ism, "Any man who changes his kid's diapers will never amount to much."[8] Japanese wives have to fend for themselves the way single mothers do in America, except that they do not have jobs and have to look after men who show up at odd hours expecting a meal and a bed. The wives are the first to get up in the morning, the last to go to bed, and are perhaps the best example of *gaman* to be found in Japan today.

For many Japanese businessmen, home is such an incidental part of their lives that they may accept a transfer to some other part of Japan and leave their families behind. They will maintain a small apartment in the new city and see the wife and kids on weekends or holidays. This is such a normal arrangement there is even a word for it: *tanshin-funin*.

Some wives might not notice the change. Says one, of her bureaucrat husband, "When we first got married, all he did was work. The only thing he ever did at home was sleep. At one point I decided to keep track of how often we actually ate a meal together. It was once every *six weeks*—and that includes weekends."

With their men away so often, women establish considerable authority at home. Men have so little time to manage household affairs that many hand over their entire pay packets to their wives. An older business contact once complained to me of how little control he had around the home. "When I was younger, I was working so hard that I didn't much care what went on at home. I was glad my wife made all the decisions. But now she's gone too far; I can hardly move the furniture without her permission. Sometimes I feel like a boarder in my own home."

The husband is, of course, supposed to be undisputed master, and in public he usually is. Women refer to their husbands as *shujin* or *danna*—both words mean "master." The charming word for widow—*mibōjin*—means "not-yet-dead person." Men of the old school address their wives as *Oi*, which means "Hey, you!"

I was once invited to dinner with several other Americans to the home of a Japanese banker. One of the other guests had just learned about the "Hey, you" school of marital relations and wanted to know what our host called his wife. "*Oi*," he said, "is two syllables. That's too long. I just call her *O*." This man, like others of his generation, refers to his wife as *gusai* ("my foolish wife"). In more progressive circles a man's wife is his *kanai* ("inside the house"). Another man's wife is called *okusan* ("person of the interior").

Wives are sometimes so much of the interior that they hardly show themselves to guests except to serve them food and drink. A guest might easily exchange no more than a few words of greeting and farewell with an older man's wife. One American who has lived in Japan for many years complains that he often must wait until an old friend dies before he ever meets the man's wife—at the funeral.

In general, husbands seem to play two different roles with their wives. As little boys men were babied and got preferential treatment from their mothers. In private, many husbands look to their wives for the same kind of mothering. After children have been born, the husband's role becomes that of a favorite eldest son. The dependent, spoiled child/husband is a stock character in TV situation comedies.

The other, more public male role is that of the gruff samurai type who is undisputed master of his woman. He calls her *Oi*, orders her around, and treats her as if she were faintly retarded. He may even beat her; until quite recently wives were little better than chattel. There are no reliable statistics on wife beating, but there seems to be plenty of it going on. Former Prime Minister Tanaka's daughter once told a magazine interviewer that her father had beaten her and had urged her husband to beat her, too, "if it makes you feel more like a man."[9]

In neither of these roles—child/husband or samurai—is there much room for the father to establish rapport with the children. In the first he is in competition with them, and in the second he ignores them. One Japanese sociologist has expressed the extreme view that in Japan the role of the father has not yet been invented.[10]

The woman generally manages to match her mood to that of her man, playing the submissive wife or doting mother according to his needs. Wives are expected not to gush with affection like Westerners but to maintain a constant level of tender admiration. This is the diet the male ego requires to maintain good health.

In his samurai mode the husband's manhood would be sullied by any admission of affection. A surefire way to get an embarrassed giggle out of a middle-aged Japanese is to ask him if he ever tells his wife he loves her. "Men just don't say things like that," he will say. One man I asked thought about the question for a moment and then said, "Once I told her I *liked* her." If pressed further, a man may say something like "If she doesn't think I love her, she wouldn't believe me if I said so, and if she does think I love her, what's the point in saying so?"

The truth of the matter is that men think it is weak and womanish to show affection. We have a serious dose of that kind of thinking in America, but we are not so badly afflicted as the Japanese.

When I was growing up, I absorbed the prevailing bashfulness about showing affection. I remember once, when I was about ten years old, my mother kissed me in front of my Japanese playmates. I would have far preferred that she slug me. For weeks afterward my little buddies teased me about that kiss.

Nevertheless, Japanese young people are getting bolder. In the big cities they now walk hand in hand or with their arms around each other and have even been known to kiss in public. More and more Japanese are willing to say, *"Ai rabu yū"* ("I love you"). The foreignness of the words keeps them just abstract enough so that they can be spoken.

One of the Japanese husband's traditional prerogatives is a little philandering. In the past this was so much to be expected that the Japanese bride's wedding apparel symbolized her acceptance of the prospect of betrayal. Her elaborate head covering is called a *tsunokakushi* ("horn hider"). It represents her determination to hide the horns of jealousy that will sprout when her husband is unfaithful to her.

These days it would be hard to claim that male infidelity is any more common in Japan than in the West, but it does seem to be different. Japanese men don't make as much of an effort to conceal their adventures, and their partners are not the same. Since few Japanese women, married or unmarried, are available for affairs, adultery seems to take the form of an occasional visit to a Turkish bath. Very few Japanese can afford the expense of courting a geisha or maintaining a mistress. Occasional flings are not a great threat to the marriage, and wives generally seem to accept them stoically. Most of the men who take sex tours to Seoul and Taipei are married. Of course, all hell would break loose if their wives were unfaithful.

Overseas business trips are a favorite opportunity for sowing wild oats. Japanese companies try to avoid the expense of sending families overseas, and many post men abroad by themselves for as long as a year. In Southeast Asia men may arrange for a live-in girl friend, but in the West they are usually too intimidated by cultural barriers to try to establish real relationships with local women. It seems they visit prostitutes instead.

"It's interesting," says a middle-aged businessman who has traveled widely for his company, "how much the price of a woman varies from country to country. But there's a good rule of thumb that can save you from embarrassment," he adds. "Find out what a pair of shoes costs in that country, and chances are, a woman will cost about the same."

Japanese are acutely conscious of how different their marital relations are from those of Westerners. They know that Japanese women permit inattention and infidelity that American wives would never tolerate. It is thus a common saying that a Japanese woman can happily marry a man of any nationality, but a Japanese man can marry only a Japanese woman. In other words, men of all nations will find Japanese women pliant and obedient, while Japanese men will find all foreign women impossibly headstrong.

A recent book that was moderately successful in Japan was titled *The U.S.-Japanese Culture Battle in My Home.* It is a self-righteous, semihumorous account of the tribulations of living with an American wife and is a warning to all right-thinking Japanese not to undertake such folly. The author, who refers to his wife throughout the book as "the enemy," is critical of nearly everything she does: the way she walks, talks, cooks, does the shopping, brings up the children. But what he resents most is her refusal to submit to his clearly superior male judgment on all things, and he blames this uppity behavior on her inferior, foreign upbringing. He feels doubly sorry for himself because his wife is of Japanese ancestry; he was counting on her to revert to the peaceable ways of the tribe once he had brought her back to the homeland.[11]

The way Japanese men feel about American wives is clear from this advice from an experienced trading company man to young fellows being posted overseas. "Your wife's job," he writes, "can be more important than your own. Especially in North America, men get pushed around by their wives and often it's the woman who wears the pants. So see to it that your wife makes friends with all your customers' wives. It can bring unexpected rewards."[12]

Nevertheless, even in Japan smart, ambitious women have always managed to break out of the traditional sex roles and establish independent careers—but not in the economic mainstream. As we noted earlier, the second tier has some openings for women. But the field of greatest opportunity has always been *mizushōbai* ("water business"), not the "hard" business of men in suits and ties. This is the world of hotels, bars, brothels, restaurants, and coffee shops, where success depends on a fickle and shifting clientele. Anyone who has walked the side streets of a Japanese city knows just how rich and varied this floating world can be. A talented woman can start as a waitress or hostess and build a small empire.

Mizushōbai often has vague gangland connections, and there is a definite stigma attached to the women who work in it. Still, many see it as nothing more than an easy way to make money and meet a lot of men. Just like the women who work for corporations, they may end up marrying men they met on the job and turn into good housewives. Others develop a taste for independence and relaxed mores. This is a world where a woman can be divorced, unmarried, or living in sin and still be as "respectable" as anyone else in the business. In a narrow sense it is a liberating environment for women who are resigned to the social stigma.

Nevertheless, if a career in *mizushōbai* means financial independence for a woman, she is still dependent on men in a different and demeaning way. The success of a *mizushōbai* establishment is directly related to the popularity of the proprietress. Japanese like to have a personal relationship with the management of their local bar or tempura stand, and a woman who can please men can make her business boom. Both the slick mama-san who runs a bar and the frowsy divorcée with a corner sushi shop must flirt with and flatter their mostly male customers to be sure that they will return.

The most extreme form of this cutthroat popularity contest is the hostess bar. Hostess bars, of which there are an astonishing number in Japan, are tiny one-room affairs with an exclusively male clientele. They are stocked with attractive young hostesses who are assigned one per customer. Each sits beside her client, lights his cigarettes, pours his drinks, laughs at his jokes, and engages him in incredibly silly, titillating conversation. Outright contact, however, is limited to a peck on the cheek, a hand on the thigh, and a little light pawing.

These women are not for sale. Though they may sometimes strike a discreet deal with a regular customer, they are under no obligation to sleep with anyone. The occasional Westerners who are invited along to hostess bars can be forgiven for finding this a little hard to believe.

All customers drink the businessman standard: scotch and water. I'm not sure hostess bars stock anything else. Every so often someone brings out a plateful of tidbits: mixed nuts; sliced pineapple; chocolate drops. No one orders these snacks; they just appear and go on the bill. A whiskey, some sliced pineapple, and a snuggle is *very* expensive entertainment. In Tokyo just to sit down in a classy hostess bar costs $100 to $150 per person, and the tab can quickly grow to double that amount. The deluxe treatment at a Turkish bath costs less than that. Not many individuals can afford these rates, so hostess bars are used mainly for corporate entertainment.

In the Ginza district of Tokyo and in similar areas in other cities, there are hostess bar department stores—ten- and twelve-story buildings with nothing but bars on every floor, all competing for the same customers. Business is directly dependent on how popular the girls are, so hostesses are rewarded by their employers if they are asked for by name. They therefore welcome their clients with whoops of joy, and make a huge fuss over them.

This form of soft-core prostitution is extremely popular. Many businessmen I know spend at least a night or two every week in hostess bars. The amount of money that changes hands is enormous. It is a common joke in Tokyo that the nightly take in the hostess bars is one of the best leading economic indicators in the country.

Even when they go overseas, the Japanese cannot do without hostess bars. All major American cities have a few, their discreet trade limited to Japanese customers. In New York City alone there are between twenty and thirty. Since there are not enough Japanese women to go around, the bars hire a few Americans, mostly aspiring actresses who are fed up with waitressing.

After all my years in Japan I am still mystified by the popularity of hostess bars. Hara-kiri makes more sense to me than spending $200 to have a woman laugh at my jokes and pat my thigh. Of the many businessmen I have asked about it, none has ever given me a convincing explanation.

"Don't you enjoy talking to pretty girls?" they ask in surprise.

"Well, yes," I reply, "but it takes some of the fun out of it to know they're being paid to be friendly."

"Why think about that? Just enjoy yourself."

"If that's the way you feel about it, why don't you just enjoy yourself at a Turkish bath? That I could understand."

"Come, come, Taylor-san, you can't take customers to a Turkish bath."

The conversation goes on at cross-purposes until they say something like "You're right, Taylor-san. It doesn't make any sense at all. We Japanese must be fools to spend so much money on pure silliness." That ends the conversation, but I haven't won the argument. "So long, Taylor-san. I've got to meet Kawashima Electric at the Ginza." I take comfort in the fact that some younger Japanese find hostess bars just as incomprehensible as I do.

There may be a clue to the mystery of hostess bars in the depression my friend Susan felt after using humble speech all day. As one asking favors, she had to heap polite abuse upon herself, a ritual that Japanese can shrug off but one which wore her down. Just as Susan felt miserable deprecating herself, I find no pleasure in the sprightly conversation of professional hostesses. Westerners expect a certain level of sincerity. When they pay money for a woman, they don't expect affection, and they don't want pseudosex; they want the real thing.

Perhaps it is long experience with suppressing *honne* and expressing *tatemae* that makes the question of the sincerity of bar hostesses irrelevant to the Japanese. It is no coincidence that many think American prostitutes are cold and unfeeling. "They don't hide the fact that it's strictly business," complains a Japanese business contact. "At a Turkish bath the girls really pamper you. They know how to make a man feel great. American prostitutes make you feel miserable." For the Japanese, a simple exchange of sex for money is unbearably "dry." The show of affection that goes with it in Japan might seem like pointless insincerity to Americans.

In a sense, hostess bars are a direct descendant of the geisha tradition. Today's bar girls have none of the cultivation of geisha, but they do supply the Japanese male with the adoring female attention he finds so gratifying. Bars provide a distinctly erotic experience, as did geisha houses, but by stopping far short of the decisive act, they offer a kind of fantasyland adultery that is entirely acceptable to society.

Also, middle-aged executives are not likely to have much time or opportunity for contact with pretty young women other than in the office. At work, relations are much more formal than in an American corporation, so the hostess bar may be a businessman's sole opportunity for a little flirtation—an experience all the more agreeable because the company picks up the tab. Moreover, there is no such thing as a business function to which wives are invited. Bar hostesses provide the only relief from the relentlessly male atmosphere of business.

Of course, no business is transacted in hostess bars. Everyone is too busy with his assigned playmate. "For businessmen," a college professor once told me, "an evening in a hostess bar is pure confidence building. It is a night out with the boys and creates an atmosphere of trust. And the more money you spend, the more trust you get. You don't develop much trust over a hamburger." While they are feeling the thigh of a young hostess, I suppose the Japanese are establishing the right "feeling" for doing business.

Along with Turkish baths and hostess bars, Japan has yet another novel institution: the love hotel. With increased use of the automobile, these have sprung up all over the country and provide privacy for irregular activities. Like Turkish baths, they can be recognized by their architecture; châteaux and Arabian palaces are favorite motifs. Rooms with mirrored ceilings and vibrating beds can be rented by the hour. However, not all customers are couples with something to hide. Many are married but live in tiny apartments with parents or children and have no privacy at home.

There seems to be a love hotel in every neighborhood. The Japanese have only the haziest notion of zoning, so a flamboyant monument to sex is likely to crop up in even the most sedate suburbs. "I think that's what I dislike about them the most," says one Westerner. "Every Japanese child grows up with one just down the street."

Nevertheless, love hotels serve an understandable purpose. In the United States as well, a motel is the classic scene for stealthy sex. But I know of none in America that looks like the Castle of Chillon or that is ablaze with giant red neon hearts. Like the infantile talk that goes on with bar hostesses, there is something distinctly adolescent about going for a romp in a love hotel. Just as the captains of Japanese industry begin to behave like junior high school kids as soon as a hostess sits down beside them, a love hotel is the sort of place I might have wanted to whisk a girl off to when I was in the eighth grade.

The conversation of Japanese men often reflects this juvenile attitude. Truck driver vulgarity is rare, but a simpering prurience is extremely common. Americans who do business with the Japanese are struck by how often they try to make off-color jokes. This is not just because they don't speak enough English to carry on a normal conversation; that kind of talk genuinely amuses them. A Western woman who is married to a Japanese puts it bluntly: "Japanese men have the sexual maturity of thirteen-year-olds."

As if sex weren't complicated enough already, in Japan it is strangely mixed up with the racial hierarchy we saw earlier, in which the Japanese are not exactly at the top. As late as 1969 a Japanese diplomat wrote a book, in English, in which he says, "Of all the races of the world, the Japanese are perhaps physically the least attractive, with the exception of Pygmies and Hottentots."[13] This is an unusually strong expression of self-loathing, and the author was eventually hounded out of the Ministry of Foreign Affairs for it. Nevertheless, it was an honest expression of the terrible sexual inferiority complex that many Japanese men feel toward Caucasians.

Size is certainly what the Japanese worry about most. They think of themselves as short-legged runts in comparison with whites and will invariably comment admiringly on tall foreigners. Particularly in the bedroom, they are convinced that bigger is better. Deep within the mind of the Japanese male lurks the fear that he simply does not measure up, that any Japanese woman who has ever experienced a Caucasian will never again be satisfied with Orientals. This fear translates into the gnawing suspicion that all Japanese women are pushovers for white men and will follow a pair of blue eyes to the ends of the earth.

In Tokyo I am reconciled to the fact that nearly every man I meet will sooner or later ask me how I like Japanese women. I usually say that I do. Then what I hear is "It must be great being a *gaijin*. Don't Japanese women fall all over themselves trying to meet you?"

I am so tired of this question I try to laugh it off: "Japan's no different from any other place. Women fall all over themselves trying to meet me wherever I go."

Back when I was still interested in investigating this curious attitude, I would ask Japanese men to tell me seriously why they thought we *gaijin* were such catnip to women. A college student tried to explain it to me. "Well," he said, "you're taller, your noses stick out farther, and your feet are bigger."

"What are you trying to say?" I asked him.

He thought some more. "Your fingers are longer, and your wrists are bigger around."

That must explain it.

One summer years ago I did some hitchhiking in Japan. For the people who picked me up, I represented an unusual opportunity: a *gaijin* who spoke Japanese and whom they could talk to for an hour and never see again. Whenever I was picked up by a young man, it was usually only a matter of time before he would ask the burning question: How many inches?

"Guess," I would tell him.

"Eight inches? Ten inches?"

"Eight inches?" I would say in mock outrage. "That's diameter, man." While they laugh nervously, I change the subject.

Fears of sexual inferiority are exaggerated by Western films.

Americans and Europeans touch and kiss casually and, at least in movieland, rush off to bed with strangers on the slightest pretext. This greater sophistication and openness easily appear to the Japanese as greater competence. To the traditionally modest Japanese, free love seems to be a Caucasian specialty for which they are just as unprepared psychologically as physically.

Some of the Japanese males' fears may have some basis in fact. A few sophisticated Japanese women seem to specialize in prowling the Tokyo night spots popular with foreigners. However, I think they either are gold diggers or are looking for men who take them more seriously than Japanese do. I suspect that a more liberated notion of sex roles is more important to them than size or brute competence.

"One thing Japanese women like about Western men is their manners," says a Japanese woman who lives in America. "After all, there are American women who really go for Europeans. They like that Continental touch—the flowers, the compliments, the attention. Just imagine what all that does to Japanese women. They think they're in seventh heaven."

Japanese men have a complex mixture of feelings for Western women. On the one hand, they are powerfully attracted to the light-skinned, long-legged, large-breasted, blue-eyed blonde, the ultimate sex symbol that is everything a Japanese woman is not. At the same time, they may be terrified that this fiendishly desirable creature, accustomed to brawny Caucasians, will laugh at their puny embrace.

Those who have gotten over that fear may think they can take liberties with foreign women that would be unthinkable with Japanese. "They have wild ideas about how *gaijin* behave," says an American woman who has lived for many years in Japan. "They have heard that there is greater sexual freedom in the West and think that means a foreign woman will sleep with anybody. At least they see no harm in trying."

When they come to America, bolder Japanese will go out and buy the Caucasian experience. The less bold will be sure to go to a topless bar or a strip show. The nude musical *Oh! Calcutta!*, which has been playing on Broadway for years, would probably have closed long ago without its faithful Japanese audiences.

Japanese women are somewhat threatened by Western women as well, but not nearly to the extent that men are. For one thing, Western men often find them very attractive, whereas few Western women think Japanese men are sexy at all. Moreover, Japanese women tend to think that even if a Japanese man is swept off his feet by a Western woman, in the long run he won't be able to handle a self-assertive partner who demands treatment as an equal.

In any case, there is a fascination with Caucasians of both sexes that has distinctly erotic overtones. Also, there is the plain fact that Caucasian features and coloring offer endless variety next to the invariable black hair and brown eyes of the Japanese. A tall redhead walking down a Yokohama street is a distinct oddity and will get a good looking over. Some of that special attention will rub off on any Japanese who may be walking arm in arm with the oddity.

Not surprisingly young Japanese go to considerable lengths to *look* Caucasian. Several years ago it was all the rage for women to dye their hair. A Japanese woman with blond hair is a fearful sight and always seems to need a root treatment. Outright blondes were therefore never common, but for a time all chic young things felt they had to be redheads. That era has passed, and now it's the men's turn. On college campuses and in show business young men are going to the beauty parlor and getting their hair set in curls and waves. Since no more Japanese men have curly hair than Japanese women are blond, there is no way to pretend it's natural, but it does make them stand out.

One radical way to look less Japanese is surgical removal of the epicanthic fold, the curve of tissue on the upper eyelid that gives Oriental eyes their characteristic "slant." This procedure waxes and wanes in popularity and is resorted to almost exclusively by women. Plastic surgeons do a brisk business in nose jobs as well, and in the entertainment business, going aquiline is all the rage.

If the Japanese are patient, they may eventually need no more nose jobs. In 1979 a major Japanese newspaper reported that compared to 1945, Japanese noses were noticeably longer and that more Japanese had oval rather than round nostrils. The article was headlined: "Rising Standard of Living Puts Japanese on Par with 'Long-nosed' Westerners."[14]

Characteristically, when the Japanese try to make themselves more attractive by looking less Oriental, they model their appearance on whites. Blacks or Latinos have no chance in the sexual sweepstakes. Blacks, in particular, are rarer and more striking oddities in Japan than any Caucasian, but to the race- and hierarchy-conscious Japanese, they are not valid role models for anything.

In Japan relations between the sexes can only improve. Sex roles are beginning to lose some of their sharper contours, and younger Japanese are beginning to turn their backs on the past. A few couples are putting off having children, and in the second tier of the economy it is now common for wives to keep their jobs after marriage. Nevertheless, a career outside the home seldom relieves these modern wives of full responsibility for domestic chores.

Women's liberation is more an idea than a movement in Japan. Few Japanese women now think of themselves as oppressed, but their consciousness will certainly change. For one thing, women's rights have been too noisy an issue in the West for the Japanese to pretend that the problem doesn't exist. There is still a world of difference between the great cities and the countryside, but social change is gaining momentum everywhere.

Strict sexual mores are giving ground to the more relaxed standards of the West. A women's magazine called *Yang-gu Re-dii (Young Lady)* reflects the changing times. In a recent issue, along with innumerable ads for bust developers, was an article titled "Shame on Men for This Kind of Sex—Does Your Man Measure Up?" What followed were brief accounts, reportedly true, by fifty women describing their most horrendous sexual experience. One, for example, complained of a man who shouted, *"Okāchan!"* ("Mommy!") in moments of ecstasy. Twenty years ago it would have been hard to find fifty single women who admitted to any sexual experience at all. Japan is changing, but it seems it must have its *Cosmopolitan*s before it ever gets a *Ms* magazine.

All of society will have to change before women can take their place beside men as anything like equals in work or at home. So long as women are kept at the bottom of the work force they will never be independent. Japan is only beginning to awaken to issues that Westerners have been wrestling with for a generation.

As for Japan's sexual inferiority complex vis-à-vis the West, it should diminish as Japan's economic success continues. As the Japanese begin to assume with whites just a touch of the arrogance they have hitherto kept for other Asians, their awe of the Caucasian will subside. Also, with improved diet younger Japanese are growing much taller than their parents. Today the average twenty-year-old is a good four inches taller than his father. The old fears may never quite die, though, until there are as many six-footers in Japan as in America or Europe.

The battle of the sexes is a terrible one in all countries. No society has a monopoly on fairness or happiness, nor is any ever likely to solve all the mysteries of gender. But Japan, where ancient social traditions are reeling under waves of Western eroticism, has a particularly hard fight. After the Islamic countries it will remain for some time to come the scene of perhaps more sexual distress than any other place on earth.

❀

CHAPTER EIGHT

CULTURE
AND
LANGUAGE

Japan has given rise to a rich, magnificent culture. Though the roots of that culture are firmly planted in China, what the Japanese took from the Middle Kingdom they fashioned into something new and splendid. Many crafts and lesser art forms did not come from China at all but are unique products of the Japanese genius.

Japan's artistic reputation is so strong and so well deserved that even today many aesthetically minded Westerners have not lost their image of Japan as a delicate world of Zen, flower arranging, and wood-block prints. Increasingly, however, this image has been lost in a haze of industrial smog. For Westerners who have fallen in love with the arts of Japan, it can be a cruel disappointment to discover how little room shipbuilding and steelmaking have left for tea ceremony.

Ever since it began to modernize, Japan has poured so much energy into economic progress that it has not always had time for culture of any kind. However, the greatest threat to the vitality of Japanese art forms has been the onslaught of culture and pseudoculture from the West. The flood has washed virtually every traditional art into an obscure corner of Japanese life where it leads a self-conscious, hothouse existence.

The Japanese have long been fascinated by the distant and exotic. Their deep-seated xenophobia has always been leavened with a keen curiosity. Since the war they have had ample opportunities to go foraging overseas and have brought home a surprising variety of Western products and practices. Christmas, for example, has been an inexplicable success in Japan, and English has made startling and often hilarious inroads on the language that the Japanese speak to each other.

This is not to say that the Japanese are becoming Westernized in every respect. In all areas of life, traditional customs survive in modern garb; Japanese thinking and behavior can still differ dramatically from ours. Nevertheless, the physical forms of art and daily life that Westerners instinctively think of as playing an integral role in Japanese life have been largely supplanted by Western forms.

A Japanese economics professor once said to me, "Deep inside, a Japanese youngster is still a samurai, but that doesn't stop him from growing his hair down to his shoulders and playing the electric guitar." I don't think there are many Japanese, even deep inside, who are really samurai, but it is this coexistence of Western form and Eastern substance that makes Japan so fascinating and so elusive.

Japan's distinctive culture has not been in steady decline ever since first contact with the West. Over the last 130 years the Japanese have veered from feelings of desperate cultural inferiority, to the most brazen cultural chauvinism, back to desperate inferiority. Far more than any Western country Japan's cultural confidence has waxed and waned with its economic and military fortunes.

Japan has felt ambiguous about its own culture ever since it sent the first emissaries to study the clearly superior culture of China in the sixth century A.D. However, the two greatest jolts to its cultural self-confidence have both come from the United States. The first was in 1853.

As Perry's black ships bobbed in Edo Bay, threatening to storm the citadels of *Wa*, temples filled with people praying for another kamikaze to blow the barbarians to perdition. When that tactic failed, the Japanese frenziedly set out, in self-defense, to learn the secrets of the Westerners. In the first dizzy decades of imitation Japan stripped itself of a great deal of ancient cultural baggage. Many modernizers thought that the benefits of the West could be assimilated only if everything Japanese were conscientiously jettisoned.

The samurai were forbidden to wear their swords, mixed bathing was banned (it went on anyway), and the Japanese were even urged to end their tradition of year-end gift giving.[1] The most resolute modernizers joined the Rokumeikan Club, which was opened in 1883 for foreigners and sufficiently Westernized Japanese. There, to the amazement of their countrymen, Japanese could be seen dressed in suits and gowns, eating with knives and forks, and dancing the polka.

Japan was going through a cultural revolution of gigantic proportions. As one recent book points out, "Neglect, decay and even discard was the alarming pattern of what the Japanese were permitting to happen to their artistic heritage during the 1870s and early 1880s."[2] For the zealots, traditional art was a symbol of the musty thinking that had to be brushed aside.

In its enthusiasm for the West, Japan turned its back on the East. Yukichi Fukuzawa (1835–1901), the famous educator, propounded what came to be known as the "Escape from Asia" theory. Writing in 1885, he argued: "Although China and Korea are our neighbors, this fact should make no difference in our relations with them. We should deal with them as Westerners do. If we keep bad company, we cannot avoid a bad name. In my heart I favor breaking off with the bad company of East Asia."[3] His views were echoed by Foreign Minister Kaoru Inoue (1835–1915), who proclaimed in 1887, "Let us change our empire into a European-style empire. Let us change our people into a European-style people. Let us create a new European-style empire on the Eastern sea."[4]

How were the introverted Japanese to be made into a "European-style" people? Even the most preposterous proposals were taken seriously. One high government official urged the Japanese to improve themselves through interbreeding. Men were to mate with Caucasian women—and not, of course, vice versa—in order to invigorate the race.[5] A different approach was favored by the ultra-Westernizers who, in their Occidental zeal, had embraced Christianity; they suggested that the nation be made to convert en masse.

One of the most astonishing proposals of those frenzied times came from the primary architect of Japan's national education system, Arinori Mori (1847–1889). He seems to have doubted whether Japanese could ever be an effective language of instruction in the Prussian-style education system he was building. He suggested that the entire Japanese language be dumped and that Japan learn English instead.[6]

These ideas all provoked a lively debate which, of course, led nowhere. Taken together, they would have amounted to nothing short of cultural and even racial suicide. A nation's language, for example, is its primary medium of cultural expression; it is an essential part of a nation's very identity. That a responsible Japanese official could propose abandoning it and not be laughed out of office shows the earnestness with which Japan embraced the West. It was this earnestness that enabled the Japanese to seize the essentials of Western power technology so much more successfully than other non-Western peoples.

Japan threw itself into its *fukoku kyōhei* ("rich country, strong military") program and soon began to reap the benefits. In 1895 it won the Sino-Japanese War and took control of Korea, and Taiwan. Ten years later Japan astounded the world by defeating Russia, a European power, and consolidated its position on the Asian mainland.

A resurgence of pride in things Japanese followed these successes, and the intellectuals of the early twentieth century began to intone a new refrain. The teacher and critic Kanzō Uchimura (1861–1930) boasted that "grander tasks await the young Japan who has the best of Europe and the best of Asia at her command. At her touch the circuit is completed and the healthy fluid shall overflow the earth."[7]

Empire building was accompanied by increasingly strident cultural chauvinism. A striking example was the Japanese Bureau of Colonization's treatment of Korea. The peninsula was the part of the empire closest to the home islands and was formally annexed to Japan in 1910. Gone by now were any worries about the adequacy of the Japanese language. It was made the language of public school instruction, and pupils were forbidden to speak Korean even during recess. At school and on public occasions, children recited the following pledge of allegiance:

1. We are the subjects of the Empire of Greater Japan.
2. We, by uniting our minds, pledge our allegiance to His Majesty the Emperor.
3. We, by perseverance and training, will become good, strong subjects.[8]

As colonization progressed, even adults were forbidden to speak Korean in public or to wear Korean clothes.

What was perhaps the crowning insult of colonization was a campaign to abolish all Korean names. The Japanese actually set out to give every man, woman, and child a Japanese name but were surprised to meet stiff resistance to this project. The Japanese felt they had clearly demonstrated their military, economic, and cultural superiority over the Koreans and could not understand a vanquished people's determination to cling to its inferior traditions.

The Bureau of Colonization operated on the assumption that Korean culture could be wiped out without a trace and that Koreans could be entirely recast in a Japanese mold. This did not mean that Koreans were to *become* Japanese. They were never citizens; they were subjects of Japan. No matter how convincingly Japanese managed to refashion Koreans in their own image, they never accepted them as personal equals.

The plan for a Greater East Asia Co-Prosperity Sphere, which Japan announced in 1940, was primarily designed to unite the occupied nations in an economic community subordinate to Japanese interests. However, it would also have served as a vehicle for the propagation throughout Asia of the Japanese values that had been forced upon the Koreans.

So effective was Japan's cultural domination that even today many elderly Koreans, from both North and South, still speak an antique prewar Japanese. Several years ago, before I was aware of this, I met a North Korean gentleman during a trip to the Caribbean. We stumbled around in defective Spanish for a half hour before I happened to mention that I had grown up in Japan. He cocked his head and asked me if I spoke Japanese. When I replied that I did, he folded his arms and looked at the floor in silence for a moment. On impulse I switched to Japanese and asked him what was the matter.

"I have not spoken Japanese," he replied in courtly language seldom heard in Japan, "since 1945. At that time I vowed never again to speak that language, and until now I have kept that vow. However, since it was in part due to the Americans that we were liberated from the Japanese, I will make an exception for you." In South Korea constant trade and contact with Japan has softened expressions of outright hostility, but there, too, the old resentments run deep.

For the Japanese, wartime chauvinism had a different effect on language. "During the war," an elderly Japanese once explained to me, "we were firmly convinced that we were going to beat the Americans and that after the war Japanese would become the language of the world. I figured I would never have to study English again.

"And do you know what I did?" He gave me a rueful smile. "I tore the leaves out of my dictionaries and used them for cigarette papers."

Japan's defeat by the United States shocked the country back into a sense of cultural inferiority not much different from the one caused by Commodore Perry almost 100 years earlier. Seen from the wreckage of postwar Japan, America was a dazzling paradise, and the Japanese rushed to copy it in every way. This mood of receptivity dovetailed perfectly with the aims of an American occupation that was by no means free from cultural chauvinism. Japan, as if of one mind, set out to learn the American way of life. Once again there was a serious proposal that the Japanese language be abolished, this time by the era's reigning literary figure: Naoya Shiga, "the god of the novel."9

By losing its war with America, Japan was ousted from its fancied place at the top of the hierarchy. No longer would it force its language and culture on vassal states; now it would take its turn at the feet of a superior power. For a generation Japan has mindlessly imitated the West, at a frantic pace that only recently has begun to slacken.

It is sadly typical of Japan that its pride in its Japaneseness should be hostage to its economic and military success. I believe that this tendency is due to two of Japan's most pronounced national characteristics: conformity and sensitivity to hierarchy. The same sense of international hierarchy that gave birth to the Greater East Asia Co-Prosperity Sphere also saw in America's victory a sure sign of American superiority. At the same time, once that superiority was recognized, it was recognized by everyone.

The cultural confidence of other major nations is not so easily shaken by defeat or misfortune. The Chinese, even when they were being bullied by foreign powers in the most highhanded way, never lost pride in their culture. Western technology was reluctantly recognized as necessary for advancement, but the Chinese took care to avoid contamination. Perhaps it was this sense of cultural superiority that prompted the Chinese to keep so much of barbarian thought at arm's length and that slowed the process of modernization. The Japanese wanted to think of Westerners as barbarians as well but, unlike the Chinese, feared, admired, and sincerely imitated them.

France offers a similar contrast. During its empire-building phase it tried to spread its culture just as diligently as the Japanese did theirs. However, in the face of adversity it never lost pride in its culture. In the twenty years from 1940 to the early sixties, France was defeated and occupied by the Germans; lost colonial wars in Vietnam, Algeria, and the Suez; and saw its empire swept away by the tide of history. Through all this the French went on trumpeting their own greatness without a moment's loss of sincerity.

At the end of the war America was so clearly the dominant world power that its influence as an occupation force was bound to be enormous. However, the other great power laid waste by the war and occupied by GIs did not suffer the same psychological damage. The author of *Japan as Number One* points out in an earlier work that ". . . whereas Germans responded to defeat by reasserting their pre-war values without seriously reexamining them, most Japanese responded by questioning their view of life and submitting it to an agonizing reappraisal from which it never recovered."[10]

Japan is now well on its way to recovery, and an increasing number of Japanese regret their disregard for their own culture. Many see the postwar decades as an inevitable reaction to the excessive cultural chauvinism of Japan's militarist period but fear that the baby may have been thrown out with the bath water. A Japanese who has studied at both Yale and Columbia writes:

> Ever since the Meiji period [1868–1912], in order to strengthen and Westernize our nation, we have abandoned our cultural, political, and economic independence. But that was only a matter of tactics . . .
> I am particularly worried that our children may be losing the forms of their own culture. They must not forget that our Westernization was only a tactical measure. If Japan is to make a contribution to the world, it will be because of Japanese culture. It is only as Japanese who prize our Japanese culture that we can be truly international.[11]

A professor at Jōchi University is expressing the same sentiments when he writes, "Of all the peoples of the earth, none have squeezed the life out of their history or been so ungrateful to it as the postwar Japanese."[12]

The well-known novelist Yukio Mishima felt so strongly about Japan's postwar aping of the West that he publicly disemboweled himself in a spectacular attempt to call attention to what he saw as national apostasy. He wanted Japan to return to the stern traditions of the samurai and saw Western influence as decadent and debilitating.

I suspect that if history is a reliable indicator of the future, the issue of Japan's cultural identity will soon begin to lose its urgency. As Japan scores one economic victory after another, it will reassert the value of its own culture. Trade war has taken the place of military conquest, so what in the past might have required the annexation of Korea can now be achieved by steady current account surpluses. Even so, renewed pride is only beginning to show itself; it will be some time before the movement firmly takes hold.

For now most Japanese are so uninterested in their own art forms that they are genuinely surprised at the Westerners who come in increasing numbers to steep themselves in the Japanese aesthetic. "They think you're crazy to be interested in that stuff," says an American woman who studied Japanese art in Kyoto. "They've lost all appreciation for the best things their culture ever produced."

In Japan today orientation to Western culture begins in kindergarten. Music classes, for example, completely ignore Japan's sophisticated tonal system and musical instruments. Children learn to keep time with simple Western instruments like the triangle and castanets and then move on to the harmonica or recorder. Once they are in grade school, probably a larger proportion of Japanese children study piano or electric organ than any other people in the world. With the traditional instruments silenced, there is no place for the Japanese dance their music accompanied.

In art classes older students draw, work in watercolors, and model in clay. The effects they are taught to strive for are Western, not Japanese. Art history classes concentrate on Europe rather than on Japan or China. Many Japanese can speak with authority about the Impressionists or the Dutch masters but cannot begin to discuss the great artists from their own past.

Student drama groups put on Western plays or works by Japanese dramatists written for the Western-style stage. Professional drama companies take almost all their material from abroad: Tokyo is always running the best of Broadway—in Japanese translation and a few seasons late. Traditional noh and kabuki drama continue as national art forms, but their attendance is small, and they have lost all dynamism. A single performance by the Berlin Philharmonic causes more excitement than an entire season of kabuki. Even more ironically, the best-known amateur kabuki performances in Japan are staged by the Caucasian students of an English-speaking high school for foreigners.

The orientation the Japanese get as students is the one they keep as adults. Japan's national museums are located in Ueno Park in Tokyo. The second-rate collection of Western art attracts masses of visitors, while the superb Japanese art museum next door is one of the most peaceful places in the city. Likewise, the shiny new museums that regional capitals have opened in competition with each other are not showplaces for local craftsmen. Instead, they house some of the world's most expensive and least admired (but no doubt genuine) Renoirs and Matisses. At one time every region of Japan had flourishing arts and crafts of its own, but they, too, have been pushed aside by the urge to copy Tokyo's fascination with the West.

The one traditional art form treated seriously in Japanese schools is calligraphy. In spite of the devastation English has wrought on the language, the Japanese cling to their inefficient but beautiful ideograms, and mastery of the subtle brushstrokes is a high art. Calligraphy is, moreover, one of the rare traditional arts with a real avant-garde movement. Perhaps because all people must write, calligraphy is an art form that is part of the life of the people.

The Ministry of Education must take a large measure of responsibility for skewing Japan's cultural consciousness. It has made Western art an integral part of the public school curriculum, while practically ignoring the arts of Japan. At the turn of the century, when the school system was founded, public education meant Western education. The government took it upon itself to introduce Western art to the people. There was no need to make any provision for the traditional arts since they were already being looked after by schools that in some cases had been going strong for centuries.

The situation is now different. While most Japanese were scampering off to taste the new delights from the West, the guardians of tradition withdrew into increasing isolation. The traditional schools of music, dance, pottery, weaving, printmaking, drama, and painting are now a cultural backwater and operate closed shops of the worst kind.

Young Japanese who show artistic talent can easily find places in Western art classes but must go through a long, uncertain apprenticeship in order to master a traditional art. The process is so arduous and arcane that now, even for Japanese, the traditional arts have an aura of mystery and inaccessibility that contrasts sharply with the familiarity of Western arts.

This aura has, of course, been cultivated by the keepers of the holy flame but has served only to seal them off in sterile enclaves. No longer an organic part of what it means to be Japanese, the traditional arts have withdrawn into the haughty seclusion of self-conscious devotees. Many have lost all forward motion, and their practitioners do no more than preserve the patterns of the past. Young Japanese—especially those who have a desire to create—feel cramped and stifled by this approach.

This dreary situation is somewhat relieved by the many cultural centers that have sprung up in Japanese cities. These offer adult classes in anything from macramé to aerobic dancing and give quick overviews of all but the most exotic traditional arts. Students are most frequently young women seeking to add a patina of traditional culture to the package they will offer a prospective husband. Even if she may never practice it, it is good that a young bride bring with her a little knowledge of the tea ceremony.

Even the kimono has lost most of its validity as a symbol for Japan. If women learn how to wear one at all, it is probably in "bride school" rather than at home. Kimonos are prohibitively expensive and are kept locked away for special occasions. Japanese men are even more estranged from their traditional dress. Most would feel as much at home in formal *hakama* or *haori* as an American would in a space suit.

Of the odds and ends that a young woman is likely to pick up in bride school, a few notions of flower arranging are likely to be her most permanent acquisition. The Japanese have not lost their love of flowers, and a sense for arranging them is probably the most common aesthetic achievement among Japanese women.

One of Japan's most striking losses is the disappearance of much of its architecture. The grinding ugliness of urban Japan is a lasting monument to the worst ferroconcrete architecture of the West. Nor is the drabness of Japan's cities due mainly to the destruction of the Second World War. As one writer points out, the Japanese have pulled down their architectural heritage with their own hands.[13] It is

Western materialism, not Western bombs, that has turned many private Japanese gardens into parking lots.

The environment for living is becoming so Westernized that even the home has become a hostile environment for traditional culture. Japanese houses are now built with far more Western than Japanese features. Few new houses have more than a room or two with floors made of traditional straw tatami matting. I have been in older homes where the tatami has been covered with rugs and the room furnished with chairs and a sofa.

Many arts can only be performed on the floor. The tea ceremony, for example, absolutely requires tatami, and no other surface is satisfactory for Japanese dance. Other arts, such as calligraphy, flower arranging, painting, and Japanese music, are also traditionally done on the floor. A rug may take the place of tatami, but the devotee would feel ill at ease in a forest of chair and table legs. Not many Japanese seem to realize how much the survival of Japanese art depends on the survival of a Japanese life-style or how important tatami is to the survival of both.

One who does realize this writes: "Feelings of frustrated patriotism well up within me when I think of the young Japanese who no longer live on tatami and who can no longer kneel properly. I am worried that if we forget how to kneel, the very basis of Japanese culture will collapse." 14

One traditional architectural feature found in older Japanese houses is the *tokonoma*. This is an alcove built into the main room of the house, where a flower arrangement, painting, or some other art object is displayed. The *tokonoma* is meant to be the center of attention so that the beauty it contains can be admired from all directions. Many Japanese have found that this is the perfect place to put a television set. "Today," complains one Japanese author, "the most common notion of a life of culture is a flush toilet and a Western-style bed. To Westernize and to modernize mean the same thing." 15

A few of the traditional forms of everyday living have survived the onslaught from the West. Even the most modern, Western-style houses built in Japan usually have a Japanese-style bath. This is a deep tub, filled with scalding water, into which a person climbs for a soak *after* he has already washed himself clean with soap and buckets of hot water. The tub is not for washing oneself in; it is for sensuous relaxation at the end of the day.

Also, whatever style of house Japanese live in at home or abroad, they always leave their shoes at the door and pad around in slippers. Many make a point of taking a pair of slippers with them when they travel to the West, so they can get out of their shoes in hotel rooms or in private homes. Most Japanese can't really get comfortable until they have taken off their shoes. It must be from all those years in Japan, but I feel the same way. Some Japanese are still more comfortable sitting on the floor than in a chair. At social gatherings held in Western-style living rooms, I have seen older women ask their hostess for a cushion so that they could sit on the floor.

Finally, I know of no people who are so attached to their native food as the Japanese. Japanese cooking is a traditional art that is very much alive. In spite of inroads from cornflakes and fried chicken, it holds its own with unchallenged vigor, and regional specialties flourish in undiminished variety. A few non-Japanese foods, such as curried rice, omelet, coffee, toast, and ice cream, have entered the dietary vernacular. The Japanese now drink twice as much beer as sake, and the world's highest-volume McDonald's outlet is in Tokyo. However, these dishes have been absorbed as new elements of Japanese cuisine and pose no threat to its authenticity.

The Japanese are, in fact, so attached to their own food that very few develop a cosmopolitan palate or really enjoy trying new foods. They expect all people to have equally limited tastes and are skeptical of Westerners who claim to like *their* food. Japanese seem to be painfully conscious of the fact that no other nation consumes as much raw fish as theirs. When I sit down to a meal for the first time with a Japanese, even if he knows how long I have lived in Japan, he will politely ask if I wouldn't really prefer to skip the *sashimi* (raw fish) or if he should ask the waiter to bring me a knife and fork instead of chopsticks.

This happens with such deadly consistency that I am often tempted to be rude. However, I usually manage the following polite exchange:

"No, thank you, Tanaka-san. I'll manage perfectly all right with chopsticks, and since the mackerel is at its best this time of year, let's start with that."

"My, how Japanese you are, Taylor-san."

"Well, not really. Would Tanaka-san care to guess how many Japanese restaurants there are on the island of Manhattan alone?"

Tanaka-san knits his brows. "Maybe twenty-five?"

"No. Nearly three hundred." I then go on to explain that although there is a large Japanese population in the New York area, it is not nearly large enough to support 300 Japanese restaurants and that *mirabile dictu*, there are many Americans who eat raw fish and were not even born in Japan.

Bill, a childhood friend of mine who has lived even longer in Japan than I have, has lost patience with the *sashimi* question. "*Sashimi?*" he will ask with a quizzical look. After a thoughtful pause he will add, "Oh, yeah, I know what that is. Bring it on. Love the stuff."

The *sashimi* arrives. Bill eyes it suspiciously. He picks up a piece in his fingers and scrutinizes it. By this time Tanaka-san is worried. "Waiter, waiter," shouts Bill, loud enough for the whole restaurant to hear, "this fish is *uncooked!*" As Tanaka-san shrivels with embarrassment, Bill explains it was all a joke and polishes off the *sashimi*.

Japan's fervent loyalty to its food only highlights its disloyalty to the other traditional arts. If the Japanese aesthetic were as traditional as the Japanese stomach, the nation would be a very different place indeed.

That the mechanics of life in Japan should become increasingly Western is an inevitable result of industrialization. All modern, complex societies must function according to the same laws of precision and efficiency. It would be patently absurd for anyone to argue that Japan should have stayed in the nineteenth century because it was more aesthetically pleasing than the twentieth. No one has the right to deny the Japanese their chewing gum, pornography, blue jeans, ferroconcrete, or piano lessons.

Nevertheless, a society that has so resolutely adhered to distinctive forms of social organization, interpersonal relations, religion, and a host of other national peculiarities could also have kept a tighter grip on its own high culture. Had it been able to maintain a cultural pride that was independent of military and economic success, I feel sure that today's Japan would have retained much more of the art and lifestyle that foreigners have found so appealing.

Some Japanese have begun to speak out in defense of Japan's traditions. Lately a few businessmen have wondered out loud to me just what sort of figure they would cut wearing traditional dress to an international conference. Japanese travelers are beginning to buy and bring back to Japan works of art that found their way overseas. The president of a small college tells me that every year more and more girls wear kimonos at graduation ceremonies rather than long Western dresses.

Neighborhoods that have kept their traditional architecture have come to realize that they are a vanishing species. Their appeals for government support prompted the passage in 1975 of a law providing for the preservation of historical areas. There are now about a dozen such designated areas in Japan, and many have become tourist attractions.

Even some corporations are trying to revive traditional aesthetics. I was once given a tour of the headquarters of one of Japan's most dynamic regional banks. My guide proudly showed me the tatami room the bank had just added to its clubhouse in the hope of encouraging the arts. The room was only a few months old, and the fresh smell of new tatami filled me with visions of splendor and delicacy.

"Has it caught on?" I asked excitedly. "Do the employees use it a lot?"

My guide's look turned sheepish. "The fact is," he said, "the men have pretty much taken the place over and use it for playing Mah-Jongg."

Still, I feel sure that Japan has turned an important corner. Its undeniable successes and its increasing wealth could make the rest of this century a time of renewal for art and tradition.

For now, Western influence keeps washing into Japan. For a nation that is constantly worrying its trade partners with export surpluses, Japan is still surprisingly subservient to foreign tastes and consumption patterns. *Hakurai* products—that is, those which have "come by ship"—still have a special magic for the Japanese.

Hakurai appeal has a long history. Before Japan was opened to the outside world, its people were fascinated by unusual products from out-of-the-way provinces. Even today they are intrigued by local specialties that are not available elsewhere in the country. Travelers returning from a trip within Japan customarily bring their family and friends distinctive gifts from the region—usually some kind of food or handicraft.

This custom has religious origins. Back when most Japanese were peasant farmers, a village might send one of its elders on a pilgrimage to a distant shrine or temple. The man went in the name of the village as a whole, which took up a collection to cover his expenses. In order to share the spiritual benefits of his trip, he would bring back charms or tokens from the shrine and distribute them among his neighbors. These tokens were called *omiyage*.

As time went on, this practice spread to all trips. Now even honeymooners have to spend a good part of their time rushing about, making sure they have picked up some local geegaw for everyone back home. The *omiyage* tradition is so ironclad that the Tokyo railway station has a large gift shop filled with foods and curiosities from all over Japan. If a businessman on a trip to Okayama doesn't have time to go shopping for the famed millet dumplings of the region, he can always pick up a few boxfuls when he gets off the train in Tokyo. *Omiyage* are valued in proportion to the distance they have traveled. Thus the perfect *omiyage* is a foreign product unavailable anywhere in Japan, which the traveler has brought back specifically to give as a gift.

The next best thing is something that has been imported. As we have seen, foreign designer-label products have a real power over Japanese consumers. This is not only because the label confers instant acceptability but also because of the prestige of imports. In many countries foreign-made products have a special cachet, but their status is particularly high in Japan. At some level it has taken the Japanese longer than anyone else to forget the era when their products were cheap and shoddy. It is a surprise for most Westerners to learn that even today Japanese products may be advertised as "so smartly designed you'd think it was imported."

It is pure *hakurai*, "come-by-ship" appeal, that manages to sell a few thousand American cars in Japan every year since the obstacles to owning them are enormous. They must be modified at great cost to conform to Japan's tough emission standards, parts and service are often unavailable, and they have the steering wheel on the wrong side. No Japanese doubts that they are poorly built, too big for Japanese streets, and uneconomical. Many Americans are surprised to see any at all in Japan.

Nevertheless, certain models have real appeal for certain Japanese. *Yakuza* ("gangsters") have a taste for Lincoln Continentals. Pimps and movie stars seem to be split over Cadillacs and sportier types like the Pontiac Firebird. There are even a few Chevy Corvettes cruising the streets of Tokyo. American cars are real eye-catchers in Japan and are the unmistakable sign of a wealthy, flamboyant life-style. They sell strictly because they are unusual and come from far away—they would make the ultimate *omiyage*.

I have no doubt that Western manufacturers of quality consumer goods could make a fortune in Japan if they took the trouble to market their products skillfully and took every advantage of *hakurai* appeal. As the Japanese shift into gear for sports and leisure, there will be an enormous market for everything from golf clubs to Aqua-lungs to backpacks to fancy speaker systems. Sears, Roebuck could practically be a designer label in Japan if its products were marketed with the right snob appeal. Toys, furniture, household goods—all could be successful in Japan if they were smartly designed and diligently marketed. *Hakurai* appeal is waning in Japan, but it is by no means too late to put it to work. A surge of high-quality Western consumer goods could revive it instantly.

The appeal of the West comes through loud and clear in advertising. I would guess that nearly a third of all models in print and television commercials are foreigners. Foreign naturally means Caucasian or Eurasian; there are no Nigerians or Pakistanis on Japanese billboards.

Part of the appeal of white foreigners is sexual, but much of it is pure exoticism. They are just as eye-catching as a Corvette or a Lincoln, and this gives them a certain authority. On TV even strictly domestic noodle products are gobbled up by salivating white models; if the *gaijin* like it, it's got to be good. Sean Connery and Paul Newman have a lot of influence when it comes to pushing radial tires or automobiles onto the Japanese.

However, most white models are complete unknowns. The Tokyo market is a windfall for hopeful Americans and Europeans who haven't yet made it back home and maybe never will. Japanese are still dazzled by Caucasian features, and funny-looking blondes who would never make the grade in the West get photographed for magazine covers.

One entirely unlikely Western import has been Christmas. Less than 1 percent of the Japanese are Christian, but the nation celebrates the birth of Christ with a materialistic fervor that rivals Macy's on Christmas Eve. Santa Claus comes to department stores, and shopwindows are resplendent with tinsel and Christmas trees. In early December all of Japan's Muzak suddenly switches to Christmas carols.

Japan has always had a year-end tradition of gift giving called *oseibo*, which may have given the postwar adoption of Christmas some of its early impetus. Now *oseibo* has been left in the snow, and Christmas has been promoted by wily retailers into an important and profitable celebration.

However, Japan's most astonishing capitulation to the West has been linguistic. English is everywhere. It is not, as in Europe, a foreign language that many people happen to have mastered but that has left the native language more or less intact. Rather, it is a mysterious power that few people have tamed but that has taken over great tracts of what was once Japanese. There are three kinds of English in Japan: first, the foreign language; second, English that has become Japanese; and third, Japanese-made English that has no existence anywhere else.

In society at large, English as a foreign language is most common on labels, signs, and T-shirts. Brand names and trademarks are almost always in English. Automobile dashboards and control knobs on electric appliances are labeled in English. Restaurants, bars, movie theaters, and even products made exclusively for the domestic market often have English names, and all young people seem to wear T-shirts with English on them. It's impossible to take a walk in Japan without being surrounded by English.

This must be very tiring for the Japanese because very few really understand English. They may remember a few phrases from school, but for the vast majority, spoken English is a string of nonsense syllables, and a page of print is an impenetrable mystery.

A Japanese may eat spareribs for years at The Rustler's Grill and have no idea what a rustler is. He might not even be able to approximate the word's pronunciation without a discreet transliteration in Japanese on a sign or matchbox cover. A Japanese who buys a stereo may have to fumble through the Japanese instruction booklet to find out what the bass and treble knobs do. There are perfectly good Japanese words for "bass" and "treble," but they never appear on an appliance. This is not because Japanese manufacturers are economizing by building the same products for both the home and overseas markets. Japanese like their appliances to have English on them.

T-shirt English is probably the most bewildering. Some of it is English translations of sentiments that may make sense in Japanese, but a lot of it is plain goofiness. "Let's go, young" is a perennial favorite. "Arabian camel" was a brief hit. "Cool elegance" was all the rage several years ago. "Passion and serenity, together by the sea" is one of my favorites. Other sentiments that have graced the Japanese chest are "Chickens of the pool," "Chocolate Club Sundae," and "Lovely Time; At first she showed disapproval but finally."

English ultimately loses all meaning and becomes nothing but a decorative pattern. Demure preteens wear T-shirts and carry handbags with the word "shit" printed all over them in tiny letters. "I got leied in Hawaii" is a shirt I have spotted from time to time. Perhaps one Japanese in 75,000 would understand that kind of English.

Misspellings are common. One summer the market was flooded with "Jimy and Emiry" T-shirts, complete with a drawing of Jimy shyly holding Emiry's hand. I have seen sleeveless T-shirts that proclaim the benefits of "weight rifting," and one that reads "How to change your PARSONARITY."

English is hard enough for Americans to spell, but it is a nightmare for the Japanese. I once heard a jazz band play a tune that the program identified as "The Old Ragged Cross." A small, regional franchise of Western-style restaurants reserves a room for its serving staff. The sign on the door reads, "Stuff." One Tokyo bar is taking no chances. It spells its name two different ways: a sign over the door says, "Bar Bolivia," while one on the window reads, "Bar Borivia."

Product names can be hilarious. One manufacturer of powdered coffee creamer decided to combine the words "cream" and "powder" and calls its product Creap. Not long ago a major confectioner introduced a new chocolate-covered cookie called Snatch. Someone must have whispered a few words into the president's ear; Snatch was quietly taken off the market. Another candymaker sells chocolates in a tin that looks just like a Band-Aid box. On the front of the box, in large red and white letters, is the product's name: HAND MAID TASTE QUEER-AID CHOCOLATE. In fine print below is a warning: "This chocolate is not medicated sweets."

The same company markets a brand of "fruits field drops" called Fanatic. On the back of that box is the following message, reproduced in its entirety: "SWEETS don't be always only for children. Grownups are ashamed of eating them. Without reference to age, everybody likes nice SWEETS. It needs to take some SWEET for everyone." Very few Japanese understand enough English to appreciate the absurdity of such deformed English, and there is little else to appreciate in it.

The reason there is so much English in Japan is that Western languages are status symbols. Brand names and labels in English suggest imports or foreign design. An American name for a restaurant adds overseas appeal. English is the language of sophistication, overseas travel, erudition, and—at some level—the conqueror. At its most basic, Japan's fascination for English is part of its cultural insecurity and its admiration of Caucasian America. It is part of a lingering *gaijin* complex.

At the same time the Japanese take a great deal of English down from its Occidental pedestal and treat it like a convenient appendix to their own language. English words, in transliteration and with comical Japanese pronunciation, turn up all the time in speech and prose. It is acceptable in learned discourse to throw in just about any English verb or noun, even if it is not one that everyone will understand. Commercial and technical terms are hopelessly Americanized even when an honorable old Japanese word has been around for generations.

Still worse are the incursions of English into everyday speech. Over the years I have seen the Japanese words for "milk," "camera," and even "Mom and Dad" pushed out of the vocabulary by *mee-ruku, kah-me-rah, ma-ma* and *pa-pa*.

Most surprising of all is the made-in-Japan English that the Japanese use among themselves. Since the Japanese are unable to pronounce most consonant sounds without adding a vowel, short English words become very long in Japanese. "Strike," for example, becomes the five-syllable *su-to-ra-i-ki*. This is a mouthful, so when Japanese workers walk off the job, they are on *su-to*. Rather than talk about "remote control" or "Los Angeles," the Japanese have invented *remo-con* and get no farther than *Rosu*.

It makes good sense for the Japanese to abbreviate words that are too long for them. I'm not sure it's as sensible for them to invent brand-new English phrases all on their own. At the ball park, for example, *full-base* means that the bases are loaded, and a successful run for the plate is a *home-in*. In business, expense reduction is a *cost-down*, and a general rise in wage rates is a *base-up*. When a car engine fails to run, its owner has suffered an *engine stop*, which is shortened to *en-su-to*. If he has to sleep over at a friend's place, he is having a *home-stay*. A recent bit of slang takes the English word "now" and adds the Japanese adjectival ending *ii* to make *nowii*, meaning "now-like" or "hip," "with it."

A few bits of suspect English have hitched a ride to the West on Japanese exports. Walkman, an awkward brand name that was resisted by Sony's American sales staff, is now almost as generic a word as Xerox. The company's pocket-size televisions have gone on sale as Watchmen. Sony has always wanted to increase our vocabularies; for years, it has tried to persuade us to play music on its Tape Corders.

In Japan some of this peculiar English has been around long enough to have a history of its own. Years ago the term "business girl" was coined to describe a single working woman. This was abbreviated BG. The English letters would appear in a block of Japanese print, and the reader would pronounce them *bee-jee*. Later, perhaps in confusion with the expression "working girl," the Japanese got the impression that in America a business girl was a prostitute. A new phrase was invented, and business girls all were promoted to office ladies. This is, of course, abbreviated OL and is pronounced *oh-elu*. The Japanese have even come up with a word for this kind of made-in-Japan English: *wasei-eigo*. Curiously, it is a strictly Japanese coinage and contains no English elements.

There is so much English floating around in the language that everyone in Japan must know a great many "English" words just to understand "Japanese." However, the Japanese pronounce these words so differently from anyone else that the same words spoken by an American or Englishman are still nonsense syllables to most of them. The reverse is also true. Furthermore, many Japanese have no idea which "English" words are homemade and which are real. A visitor to America might ask directions to the *sū-pā* ("supermarket") and be shown the janitor's (superintendent's) room.*

In the English-speaking world our language is still being enriched by learned borrowings from the Greek or Latin to make words that never existed in those languages. "Telephone" and "subcutaneous" are examples. However, I know of no other modern language that takes elements from another, completely unrelated modern language and combines them in entirely new coinages. The people who invented the electric toothbrush didn't name it the Dentomatique. If Japanese had invented it, they would probably have called it Brushman.

Actually, in spite of the sometimes barbarous results, I find a certain charm in the Japanese disregard of English grammar and syntax

---

*The Japanese have a similar but little-known problem with Chinese names. In addition to their own phonetic writing system, they use ideograms originally borrowed from Chinese but pronounce them differently. The Japanese pronunciation for the characters *Deng Xiaoping* is *Tō Shōhei*. No one else in the world, not even the Chinese, has ever heard of Tō Shōhei, and the Japanese have never heard of Deng Xiaoping! Japanese thus have a terrible time talking to anyone but each other about Chinese people and place-names.

when they build new words. After all, they are making up new Japanese words, not new English ones. The outright replacement of Japanese words by English, on the other hand, strikes me as a kind of linguistic servility that few nations would tolerate. The French have made a huge fuss over the penetration of their language by English. The situation in Japan is ten times worse, but hardly anyone seems aware of this desecration of one of the world's richest, most beautiful languages. Many Japanese can still write prose that is unadulterated by English—but it takes a deliberate effort.

Foreign visitors often express dismay to the Japanese about the sad remains of other art forms, but few Westerners are familiar enough with the language to understand the depredations made by English. Japan's sensitivity to Western criticism, which has certainly shamed some Japanese into reevaluating their own culture, is thus not much help in preserving the purity of the language. A professor at Gaku-shūin University is a voice crying in the wilderness when he bemoans the loss to foreign incursion of "our beautiful, subtle Japanese words."[16]

The English boom is all the more curious because at heart the Japanese have very equivocal feelings about English or any other foreign language, though this is not apparent at first glance. The more than 90 percent of all Japanese who have graduated from high school have had six years of a foreign language, usually English. Radio and television air regular *Let's Learn English* programs to devoted audiences. Even small corporations often hire outside English teachers to conduct weekly classes. Ambitious parents send their children to special after-school English sessions to give them a leg up in this important skill. School students are encouraged to stop foreigners in public places and politely ask if they may practice their conversation. The whole country seems to be beavering away at English.

However, the results of all this effort are pitiful. Some Japanese learn to read English haltingly, but very few ever learn to speak it fluently. I would guess that if someone were to take a random sample of Japanese and Americans, he would find almost as much fluency in French among the Americans as English among the Japanese—that is to say, not much.

The dismal results of all this language study have mystified Westerners for a long time. One enduring problem is that what is usually taught in schools and university is not what English speakers think of

as English, but an antique dialect that is the language of college entrance examinations. It is strictly a written language and is as alive
and dynamic as Linear B. "How many brothers has he?" a Japanese
would ask if he tried to speak this dialect. Exam English is taught in
the most stilted, unimaginative way, and classes are a grinding bore.
Not many teachers could keep a real English conversation going even
if their lives depended on it.

Fortunately the Japanese have discovered that what it takes to pass
the Tōdai English exam is not what it takes to clinch a deal with the
Australians. "English Conversation" is now an important subject of
study, but it goes on *outside* the school system because it doesn't help
anyone get into university. Any attempt to change the examinations
so as to test a real command of spoken English would be tampering
with a semisacred tradition. Moreover, since foreigners are the only
people who can assess a command of real English, it would mean
allowing non-Japanese to mess with the rites of passage.

English teaching, like all instruction in Japan, must face another
serious problem: the infallibility of *sensei*. I know an American woman
named Alice who used to work on an English conversation television
show for the prestigious national broadcaster NHK. The show was
always hosted by a Japanese professor, but Alice and three or four
other Americans were hired to give the show an authentic accent. At
one point the original *sensei* left the program and NHK brought in a
new one who had studied at Harvard.

This man started writing out scripts for what had until then been
a more freewheeling show. "That was boring," says Alice, "but it
would have been all right if he hadn't written so many mistakes into
his scripts. We told him he was putting bad English on the air, but he
wouldn't listen to us. He insisted that we memorize our lines, mistakes and all.

"We finally decided to go to the management of NHK and tell
them what was going on. We appealed to their pride as national
broadcasters. We told them that people would lose confidence in
NHK if their show was full of mistakes. It didn't do any good. 'We
have a contract with this man,' they said, 'and we can't fire him or
interfere in what he does.' They were more interested in keeping good
relations with that man than in putting on a good program." Alice and
her friends eventually took dramatic steps to get the program off the
air: They resigned en masse.

Only in Japan can I imagine a language teacher ignoring the opinions of native speakers, but *sensei* had been to Harvard and was not about to listen to female underlings. After all, not even management dared challenge him.

In the more pragmatic business world fewer Japanese think they speak better English than Americans, and *gaijin* can turn a quick buck teaching English conversation. The native speaker is now in great demand, and companies will snap up almost any paleface to run their weekly classes. This is an improvement over learning exam English, but it has occurred to few Japanese that language teaching is a specialized skill. Most Americans haven't the slightest idea how to teach their own language, but in Japan a college degree and a U.S. passport are ample qualifications for private instructors. Some of the more enterprising *gaijin* have set up full-blown schools to meet the demand.

Still, the Japanese do not learn. Virtually the whole population is convinced it has the sort of mental block against languages that some Westerners claim to have against calculus or physics.

The now-famous Dr. Tadanobu Tsunoda was mining a rich lode of irrationality when he announced that the Japanese brain copes with sounds and languages differently from Western brains. He claims to have demonstrated experimentally that Japanese process natural sounds, such as the wind, flowing rivers, and animal cries, in the left hemisphere of the brain. All other people process those sounds in the right hemisphere. Even more mysteriously, Japanese are supposed to process the sounds of *Japanese* musical instruments in the left hemisphere and the sounds of Western instruments in the right. Everybody else processes *all* kinds of music in the right hemisphere.[17]

Tsunoda goes on to say that the Japanese brain is simply not equipped to deal with foreign languages, that the attempt to master them only debilitates the Japanese. He even suggests that Japanese athletes at the Olympics refrain from speaking with the other athletes for fear that language-induced fatigue will impair their performance![18]

Although no one else has apparently been able to duplicate Tsunoda's findings,[19] that has not stopped the Japanese from making him a minor hero and his book a best seller. However, the doctor gives us an unwitting clue to the real reason the Japanese don't master foreign languages when he writes, "Japanese who feel out of their element in English, including myself, are somehow relieved when they hear the comment 'So many times when a person speaks really good English, he's also a real drip.'"[20]

Many Japanese openly admit their instinctive distrust of any fellow countryman who speaks a foreign language fluently. I know a college professor who has spent many years abroad and who speaks excellent English. "I make an effort," he once told me, "to avoid having to speak English in the presence of Japanese. It upsets them."

I asked him why he thought this was so.

"I used to think it was an extreme form of professional jealousy, but that's not the whole story. If I were Japan's most brilliant physicist, say, I could talk about physics all day and would be respected for it. There's something different about foreign languages."

"Part of the problem," says the wife of a Japanese businessman, "is that for us, it is as much of a shock to hear another Japanese speak fluent English as it is to hear an American speak fluent Japanese. It's just not supposed to happen; there's something eerie about it."

One reason it's eerie is that real fluency comes only from immersion in a foreign culture, something Japanese view both with longing and with suspicion. Foreign travel or an assignment abroad is still glamorous to many Japanese, but anything more than a patina of cosmopolitanism is an unhealthy sign. Real familiarity with a foreign culture or language is a dazzling achievement for a Japanese but can come only from an excessive, perhaps faintly disloyal zeal for foreignness. It goes too far beyond the bounds of Japan's simpleminded fascination with the West.

Just as the Japanese tend to travel in groups, those who go overseas for business tend to live in close-knit communities and are not comfortable in any but a Japanese context. They may speak with foreigners at work, but it is the rare Japanese businessman who develops real friendships with locals and seeks their companionship. Any Japanese who has broken this pattern and who has even temporarily lost himself in a foreign life-style is a nail that protrudes, and he may be tainted with untrustworthy sentiments.

The Japanese know, therefore, that fluency will bring them great prestige but will also label them as eccentrics or perhaps even worse. A Japanese who seeks real competence in a foreign language runs certain risks and must overcome psychological barriers that do not exist in less parochial societies.

Thus, for most Japanese, English is not a key to novel experiences or a means to gain access to unexplored reaches of human consciousness. It is strictly a business tool, a technical specialty, and one goes about learning it with the same joylessness with which one might learn accounting. The great Japanese trading companies sprang up in part because their men had some knowledge of this technical specialty; other companies had no idea how to cope with barbarians. Now many Japanese companies deal directly with the outside world, but for their employees, English is for making money, not friends.

Even businessmen who have been loyal members of the overseas Japanese community and whose English has not advanced past the bare essentials may have trouble shaking off the foreign stigma when they return to Japan. They face problems substantial enough to have given rise to a new word: *kikoku mondai* ("homecoming problem"). They may find themselves subtly pegged not only as foreign experts but as somehow foreign themselves. Their former colleagues may check them over carefully for anything they might have picked up "over there." The slightest change in tastes or behavior is attributed to "putting on foreign airs."

Unsophisticated Japanese are more straightforward in their reactions. The wife of a Japanese businessman once told me about returning with her husband to his hometown after a stay of several years in America. Brothers, cousins, aunts, and uncles gathered to greet the intrepid adventurer, home from abroad. She reports that the family members looked him over from head to toe and exclaimed in surprise, "Why, you don't look a bit different from all that time in America."

Japanese who enjoy dealing with foreigners and who have resigned themselves to the notoriety of such behavior may go on to establish reputations as interpreters of the outside world to their companies. They may carve out pleasant, independent niches for themselves, but they give up any chance at top management.

The president of a successful Japanese company once explained the secret of his advance to the top. "It's because I don't speak English," he said. "If I did, I would have become the boss's interpreter and would have gotten no further."[21] Communication with foreigners is still so specialized a skill that those who can manage it may find themselves boxed into a limited career.

Japanese returning from overseas assignments may prefer to downplay their experience so as to be readmitted to the company mainstream. They work hard at behaving just as Japanese as their company "classmates" and at rebuilding their network of personal contacts. Careful maintenance of group ties is essential for success, and three years in Frankfurt can damage those vital ties. In companies that are primarily export-oriented, a foreign assignment may be a necessary step to the top, but elsewhere it can easily be exile.

Problems for children who have lived overseas can be even more severe. They adapt much more quickly to new cultures but then return to schools and classmates that demand even greater conformity than adults do. American newspapers have even reported incidents in which former neighbors thought that youngsters must be retarded for having forgotten some of their Japanese. In 1978 International Christian University High School was established in Tokyo mainly to meet the needs of children who had trouble fitting back into the Japanese school system.[22]

What parents fear most, however, is that children will fall behind in their studies and end up losers in Japan's rigid examination system. Overseas Japanese thus worry a great deal about their children's education. The Japanese government maintains 140 schools in foreign countries, half of them with full-time curricula identical to schools in Japan.[23] Where there are no such schools, children must be educated in local institutions, though their parents may coach them in Japanese subjects on weekends.

Recently I visited the suburban home of a Japanese friend whose company has twice assigned him to the United States. His daughter, Sachiko, is happily attending Catholic junior high school and seems to be perfectly bilingual. I asked her mother how the girl was doing in school, and with a smile, she showed me Sachiko's report card. It was mostly A's, a B or two, and a note complaining that Sachiko didn't show much interest in religion class.

"This is a great report card," I said. "Does Sachiko have to study much to get these grades?"

"Study?" said Sachiko, who was just zooming by, chasing her little brother. "I never study."

"It's true," her mother added. "In Japan she would have to come home and work five hours a day to be sure of getting into a good high school. We're worried about what's going to happen to her when we go back to Japan."

"I don't want to go back," said Sachiko, for obvious reasons.

In America it is an asset to have grown up abroad, and university admissions committees welcome applicants with unusual backgrounds. Not so in Japan. Its well-regulated, conformist society has no room for anything so disorderly. A Japanese who graduated from an American high school would be far behind on college entrance examinations and would get no recognition for his experience abroad. If he managed to pass the exams, he could have trouble being accepted by his classmates. They would be envious of his exposure to the West but suspicious of it as well. Potential employers would be just as wary about hiring such a person, for no matter how useful his fluent English would be, he might never conform to the corporate culture.

No Japanese assigned abroad wants to turn his children into outcasts. Therefore, by the age of twelve or thirteen, when competition for grades is already quite stiff in Japan, boys, for whom education is important, are often sent home. Mothers—*kyōiku mamas*—often go with them, and the parents live apart until the husband's assignment ends. When sent overseas, Japanese executives with adolescent children often leave them behind.

Those rare Japanese who live abroad and melt into the local community may find they have lost too much of their Japanese personality ever to fit in again back home. Artists, musicians, or teachers who have lived for years in America begin to lose their subtle sense of hierarchy and conformity and no longer feel comfortable in Japan. Some complain that they are made to feel even more different than they really are, by family and friends who either make a special fuss over them or give them the cold shoulder. They are strangers in their own country. "I couldn't live in Japan anymore," says a man who has taught judo for many years in Washington, D.C. "There's no use even trying."

The predicament of Japanese who have made a reputation overseas is heightened by their very celebrity. Seiji Ozawa, conductor of the Boston Symphony, is received like a *foreign* celebrity even if he might prefer to be treated like a Japanese. When I ask about John Lennon's wife, Yoko Ono, Japanese will cock their heads and say, "Oh, yes, she *was* Japanese, wasn't she?" A Japanese who is acclaimed abroad and who cuts a figure on the world stage somehow ceases in the minds of his countrymen to be entirely Japanese. Americans or Europeans would never give up their claim to a famous citizen simply because he lived, or first became famous, abroad. They would probably insist he was theirs even if he had lost all loyalty for his homeland.

Japanese who have more than a nodding familiarity with foreign cultures are thus extremely rare. Many may be well informed by the press about world events, but very few have direct, authentic experience of the texture of life outside Japan. In this they are perhaps no different from most other nationalities. Except for a few small countries in Europe, multicultural sophistication is still an unusual achievement. What sets the Japanese apart from other people is their conscious refusal to dip more than a toe into foreign waters and their abiding mistrust of any Japanese who have taken the plunge. The result of this xenophobia is that in spite of their important role in the world economy, the Japanese are still among the most parochial people in the world.

English is the lingua franca of both business and diplomacy, but because they speak it so poorly, the Japanese are severely hampered. Ministers and heads of state cannot fall into informal discussion with their foreign counterparts because they must speak through interpreters. Japanese delegations to international conferences act like stiffs because they are so uncomfortable with foreigners and foreign languages. There is an old joke about the Englishman who reportedly sat through a speech delivered in halting English by a Japanese and later remarked, "It's really rather striking how at times the Japanese language actually sounds a bit like English."

For the same parochial reasons Japan is badly underrepresented on the staffs of international organizations. Few Japanese would be comfortable or effective in such a diverse, polyglot setting. Furthermore, a Japanese businessman who takes even a temporary assignment at an international organization puts his career in serious jeopardy. If his original company agrees to take him back, he will have lost seniority and will have to rebuild his personal contacts. Naturally no other top-tier company would dream of hiring such an obvious maverick.

Foreign languages and cultures are a vicious circle for the Japanese. They fail to learn languages because they are badly taught and because foreign languages are difficult for all people. Some Japanese now fail to learn because they are convinced that their brains operate differently from everyone else's or because they think any Japanese who speaks a foreign language is a "drip." Language is, of course, the key to understanding any foreign culture. Without it the Japanese will continue to fear the corrupting influences of foreignness and to doubt the character of any Japanese who has mastered a foreign idiom.

Simultaneous feelings of attraction and repulsion for what is foreign are a fundamental Japanese contradiction. Nearly 150 years after

Perry sailed into Uraga Bay, the principle of *wakon yōsai* still rules Japan's stormy love affair with the West. The Japanese have taken a saturation dose of Mozart, Charles Bronson, Louis Vuitton, and Ernest Hemingway, but the Japanese soul has survived unscathed.

Masao Miyoshi is one of those remarkable Japanese who are completely at home in an alien culture. He is a professor at the University of California, Berkeley, where he teaches not Japanese but English literature. He was not far off the mark when he wrote recently, "America and Japan, one might stop to reflect, lie as far apart now as they did a century ago."[24]

CHAPTER NINE

✿

JAPAN AT PLAY

General Douglas MacArthur ran the occupation of Japan from 1945 until 1951. Not long after his return to the United States the general made a speech in which he outlined the shape of America's future relations with its former enemies. Germany, he said, was a mature nation which could be expected to develop politically and economically in much the same way as Britain or America. Japan, he cautioned, was a twelve-year-old by comparison and would have to be reared carefully before it could take its place among the adult nations of the world.

These remarks caused great consternation in Japan, where the general had been greatly admired and honored. To this day the Japanese have not forgotten this slur on their maturity, though they sometimes exaggerate it: It is commonly thought that MacArthur called the Japanese a nation of twelve-year-olds. Today few people would call the Japanese economic or political adolescents. However, when they take a break from work and decide to play, the general's words—and their Japanese interpretation—sometimes cross my mind.

The Japanese have not had the same traditions of sport or fun as in the West. They have amused themselves in a variety of ways, but to *gaijin*, traditional Japanese diversions often seem like an excuse to behave like children. When Japanese really want to have a good time, they must throw dignity to the wind and escape from the stiff everyday demands of their society.

With increasing leisure the Japanese have added Western sports and hobbies to their repertory of pleasures but have given these imports a distinctively Japanese flavor. Golf and tennis rarely seem "fun" for Japanese as they are for Western amateurs; they are serious undertakings that require expensive equipment and elaborate preparation. They are important symbols of wealth and leisure and are pursued as much for prestige as for enjoyment. The spirit in which they are "played" is akin to the determined zeal of the workplace.

A Japanese writer describes the prewar background to Japan's stunted sense of fun: "Enjoyment for its own sake was frowned upon. This notion, together with the idea that any free time that came one's way should be used for work, was widely held throughout the country—a mode of thinking that continued, indeed, right up to the Second World War; . . . people had little notion of any concept of life extending beyond the one of work."[1]

The immediate postwar period was hardly one of fun and frolic either, but as Japan moved into the more prosperous 1960s, attitudes began to soften, and language began to change to keep up with the times. The Japanese adopted the English word "leisure" and the French *vacance* partly because they did not have satisfactory equivalents of their own. The Japanese word *yasumu*, which means "to take time off from work," also means "to rest" or "to recover from illness."

Perhaps this concentration on work explains why the Japanese can hardly be said to have invented a single sport or game. Judo, karate, kendo (sword fighting), and the like are martial arts, not sports. Originally they had nothing to do with sportsmanship, fun, or camaraderie but were pursued as a means to power and enlightenment. They had a life-and-death seriousness about them that is far removed from the spirit of baseball, golf, or even wrestling. Today, even in Japan, the mystic, spiritual aspects have been toned down for the more popular martial arts, but an American who signs up to learn karate at his local health club may have to swallow a stiff dose of chanting and meditation along with it. Until contact with the West, Japanese did not even have a word for sports and imported the word *spōtsu* along with the concept.

If the Japanese have invented a sport at all, it is sumo wrestling. Television coverage and the example of Western-style spectator sports have turned the tournaments into big-time sporting events, and the near-naked behemoths tangle in sweaty concentration before packed halls. However, sumo is still a stately, dignified spectacle, rich in trappings that point to its religious origins. In its emphasis on ritual and purity, sumo is more martial art than sport.

The Japanese have not produced many games either. Shogi and go are board games that have long been played in Japan, but both came originally from China. Mah-Jongg is now Japan's most popular indoor game, but it did not arrive from China until the 1920s. Playing cards are called *karuta*, from the Portuguese word *carta;* they, too, are imported.

Japan has, of course, given rise to many refined art forms, which have always attracted talented amateurs. Nevertheless, tea ceremony, haiku writing, calligraphy, brush painting, and the like are sober undertakings that rarely so much as hint at playfulness. For those who practice it devoutly, even the tea ceremony is formalized as "the way of tea." Mastery of "the way" requires a dedication to form and etiquette that can lead to spiritual purity, just as devotion to the martial arts was meant to bring enlightenment.

Traditionally what passed for simple fun in Japan was religious festivals. Shinto observances can be high-stepping frolics, and in many parts of Japan festivals are still times of great excitement and activity. Women break out their kimonos, and in the summertime even men may walk about in simple traditional dress. Townsfolk and tourists pour into the streets to patronize an endless variety of food and souvenir stands, to join in the folk dancing, or just to gawk. Sometimes the Shinto images themselves are marched through the streets in elaborate palanquins on the backs of chanting high-spirited men.

Drinking has long been associated with Shinto festivities because it was thought that an offering of sake would make the gods as happy as it makes men. Moreover, a certain degree of inebriation was justified on the belief that the surprising utterances of drunks had a godly sort of authenticity. In feudal times, when the Japanese were even more constrained by social codes than they are now, they must have thought that the unspeakable truths that only a drunk would pronounce must be the voice of a god.

Drinking is still a vital safety valve in Japan because it allows the stiff, reserved Japanese to behave like children. It is an escape from the harsh demands of hierarchy and group etiquette, and a man may do or say virtually anything so long as he is in his cups. No matter how subtly the Japanese manage to "read" each other's bellies, they still need the relief of telling off the boss over a few stiff drinks.

Probably because of its therapeutic function, drinking is perhaps the most important form of recreation for Japanese men. Alcohol is the major social lubricant in most parts of the world, but drink, and the little ceremonies that surround it, are as necessary to the Japanese as they are, say, to the Irish.

Bars, whether or not they employ hostesses, are an essential part of Japanese life. Bars and nightclubs dominate whole districts of Japanese cities, and after work, men flock to their neon lights. Regular drinking sessions are the basic form of corporate *otsukiai*, and a rowdy bar is the ideal place for letting off steam or for frank exchanges that would be difficult for two sober Japanese.

Drunkenness, as an excuse for all manner of otherwise inexcusable behavior, is an accepted fact of life.* But since regular *otsukiai* only goes on with one's *nakama* and immediate superiors, a drunken exchange with the real big shots of a company must sometimes wait until the year-end *bōnenkai* ("forget-the-year party"), when the Japanese usher out the old year by drowning it in drink.

An American I know who taught briefly at a Japanese college soon learned the significance of *bōnenkai*. "In the fall one of the junior faculty told me he was already looking forward to the *bōnenkai* because he had a bone to pick with the dean," he said. "It was something he couldn't bring himself to discuss without fortifying himself with booze, and the *bōnenkai* was his only chance to get smashed with the dean. I don't even remember what the problem was, but he had to keep it to himself until he finally got it off his chest at the end of the year."

Since drunkenness is such an important release mechanism for the Japanese, they often act drunker than they really are, for the mere

---

*An important exception to this rule are the stiff criminal penalties imposed on drunken drivers. Offenders frequently go to jail.

appearance of having been drinking is a permit for otherwise scandalous behavior. Many Westerners have had to track down a Japanese colleague at a party to discuss some matter of urgent business. Tanaka-san, who has been reeling around the room, chasing waitresses, is all business and sobriety when led aside and told what is happening. Once the problem has been taken care of, he charges back to the party to chase more waitresses.

Japanese also act drunk in order to join in the spirit of the group. A late arrival at the local bar will soon be just as boisterous as his *nakama* who have been drinking all evening. Westerners take a different approach. They often try to appear as sober as possible even if they can hardly stand up. Japanese call this killing the sake and think that it kills the pleasure as well. Therefore, even if some of the whooping, tottering stragglers on the last train to the suburbs actually are incoherent, it is often a safe bet that Japanese are not nearly as drunk as they seem to be.

In Japan an important part of the ritual of drinking is the establishment of rapport with a bar's proprietors. Far more than in America, men have "their" bars where the waitresses and bartenders welcome them by name—or title—when they walk in the door. Work groups that drink together are familiar faces in nearby bars, where they are regular, valued customers.

Many Japanese bars operate a *bottoru kiipu* system ("bottle-keep"— another example of homemade English) to help customers establish privileged status. According to this plan, a man pays for an entire bottle of scotch—at wildly inflated prices—which stays at the bar with his name on it. Whenever he comes in, the bottle is brought to his table and he is charged only for food and mixers. This is clearly good business for the bar; most of its stock of liquor is paid for before it is drunk. It is also good for the customer; a kept bottle, the next best thing to a kept woman, is a tangible sign of good relations with management. The bottle is a symbol of a new "group," a focus for the personal attachments so important to the Japanese.

This is one group that does not demand exclusive loyalty. There is nothing to stop a man from setting himself up as a privileged customer in bars all over town. I know many Tokyo businessmen who keep bottles in six or eight different places. They choose a few spots near the office for regular *otsukiai* and the rest for a variety of ambiences to suit different occasions.

Once I was taken to a fancy hostess bar by a banker who told me that this was his top spot. It had only one drink in stock: Chivas Regal. Several walls of the tiny place were covered by shelf after shelf of kept bottles of Chivas Regal—an impressive sight.

Many Japanese men freely admit that they could not survive without their bars. Wherever they live, they establish themselves as regular customers in a few places where they can always go for relaxation and recognition. When I was living in Tokyo, Japanese friends often asked me to take them to one of "my" bars and were surprised to learn that I didn't have any.

Choosing a bar can be risky business. Prices vary wildly, but in Japan it would be a shameful admission of poverty to ask the price of a drink in advance. A new customer orders a few rounds and prays silently that the bill won't come to $30 per drink. Often the decor and style of a place are a fair indication of the price range, but even the locals can be fooled. Friends have told me they have had some anxious moments waiting for the bill after a few drinks in an unfamiliar bar.

Some nervy establishments take advantage of this no-price-list system and shamelessly charge hundreds of dollars for a brief carouse. They are called *bōryoku* ("violence") bars and keep a thug or two in the back room to persuade surprised customers to pay up. In the summer of 1981 there was a scandal over an incident in which a man wandered into one of those places, jumped out a window to avoid paying the bill, and broke both legs. The Japanese wouldn't have this problem if asking the price of a drink did not cause such a terrible loss of face.

In Japan a man who worries about expenses or studies the bill for addition errors is dismissed as womanish and petty. A real man glances at the bottom line, drops a few large bills on the table, and pockets the change without counting it. I know Americans who think nothing of whipping out pocket calculators to check their restaurant bills.

A favorite barroom activity in Japan is singing. The Japanese love to sing and be sung to under practically any circumstances, but the bleary atmosphere of a bar is ideal, and many are specially set up to accommodate this mania for song. Even the tiniest will shove a two-piece band and a mike stand into a corner, so customers can serenade each other. Recently live accompaniment has been widely replaced by *karaoke* ("empty orchestra"). This is a library of cassette tape recordings of only the background music to popular songs. The customer chooses a song, a bar girl plugs in the tape, the "empty orchestra" strikes up a tune, and for a few minutes Tanaka-san is Old Blue Eyes. Most of the time customers listen indulgently to each other, but there are occasional reports of bar singers' being stabbed or beaten up by other customers who couldn't stand their screeching.

A group of drinkers will get up to sing in definite rank order—scotch and water can dim the hierarchy but not obliterate it entirely. Junior colleagues must get up and make fools of themselves before senior colleagues will. The whole process is accompanied by much laughter and exaggerated applause. Westerners are usually stumped by all this. The last thing they expect their important customers to do is break into song. Americans are urged to follow suit, and sure enough, many bars stock *karaoke* versions of "My Way" and "Love Me Tender."

Obviously what matters is not how well anyone sings but whether or not he cuts loose and makes a manly go of it. Still, most Americans, no matter how drunk, are a little leery of belting out "My Way" to a roomful of giggling Japanese. It was always a tremendous hit with customers when I would grab the mike and croon a few tender Japanese ballads I remember from my youth. Even for someone who doesn't know Japanese, these songs are easy to learn. I am sure that if the President of the United States were to knock off "Tokyo Blūzu" in a *karaoke* bar, it would do more for Japan-U.S. relations than years of patient diplomacy.

Although bars often give Westerners their first glimpse of a genuinely relaxed Japanese, most Japanese men are not at their most impressive after a couple of highballs. Even if there are no hostesses on hand to bring out the adolescent in them, one of Japan's foremost sociologists—who happens to be a woman—complains: "[In a bar] much of the talk is so stupid as to make one wonder that it can come from the lips of adult men."[2]

Despite semi-obligatory rounds of *otsukiai*, alcoholism is not a big problem in Japan. Many Japanese men turn pink and goofy after only a few beers, so perhaps they can enjoy the effects of alcohol without having to consume too much of it. Several have told me that they are metabolically different from Westerners and that the absence of a certain enzyme makes them more sensitive to alcohol but reduces the risks of alcoholism.

A unique form of entertainment that baffles me almost as much as hostess bars is pachinko, a word that derives from underworld slang for a pistol. Pachinko is a kind of vertical pinball in which steel balls the size of a large pea are fired into the top of the machine. They then bounce down through a series of chutes and gates either into a scoring pocket or into the trap at the bottom of the machine. The right shot scores a jackpot of new balls, but the player has no control over a ball once it is fired, so pachinko is a game of almost pure chance. The steady tinkle of hundreds of steel balls bouncing down behind the glass has a mesmerizing effect on players, who may stand, glassy-eyed, at their machines for hours.

Pachinko is not a game for children. Since winnings can be turned in for prizes, it is a form of gambling and can be played only by adults. In 1979, 24,490,000 Japanese played pachinko at least twice. If that sounds like a lot, it is still down from 30,240,000 in 1976.[3] Pachinko, the immense popularity of which has always mystified me, is losing ground to video games, which at least require some kind of interaction. Pachinko is not popular in any other part of the world, nor do I expect it to become so.

The nation that plays pachinko also reads comic books. There is something for everyone in Japan's vast comic book culture. There are adventure comics for boys, romance comics for girls and housewives, sex and violence comics for businessmen. The best-selling magazine in Japan is *Shūkan Shōnen Janpu* (*Boys' Weekly Jump*) with a circulation of 2.5 million. Not all those 2.5 million readers are boys. Many adults pick up the *Weekly Jump* for its rich brew of action, adventure, and adolescent prurience. The highest-circulation noncomic magazine in Japan weighs in far down the list with a readership of 650,000.[4]

For an authentic taste of Japan's comic book culture, one need only pay a visit to Kinokuniya, a Japanese bookstore that recently opened in New York City's Rockefeller Center. The most crowded part of the store is at the back, where a tight cluster of men invariably gathers to leaf through the latest issues of *Boys' King, Boys' Magazine*, and *Boys' Sunday* as well as the *Jump*.

Of course, not all Japanese pastimes are as mindless as pachinko or as questionable as hostess pinching. Nevertheless, wine, women, song, and pachinko are Japan's indigenous forms of entertainment, and each allows the Japanese man to behave in ways that Westerners might find childish. Along with Mah-Jongg and television, they are still the only real fun and relaxation that many businessmen ever get.

However, with increased leisure and broadening horizons Japanese are taking to other forms of entertainment with ever-increasing enthusiasm.

Team sports are, of course, a perfect activity for the Japanese. That such a group-conscious people never invented any has always struck me as a strange oversight. Unlike their elders, Japanese children have always played team games, and when I was a child, my Japanese playmates taught me a great many. Twenty-five years ago, when Japan was still poor, we could amuse ourselves for hours on end with nothing more than some broken tiles and a few lines drawn on the ground. When we could get our hands on a ball, we played a variety of team games that I have never seen anywhere else. These complex, challenging games are now slipping into oblivion as Japanese children—like American children—are pampered with elaborate store-bought toys and distracted by television.

Adults, however, avidly took to team sports as soon as they arrived from the West. Now, except for a few oddities like jai alai, curling, and lacrosse, virtually every Western team sport is played in Japan. There are even a few colleges that play American football. As one might expect, teamwork is more important than individual skill, and even the rare Japanese superstar is never a hot dog or grandstander. Victory is always *okagesama-de:* thanks to the teammates and the fans.

Baseball is by far the most popular spectator sport. Introduced in 1873, it rapidly won fans and was played professionally even before the Second World War. After Pearl Harbor it suddenly became an enemy game. The government tried to discourage it, but there was no stopping the fans; soldiers took along their bats and gloves so they could practice behind the lines. The best the authorities managed to do was circulate new, strictly Japanese words to replace American baseball lingo.

After the war, as Japanese professionals steadily improved their game, league officials began to grouse about how unfair it was for Americans to call their national championships the *World* Series. Japanese confidence was built up by postseason games with touring American teams that usually showed up without their star players and lost as many games as they won.

Early in 1971 the Baltimore Orioles were selected to make a postseason tour of Japan. This was exciting news for Japanese baseball because Baltimore had won the previous year's World Series and seemed a good bet to win it again. The Japanese were itching for a shot at the best team in America so they could prove to the world what a baseball powerhouse they had become. Baltimore proceeded to win the Eastern Division pennant but, to the chagrin of all Japanese baseball fans, lost the Series, three games to four, in a hard-fought contest against the Pittsburgh Pirates. The Japanese were so desperate to play the champions that they even made a last-minute attempt to bring over the Pirates.

When the Orioles finally arrived for their first game, the stadium was packed to capacity, and practically the entire nation gathered around TV sets to watch Japanese baseball come of age. Kimono-clad beauties presented bouquets of flowers to the visiting team, and the Japanese foreign minister made a pregame speech. All the razzle-dazzle finally got through to the Orioles; it dawned on them that the Japanese were challenging American supremacy. They rose to the occasion and beat the best team in Japan, 8 to 4. They then went on to demolish every other team the Japanese sent against them.

It was a chastening experience for the Japanese. "They must be the best team in the world," marveled the sportswriters. "How could they have possibly lost to Pittsburgh?" Since then there has been no more disgruntled talk about a "real" World Series. However, someday the Japanese will be back. They are not happy being second best at anything, and in the meantime, they are raising a new generation of some of the most dedicated ballplayers anywhere.[5]

In fact, the Japanese get so excited over *high school* baseball that the national championships stir up almost as much emotion as the Olympics. The winners of fierce regional eliminations meet at a professional stadium for a week of nonstop play. Business practically grinds to a halt as the whole nation tunes in to watch dazzled kids play their hearts out on live coast-to-coast TV. Months before the tournament begins, the fans are primed with stories about last year's winners and this year's dark horses. Newspapers run pictures of baseball players snoring through geometry class after their grueling 5:00 A.M. practice sessions.

There is something about the whang of an aluminum bat, the face-down slide into second, the unashamed tears of the losers that captures the imagination of the Japanese. High school baseball embodies Japan's old-fashioned virtues: teamwork, discipline, obedience, hard work, and fighting spirit. The best players are swamped with job offers from admiring corporations.

However, if Japanese businessmen relive their childhood watching high school baseball on TV, the sport they play for themselves is golf. In many companies, like it or not, golf is almost as much a part of the job as wearing a suit. It is required behavior for the compleat businessman; many companies even recommend to their new men what brand of clubs to buy. A few determined eccentrics manage to get out of it, but in Japan golf is such a direct extension of the workplace that refusing to play is a little like not showing up for work.

Golf with colleagues builds solidarity, golf with customers makes sales, and the Japanese are just as dedicated on the links as in the office. A business contact once told me about the care he puts into a round of golf: "In my company we always take a bath and wash our hair *before* we pick up the customers. That way we can just rinse off after the game and be out in the clubhouse, preparing drinks, while the customers are still in the shower."

Part of the appeal of golf is pure snobbishness. A golf course takes up lots of valuable acreage in land-scarce Japan, and club memberships can easily cost $4,000 or $5,000 a year. Some courses charge several hundred dollars just to play one round. There are double- and triple-decker driving ranges in Japan which may charge up to $40 an hour. Golf is not a sport for the poor and is a sinkhole for enormous corporate entertainment expenses.

Japanese pursue the game with incredible determination. I have known more than just a handful who played every Saturday and Sunday, weather and job permitting. On weekdays they might stop off at a driving range after work. It is not uncommon to see men swinging rolled-up magazines as if they were 5-irons or putting pebbles with an umbrella as they wait for a bus.

The Japanese are slightly touched when it comes to golf. Once, over lunch with a customer in New York, I was treated to a litany about how hard a time Kondō-san was having adjusting to America. His wife had no friends, his kids were confused in school, his English wasn't improving, his American secretary was cheeky to him, etc., etc.

"My gosh," I said, "you must wish you had never come."

"Not at all. I'm very happy I was sent to America."

"What? I thought you were just telling me how miserable you are."

"Oh, no," he said. "I knew about all those things when I applied for the transfer. What I really came to America for is the golf—and the golf is marvelous."

Courses are more plentiful in America, and the game is far less expensive than in Japan. Men like Kondō-san don't understand why Americans aren't as excited about golf as they are.

In Japan Western sports and hobbies are pursued with the same grim seriousness as increased market share. Jazz fans, for example, are just as fanatical about jazz as businessmen are about golf. They may pay no attention to classical music or rock and roll, but they know everything there is to know about jazz. When they come to America, they will dash from one jazz club to the next just as frantically as other tourists dash from Disneyland to the Grand Canyon.

Clothes and paraphernalia are part of Japan's seriousness about having fun. Owning the proper equipment is a vital and self-conscious aspect of participation. Japanese hikers, for example, must be the best equipped in the world. They will reach for their boots, alpine socks, backpacks, and rock axes just to walk up a nearby hill. Amateur baseball players are quick to shell out for uniforms; they like to wear them to practice, not just in a game, the way Americans would. Tennis players would not be caught dead on the court in anything but crispy white tennis togs. Many courts will not even allow players to wear anything else. Golfers are just as uncomfortable teeing off in improper attire. Japanese are surprised to find Americans hiking, golfing, skiing, jogging, or playing tennis in whatever is comfortable.

Japanese sometimes tell the story of one of their former prime ministers who was invited to a duck shoot by the British prime minister. The Japanese, who had never shot a duck in his life, went out and bought the Savile Row equivalent of a hunting outfit. He was chagrined to find the British PM wearing faded corduroys.

The right clothing is, of course, part of Japan's concern for proper form. Japanese do not just get out and have a good time. They take great pains to learn the rules, observe the etiquette, and look the part. They approach new activities with great caution, and the clearer the rules, the more comfortable they are. A little alligator on their shirtfronts or three stripes on their tennis shoes set them at ease.

Sometimes appearance is everything. These days in Japan there are quite a few sporty cars cruising around with surfboards strapped to their roofs. I had never given them a second thought until one day when I wandered into a chic sporting goods store in Tokyo. As I ran my hand over the sleek surface of an American-made surfboard, it occurred to me that there are hardly any waves on Japanese beaches. I asked an attendant where people go to surf in Japan.

"There's no good surfing in Japan," he said. "Most of our customers go to Guam or Hawaii."

I thought for a moment. "Does that mean that all the guys driving around with surfboards on their cars are on their way to the airport to catch a plane to Hawaii?"

"I don't believe so," said the clerk. "When they go to Hawaii, they rent boards there. I think a lot of people buy them from us and put them on their cars just for show. There is a surfing boom now."

The surfboard seems to be the latest snazzy accessory to another very high-toned Western "sport," the *doraibu*. Cars mean status in Japan, and in a nation that still feels the passion for automobiles that Americans had in the 1950s, many young Japanese will list "driving" as one of their sports or hobbies.

The *doraibu* experience requires that cars be kept spanking clean and that the tiniest scratch or dent be fixed immediately. A feather duster is standard equipment in most cars; the proud owner uses it to flick off the lightest accumulation of dust. Japanese are dumbfounded at the battered old jalopies that some Americans drive. They may never have seen a car with a color-contrasting fender from the junkyard or even one with missing hubcaps. In Japan cars are part of that serious field of Western status and endeavor that is sport and are just as important an accessory as Bjorn Borg tennis togs.

Automobiles are magic for the Japanese because the middle class has only recently been able to afford them. They also confer instant status because so few people really need one; Japan's public transportation system is probably the best in the world, while the same cannot be said for its highway system. Recently I was invited to dinner at the home of a young Japanese couple who live in a Tokyo suburb. At the end of the evening I was getting ready to stroll down to the subway station when my host insisted on driving me home in his car. I pointed out that the train would probably get me there quicker than he could and that afterward he would have to drive back home. I wasn't listened to. As my host rushed out to get his car keys, his wife explained to me, "It's all right. He hasn't had the car for very long, and he's still excited by every chance he gets to use it."

That man's automobile is somehow a symbol of Japan's newfound wealth and increasing leisure. Japanese are excited by the free time that prosperity has brought them, but they are not always sure what to do with it. Unselfconscious Western-style enjoyment of the kind that Japan is increasingly seeking requires a sense of relaxed self-satisfaction that is still rare in a nation where poverty was widespread only a generation ago.

It may be that Europeans and Americans have become so devoted to the enjoyment of leisure that they are increasingly inclined to shut their work off into a corner of their lives and to assume that no pleasure or satisfaction can come from it. If, for the Japanese, play sometimes seems to be nothing more than an extension of the spirit of work, for Westerners, it is more often a negation and an escape from it.

A Japanese banker writes of his surprise at the way Westerners enjoy themselves. He points out that even when they go to the beach, Japanese seem to feel that the only way to have fun is to go at it full tilt, just as if they were still at work. He wonders what it says about the Japanese that they are not happy unless they are running up and down the beach, playing volleyball, or splashing in the breakers, while Westerners may be perfectly content to lie motionless in the sun.[6] We could just as well ask ourselves what it says about Westerners. Nevertheless, this man is not alone in wondering when Japanese will ever learn to relax and enjoy themselves.

Kiyoshi Nasu, a Japanese newspaper reporter, tells a story about former Premier Takeo Miki, who visited New York in 1975 and was made an honorary citizen of the city by Mayor Abraham Beame. During the ceremony Beame, who was at the time struggling to save the city from bankruptcy, cracked that since Miki was now a citizen, he was going to have to pay city taxes. To Nasu's chagrin, Miki answered in all seriousness, "If they are not too high, I will pay."

"Why," moans Nasu, "don't the Japanese know how to take a joke?" He goes on to guess that it must be because they are so preoccupied with rank, form, and all the other burdens of living in Japanese society that they do not have "room in their hearts" for a sense of humor.[7] Sometimes I wonder how much room in their hearts Japanese have for a simple good time.

Except when they stumble into the forgiving world of whiskey and bar hostesses and have drowned their inhibitions in scotch and water and a song, Japanese are rarely at ease. Relaxation is something Americans may be a little too good at, but it is an elusive, unfamiliar activity for the Japanese. It has not been compatible with the "crisis consciousness," the "hunger mentality," the *oitsuke, oikose* ("catch up and pass [the West]") that have driven postwar Japan.

Fortunately they may not drive Japan forever. Younger Japanese are not nearly so crisis-ridden as their parents. Predictably, as they begin to learn how to switch off the hunger mentality at 5:00 P.M. and relax, their elders have begun to rail about how soft they have become. "It seems to me that our youngsters have developed a distaste for risk and hard work, and that this has to do with material abundance," writes an economics professor. "With advances in wealth, our children have become . . . unwilling to toil. . . ."[8] I suspect it has a great deal to do with material abundance. But then what is the point of material abundance if it does not allow people to toil a little less?

Japanese young people are not turning into layabouts, but they are no longer willing to devote themselves entirely to their jobs either. They are more accustomed to leisure than their parents ever were and are getting more practice at using it. If the professor thinks he can teach his students to toil for country and company the way their parents did, he is fighting a losing battle. The Japanese have worked very hard and they will continue to work hard—but they are finally learning how to play.

CHAPTER TEN

❀

JAPAN AND
THE WORLD

As we have seen, Japan is a nation which has pursued commerce to the ends of the earth, yet cannot shed its age-old mistrust of what lies beyond its shores. It has become an economic superpower but has so far refused to take an active part in running the affairs of an increasingly complex and politically fragmented world. Since its crushing defeat in the Second World War Japan has been content quietly to amass wealth and has watched from the wings as other powers jostled each other for center stage.

It is businessmen, not diplomats, who have shaped postwar Japan. If Japanese diplomacy since the war has had a motto, it is "Offend no one, especially not the United States." Japan has passively followed world events, always careful to support the right causes and pick the right friends. In the rueful words of one scholar, it "has repeatedly followed the pattern of waiting to see how world opinion will shape up toward any incident that occurs and then jumping on the bandwagon."[1] The Japanese have vigorously exploited opportunities that presented themselves but have waited for America to set the example.

Thus they have not tried to direct world events according to their own purposes, but they have also shirked responsibility for them. The result has been an historical anomaly: a nation that is both economic giant and political dwarf.

Nevertheless, no nation with an economy as large as that of the Soviet Union can tiptoe through the postwar world forever. Like it or not, the Japanese are now at the center of the world economic system and can no longer pretend that they are industrial underdogs, struggling to give their poor island nation a subsistence income.

The Japanese cling to this pretense for a number of reasons. For older people, the devastation and poverty of the immediate postwar years are such vivid memories that many still cannot believe Japan is a wealthy nation. Japanese who did not live through the war, and who have grasped the reality of their country's extraordinary success, have other reservations about shouldering the responsibilities of greatness.

Japan's relations with the outside world are still colored by distaste for the fact that it must have relations at all, by the secret fantasy of Japan as a sheltered enclave where understanding and harmony might flourish undisturbed. As the authors of a recent study of American policy in the Far East have written, "[The Japanese] still regard . . . foreigners as exotic creatures to be kept at a distance, the outside world as a 'zoological garden' to be observed with detached curiosity. They sally forth into this dangerous environment only to scurry back home to the embrace of a highly integrated and protective society."[2] An opinion poll taken in 1980 showed that three out of four Japanese do not associate with foreigners and, what's more, don't want to.[3] This is not the gregarious cosmopolitanism on which effective peacetime foreign policies are built. It is, instead, an aloofness that breeds suspicion and misunderstanding.

Today Japan is wrestling reluctantly with the two foreign policy issues that shape its relations with the rest of the world: trade and defense. As recession drags on, trade is a vital concern for Japan's commercial partners. Relentless unemployment at home has tempted Western politicians to turn their backs on free trade and to save jobs by shutting out imports. Mounting trade deficits with Japan are hailed as proof that it is not playing fair.

In the past Japan has certainly been guilty of unfair trading practices, and a few inefficient industries continue to thrive in the shelter of trade barriers. However, in response to mounting foreign pressure,

Japan has made a good-faith effort to open its markets and is now, in my view, more sinned against than sinning. It would never have reformed voluntarily, but as we shall see, Japan has finally been dragged kicking and screaming into the world of free trade.

The Japanese debate on rearmament, which should be only simmering quietly, has been brought to a rolling boil by the United States. America has long wanted to shrug off a larger share of the defense burden onto Japanese shoulders, and as the economic gap between the two countries narrows, its requests have become increasingly ill-tempered. American resources are stretched thin, and rich Japan may at first seem like a good candidate to help defend capitalism. Armed to the teeth, Japan might give the U.S. Seventh Fleet a temporary breather. Full rearmament, however, would rekindle the fears of Asian nations that were brutalized by the forces of imperial Japan and would drastically alter Japan's role in Asia.

Opponents of rearmament are also haunted by the specter of resurgent Japanese militarism. I think such fears are exaggerated. Still, Japan is already handicapped by insular habits and inveterate xenophobia. Military power on the same scale as its economic power would only widen the psychological gulf between the Japanese and their neighbors.

Japan's current trade problems have two causes: its extraordinary success as an exporter and its history of protectionism. For those who think of Japan as pouring practically all its industrial production onto world markets, it is a surprise to learn that its exports amount to only 14 percent of its GNP. This puts it well below Holland's 49 percent, Taiwan's 48 percent, and South Korea's 33 percent. Germany at 26 percent and France and Britain at just under 20 percent all have more internationalized economies than Japan's. Of the world's major trading nations, only Brazil and the United States, at less than 10 percent, export proportionately less than Japan.

What makes Japan so troublesome to its trade partners is its tendency to concentrate so successfully on manufactured exports that foreign competitors are pushed to the wall. Japanese cameras, motorcycles, and tape recorders have nearly cleared the world of rivals, and steel, ships, and autos could have done the same had manufacturers not been restrained for political reasons. Throughout the Western world people have been put out of work by the Japanese.

Extraordinary success in certain export markets would not be so galling if Japan would only import as many industrial products as it exports. Exchange of manufactured goods between developed nations makes up the real bulk of world trade, and for such countries as France, Germany, and the United States it accounts for about 60 percent of all imports. Japan is an irksome exception to this rule: only 25 percent of its imports are manufactured products. It thus runs trade deficits with some of its raw materials suppliers but has racked up huge surpluses with the industrialized nations. Its surplus with the United States has climbed from $8 billion in 1979 to $10 billion a year later to $15.8 billion in 1981 and to $20 billion in 1982. With the European Economic Community (EEC), Japan's surplus has increased each year for the past decade, and in 1981 it stood at $10.5 billion.

Western governments have refused to believe that free market forces could give rise to such massive imbalances. They know that their exporters are not all lazy or incompetent, and it is tempting to assume that if Western exports are not selling in Japan, it is because they are barred from the market. There is no doubt that Japan has been blatantly protectionist in the past. The auto and steel industries grew up in a closely guarded domestic market, in which they first established themselves before taking aim at the world. Today, systematic protection of entire industries is mostly a thing of the past. The United States and the EEC have chipped away nearly all of Japan's tariffs and a great many of its nontariff barriers. Those that remain are supported by constituencies that are so politically powerful that the Japanese government is not willing to pay the price for their removal.

The one sector of the economy that is still shamelessly protected is agriculture. Japanese farms are, on average, less than one one-hundredth the size of American farms and are woefully inefficient. However, as a result of unequal political representation of town and country, farmers have more than their share of electoral power. Also, as in most countries, farming is part of enough people's recent past to give it a special place in the national consciousness. Those who work the land somehow symbolize a purer Japanese spirit than those who have sold their souls to industry. Finally, no country can afford to be entirely dependent on foreign food. As Richard Nixon clearly demonstrated in 1973, when he peremptorily halted soybean shipments to Japan, even the friendliest food suppliers cannot always be trusted.

Thus Japan still flouts the laws of the General Agreement on Tariffs and Trade (GATT) by slapping annual quotas on twenty-two imported products. These are mostly foodstuffs, such as beef, milk, cheese, fruit juice, and oranges. Also included are raw leather and leather shoes, in order to protect Japan's feeble tanning industry. Thanks to quotas, Japanese consumers pay many times the world price for some of these products.

The powerful farming groups that benefit from protectionism don't hesitate to flex their muscles. In May 1982 they ran a full-page ad in one of Japan's best-selling newspapers, the *Asahi*. It was entitled "That Troublesome Beef" and was anything but subtle:

> Some people are telling you that free trade will bring us cheap and tasy beef and oranges. Watch out. Tasty talk always has a catch.
>
> What those foreigners are trying to do is use some tasty tidbits as bait to throw open Japan's entire agricultural market. The camel's nose is sniffing around the tent. . . . Do you really want foreign goods when it means that the farmers of your own country will suffer?
>
> Think about it, Mrs. Housewife. Don't be fooled by what looks cheap to you now.[4]

Farmers are so dependent on protection that in January 1983 some ten thousand took to the streets of Tokyo to demonstrate against the mere possibility that the government might propose an increase in imports.[5]

With Americans, the farmers argue a different line. They admit that if Japan were entirely unprotected from beef imports, the domestic cattle industry would probably disappear. They point out, though, that 90 percent of the corn consumed in Japan comes from the United States, and much of this is fed to cows. If there were no Japanese cows to feed, they claim, corn imports would drop, and the trade imbalance would be just as bad as before. It's not hard to imagine the colorful language with which American cattlemen respond to that argument.

Inefficient agriculture is also openly protected by the Japanese Tobacco and Salt Public Corporation (JTS). JTS is a government monopoly that has complete control over production and distribution of all tobacco products in Japan. There is no confusion about its mission.

When asked by a journalist why JTS was not run as a private concern, one of its executives reportedly replied, "Because this would result in only imported products being sold in Japan."[6]

JTS buys primitively produced Japanese tobacco at three times the world price but still manages to sell its cigarettes at a fat profit. It does this by strictly rationing the availability of foreign cigarettes. Of the 250,000 retail tobacco outlets in Japan, fewer than 10 percent are allowed to sell foreign products, and these are sold at inflated prices. Cigars that sell for 8 cents apiece in America cost 35 to 40 cents in Japan,[7] and a pack of U.S. cigarettes sells for a hefty 40-cent premium over local brands. JTS jacks up the price so foreign tobacco won't compete with its own and then pockets the difference. This provides extra revenue for the government and has also kept American products to less than 1.5 percent of the market.

When R. J. Reynolds tried to launch its new cigarette More in Japan, it ran into a special set of obstacles. The Japanese did not make a long brown-wrapper cigarette like More, and the new product seemed poised to take a substantial share of the market. JTS countered by keeping More in a limited test market for two years, during which time it developed its own brown-wrapper cigarette. By the time More was released to the general market it faced a direct competitor that was already firmly entrenched.[8]

To make things even harder, foreign tobacco companies are not allowed to advertise in the Japanese media but are restricted to the minuscule English-language press. When challenged on this point, Japanese officials have claimed that they are opposed to advertising that encourages bad habits. Smoking foreign cigarettes must be a worse habit than smoking domestic brands; Japanese cigarettes are advertised everywhere.

Back when the U.S. surgeon general first announced the dangers of cigarette smoking, the press assured its readers that Japanese cigarettes couldn't possibly be harmful even if American cigarettes were. Perhaps the JTS men who are reported to have torn down perfectly legal point-of-sale ads for American cigarettes[9] still believe this.

JTS is driven to protectionism because the Japanese clearly prefer American cigarettes. They smoke $10 billion worth of tobacco every year, and the more optimistic U.S. trade officials have estimated that American producers could increase their annual sales by $2 billion if the Japanese market were opened to real competition.

Recently the United States extracted a promise from JTS that it would increase the number of retailers permitted to sell foreign tobacco, and in January 1983 the Japanese announced a cut in the cigarette tariff from 35 percent to 20 percent. This was meant to reduce the premium that consumers were paying for American cigarettes, but JTS undercut the measure by hiking its retail markup. The storm of protest that greeted this bit of trickery reached as far as the prime minister. Retail prices were quickly dropped, and the Japanese labeled the episode a "misunderstanding."[10] In the past, JTS has been more prone to misunderstandings than perhaps any other government agency, and U.S. negotiators are keeping close watch on it.

The quota on leather shoes offers a similar opportunity for officially sanctioned profiteering by allowing domestic producers to control access to foreign goods. Import quotas for shoes are parceled out to Japanese shoe companies as a reward for successful exports. Since these companies have sole access to strictly limited quantities of a desirable product, they can buy inexpensive Italian shoes and sell them at whatever markup the market will bear. Thus, Japanese shoe manufacturers not only are protected from foreign inroads but are able to add to their own profits by selling small amounts of the very product they are being protected against.[11]

Manufactured goods generally face obstacles more subtle than GATT-illegal quotas. A favorite way to protect domestic manufacturers has been to choke the import process with complex regulations and to require interminable testing before a product is approved for sale. For example, every imported automobile must be individually tested to be sure it meets Japan's stringent emissions requirements. In other countries only a few sample vehicles need be tested. Until 1978 every large foreign-produced marine diesel engine had to be disassembled, and various parts submitted for testing, before it could receive a Japanese government rating. This discriminatory requirement was abolished only in the face of vigorous EEC protests.[12]

Often the laboratories that test imports are run by the very Japanese manufacturers with which foreign companies are competing. A small American producer of auto battery testers has described its struggle for Japanese import approval:

This can take years. You send them a unit for testing. Then months go by. After many letters, telexes and phone calls, you are finally told the product failed the test. You request information on what caused the failure. They are unable to give you an explanation.

If you ask what voltage was used in the test—the reply is 'standard' voltage. But they are unable to define 'standard' voltage, and promise to mail you the information at a later date.

In the meantime, they request two additional battery testers and explain the original testers were destroyed while testing.

This time you stipulate that the new samples be tested one at a time so if one is destroyed the second can still be tested to the point prior to the destruction of the first tester. You also request that it be returned so that you can have a better idea of what the failure mode is. However, the Japanese either destroy both samples or claim they lost the second tester. This goes on and on and on.

You can waste years trying to crack the Japanese market.[13]

As another means to keep out imports, Japanese industry standards have been cynically manipulated to the direct detriment of foreign competitors. In 1973 and 1974 an American company introduced a tabletop electric griddle that began selling very well in Japan. The next year Japanese safety standards were changed so that the hottest the griddle's hand controls could get during cooking was two degrees Centigrade *lower* than the maximum temperature reached by the American product. This immediately shut out the U.S. company, and by the time it redesigned its product and got new approvals Japanese manufacturers dominated the market.[14]

Foreign detergent makers were caught in a similar snare. Japanese authorities, working closely with domestic companies, established a timetable for the introduction of phosphate-free detergents, but did not include non-Japanese companies in their talks. Thus, when the phosphate ban was announced, Japanese producers were ready with new products and gobbled up market share, while foreign competitors scrambled to meet the new regulations.[15]

In another famous case a U.S. exporter of potato chips found that its tariff bracket rose as sales increased. During the test market phase Japanese Customs classified the product as "vegetables, prepared or preserved," with a tariff rate of 16 percent. When the company started selling successfully across the country, its potato chips were reclassified as "pastry, biscuits, cakes and other fine bakers' wares" and hit with a 35 percent tariff. Only after an impassioned appeal to the Joint U.S.-Japan Trade Facilitation Committee, which had been established in 1977, was the company able to have the 16 percent rate reinstated.[16]

The inability of foreign firms to invest freely in Japan has been another serious obstacle to their penetrating the market. Until 1980, when foreign exchange and investment laws were liberalized, potential investors had to meet rigorous government requirements, and before 1976 each investment had to be approved on its own merits, case by case. Only those companies willing to share know-how and technology were allowed to set up shop. Just after the war potentially useful companies such as Dow Chemical and Caterpillar Tractor were permitted to start joint ventures, and IBM and Burroughs, which could offer entirely new technology, were allowed to establish wholly owned subsidiaries. However, as Japan's own technology improved, foreign investment was slowed to a trickle.

It was largely due to tariffs and restrictions on foreign investment that the Japanese electronics industry made such impressive progress. Back in the 1960s, when American companies had a clear lead in integrated circuits (IC), a number of U.S. manufacturers applied for permission to build and sell them in Japan. The Japanese, who were actively promoting the domestic electronics industry, responded with high tariffs on ICs imported from America and systematically refused to allow U.S. companies to establish wholly owned subsidiaries. American companies found that the only way to make money in Japan was by selling their technology—precisely what the Japanese wanted them to do.

The only U.S. company to skirt this dilemma was Texas Instruments (TI). It refused to sign licensing agreements and held out for at least fifty-fifty participation in a Japanese joint venture if it could not get approval for a wholly owned subsidiary. TI was in a strong position because some of its technology was the best in the world. Still, it took years of dickering before MITI allowed it to establish a joint venture with Sony in 1968, and even then, only on the condition that it agree to license its technology—not just to Sony but to its direct competitors: Hitachi, Matsushita, Toshiba, and Nippon Electric. Four years later TI was able to buy out Sony's share of the joint venture, and until restrictions were relaxed in 1980, it was the only American IC maker to have a wholly owned subsidiary in Japan.[17]

The United States, by contrast, has been wide open to the Japanese electronics industry. Not only have foreign manufacturers been able to sell their circuits unhindered, they have been able to buy up some of the small, innovative companies that gave the American industry its early edge. Electronic Arrays, Micropower Systems, and Maruman IC are now owned by Nippon Electric, Seiko, and Toshiba respectively.[18]

Very recent changes have vastly increased the possibilities for foreign investment in Japan, but there are still areas that are off limits. Theoretically it is possible for foreign interests to take over a high-tech Japanese company, but approval would be only slightly more forthcoming than on a request to buy out the Bank of Japan. Strictly speaking, foreign banks are now permitted to buy small Japanese banks, but all attempts so far have been thwarted by the authorities for "technical" reasons. Nor can foreign interests buy a Japanese company with a seat on the Tokyo Stock Exchange; the exchange is still an all-Japanese club. In America several Japanese banks have established branch networks by swallowing up small U.S. competitors, and seats on the stock exchange are for sale to whoever can afford them.

Tight restrictions have succeeded in keeping foreign capital out of Japan. The roughly $3 billion that Japan invested overseas from April through September 1981 was nearly equal to all foreign investment in Japan for the past *thirty years*.[19]

Another long-standing source of trade friction is the requirement that goods brought into Japan be handled by a *Japanese* company which acts as the authorized import agent. Foreign goods flow into Japan not because the exporter has been authorized to send them over but because a particular Japanese company has been given permission to import them. At its least offensive, this rule adds trouble and expense to the efforts of small exporters who cannot afford to set up an importing subsidiary in Japan. At its worst, it can snarl the whole process because import permission cannot be easily transferred from one agent to another. If an exporter wishes to change agents, it may have to go through a lengthy reapplication while its product is tested and approved all over again.[20]

Finally, even when a foreign company has managed to meet all the legal requirements for export, it must learn the complex ceremonies and traditions that surround commerce in Japan. The fact that they all are conducted in Japanese makes them particularly difficult to untangle. Japanese is a notoriously difficult language, and only a tiny minority of Westerners posted to Japan can speak it. A French company trying to sell in America would never dream of sending over people who spoke no English; they would be hopelessly cut off from their customers. Yet that, in effect, is how Western companies have tried to operate in Japan.

Another thorn in the side of any exporter is Japan's rickety, old-fashioned distribution system. Most Japanese wholesalers handle only a few products and cover a small part of the country. They are bound together in a multilayered lattice, and half their trade is among themselves rather than with suppliers and retailers.[21] Unless a foreign producer is able to establish its own distribution network, as Coca-Cola did, its products will be handled by many hands before they reach the consumer. At every step of the way middlemen operate in the clubby atmosphere of personal connections that the Japanese like best.

Some frustrated exporters have found the system so Byzantine that they think of it as a particularly invidious nontariff barrier. There is no doubt that it is clumsy and inefficient by Western standards. However, Japanese producers use the same system, and its complexities were not cooked up just to bamboozle outsiders. Even Sony and Honda had more trouble with domestic than foreign distribution because they came to prominence after the war and were relative latecomers to the Japanese market.

Insiders, of course, benefit from long familiarity with the system and from contacts built up over time. As a MITI official once explained to a foreign journalist, "To really get access to this market, you've got to learn Japanese and drink sake in nightclubs for three or four years."[22] Japanese businessmen have the advantage of speaking Japanese, but they, too, have spent many a bleary-eyed evening building up contacts. What appears to Americans as an antiforeign prejudice may be nothing more than reluctance to do business with unfamiliar customers.

Even the best-laid plans of foreign companies can fall afoul of cultural quirks. Unsuspecting Americans once introduced a product endorsement ad campaign that had been a success all around the world but was a failure in Japan. The ads featured Muhammad Ali.

The company didn't realize that the Japanese don't like to take advice from blacks, no matter how famous.

Another classic failure was the rice-cooker cake. Betty Crocker had discovered that there was no market for cake mixes in Japan because few Japanese homes have ovens. However, practically all have electric rice cookers, and the company cleverly designed a cake mix that could be cooked up just like a pot of rice. The product flopped. Betty Crocker had underestimated the ritualistic importance of rice to the Japanese and had not suspected that housewives would worry about the purity of their rice once they had polluted their cooker with cake.[23]

In the past Americans used to swagger into Tokyo convinced that they had "written the book" when it came to business and management. After all, the Japanese were a nation of imitators, who could learn a lot from a two-fisted, no-nonsense American approach. Many a two-fisted American was laid low by legal and cultural barriers and gave up on the Japanese market entirely.

More patient companies have tried to minimize problems by staffing their subsidiaries almost entirely with Japanese. This approach can be successful but has problems of its own. If foreign companies want to hire anything but the dregs of the labor market, they have to be prepared to offer lifetime employment and a family environment, and it may still be hard for them to attract topnotch people. In the hierarchy of corporations no *gaijin* company has anything like the prestige of Japan's old-line domestic firms. Only a few American giants like IBM or Citibank, which have had substantial operations in Japan for years, can attract the best people.

Nonetheless, the dice may still be loaded against them. A foreign company, even staffed entirely by Japanese, remains in some sense an interloper. Muckraking lowbrow weeklies can get far more mileage out of a scandal at Caterpillar than one at Komatsu Tractor. When Hitachi and Mitsubishi Electric were stung for buying trade secrets stolen from IBM, their images suffered and their stock prices fell— but it was IBM Japan that lost sales.

All this is not to say that the Japanese market is impenetrable. It is difficult and extremely competitive, but for companies that are willing to make the effort, it offers great rewards. As Japanese trade officials like to point out, some American manufacturers have done very well in Japan. Coca-Cola has a commanding 33 percent share of the soft drink market, Warner-Lambert sells 70 percent of Japan's razor blades, IBM makes 30 percent of the computers, and Borg-Warner sells 54 percent of the automatic transmissions. Japan Procter & Gamble is practically unopposed in the disposable diaper business, and S. C. Johnson & Son of Racine, Wisconsin, has a 30 percent share of the floor wax market.[24] There are now 160,000 Japanese Avon ladies knocking on doors, selling cosmetics.[25]

These companies have gotten where they are through patience and hard work. When P&G introduced Pampers to Japan, it launched what was probably the largest sample giveaway campaign in Japanese history. The company could afford it; it was firmly established in Japan and already had 20 percent of the detergent market. Still, it takes sustained efforts to get results. As a strategist for the company explains, "Getting and holding onto a piece of this market takes a lot of money up front. The payout may be longer but you can eventually make a mint in this country."[26]

As time goes on, it will still take determination to sell in Japan, but real progress has been made in eliminating some of the most glaring trade barriers. Americans and Europeans have joined forces in storming the barricades, and in January 1982 Japanese officials acted on sixty-seven of ninety-nine trade complaints that the United States and the EEC had presented jointly. They promised to streamline and liberalize product testing and import authorization procedures. They also agreed to drop some of their more obstructionist licensing and customs clearance procedures in a series of moves that should affect everything from automobiles to cosmetics.

At the same time an Office of Trade Ombudsman was set up within the Cabinet to act on trade complaints. Unlike the bureaucrats who used to handle grievances by "studying" them until they went away, the ombudsman has been given real power and shows signs of being willing to use it. In the first six months of its existence it took up fifty-one trade complaints and resolved twenty-nine of them.[27] The U.S.-Japan Trade Facilitation Committee has already proved its usefulness in championing American trade interests.

Since the late seventies the Japan External Trade Organization (JETRO) has shifted its emphasis from the promotion of Japanese goods overseas to the encouragement of imports to Japan. Its offices, located in major cities around the world, distribute free literature and advice on Japanese markets. In recent years an increasing number of

Japanese trade missions have been sent to the United States and the EEC in search of goods that could be sold to Japan. Even Japan's new prime minister, Yasuhiro Nakasone, flew off to Europe and America for trade talks only weeks after taking office late in 1982. As a sign of the new leader's good intentions, tariff reductions on a further sixty-eight products were announced just before his departure.

The Japanese would never have taken these steps if they had not been bullied into them by resentful Americans and Europeans. Americans are right in complaining that ". . . Japanese negotiating practice historically is to resist pressure until a crisis, negotiate minimally acceptable levels, and then continue to pursue Japanese goals."[28] Nevertheless, I believe that there has been a significant change of heart at the top levels of Japanese business and government and that the Japanese are well on their way to dismantling the worst of their legal barriers to trade.

A sign of the times is the experience of the Materials Research Corporation, a producer of equipment for manufacturing semiconductors. It breezed through every step of the way when it set up a plant in Japan, which was dedicated in March 1982. Far from being harassed by Japanese officialdom, the company's president says, "We are being helped tremendously by the Japanese government."[29]

Japan is making such progress in opening its markets that there is now some question as to how much difference it would really make if every remaining Japanese nontariff barrier were removed. Even the most optimistic American trade officials would not expect an increase in U.S. exports of more than a few billion dollars, and private estimates of the net effect run as low as $1 billion[30]—a mere fraction of the $15 to $20 billion trade imbalance between America and Japan.

The U.S.-Japan Trade Study Group is a cooperative project of Tokyo-based American businessmen working with Japanese industry and the government. In a report written before the latest Japanese efforts at liberalization, the group stated plainly that "any long-term improvement in the bilateral trade imbalance will depend more on improved performance both by U.S. business and government in promoting exports than on the removel of remaining Japanese non-tariff barriers."[31]

Even William Brock, the U.S. special trade representative, who can usually be counted on to bash the Japanese, has admitted that "we've talked so much about Japanese barriers that I'm afraid some business people have said that it's not worth making the effort. That's not an accurate evaluation. There are sectors where the opportunity exists today and has not been fully seized."[32]

Furthermore, the other industrial nations have in many cases taken openly discriminatory measures to shut out Japanese products. The United States has forced the Japanese to establish "voluntary" restraints on fully 30 percent of its exports here. Cars, steel, textiles, and color television sets all are restricted. Even in agriculture the American record is far from unblemished. In fiscal year 1984 the "free-trading" Reagan administration planned to spend more than *$15 billion* on subsidies to American farmers.[33]

EEC countries are even more liberal to their farmers and just as high-handed toward Japanese manufacturers. Late in 1982 France decreed that all imports of Japanese video recorders would henceforth be processed through a tiny customs office in Poitiers that is staffed only a few hours a day. Italy has thirty-eight bilateral restrictions on Japanese imports, France has twenty-seven, and the Benelux countries have nine.[34] These measures are even more in violation of GATT rules than Japan's quotas, for they discriminate against only one country. Japan's quotas apply to everybody. If *all* restrictions on trade were removed, both Japanese and Western, Japan would probably *increase* its trade surplus.

Americans have started resorting to the same devious tactics of which they have long accused the Japanese. In 1981 AT&T accepted proposals on a fiber optics contract for its new Boston–Washington telephone network. A bid from Fujitsu, at $56.5 million, was nearly $20 million lower than the best American offer, and the company fully expected to get the contract. At the last minute a coalition of congressmen organized by one of the losing American bidders persuaded AT&T to give the contract to a U.S. company for "national security" reasons. Pentagon officials later torpedoed this reasoning by pointing out that the fiber optics communications system for the NORAD (North American Air Defense Command) installation in Colorado is supplied by the Nippon Electric Company.[35]

The Japanese national telephone company was attacked for years by foreigners because of its stubborn buy-Japanese policy. Ironically, it has recently done an about-face and has been practically begging U.S. companies to bid on its contracts.[36]

It is no surprise that many Japanese are angry about what they see as hypocritical criticism from the West. "[W]e are being subjected to a torrent of complaints from abroad about our trade being in the black. But most of the arguments appear to me as nothing more than outrageous nitpicking," writes a typical Japanese commentator. "Business," he adds, "is not charity."[37]

Japanese have no patience with complaints that their language, culture, and distribution system are nontariff barriers. As they are quick to point out, they have had to learn their way around in countries that were just as mysterious to them as Japan is to Westerners. Furthermore, while Westerners gripe about Japanese safety and testing standards that differ from their own, the Japanese have been quietly adapting their products to a thicket of foreign requirements that are just as annoying to them. Japanese automobiles, for example, do not have safety-glass windows, but every Japanese car shipped to America must be fitted with them. The United States, they also complain, is one of the few countries left that refuse to classify goods according to the Consultative Committee on Customs Nomenclature (CCCN). If Japan were to do anything so eccentric, it would immediately be accused of obstructing imports.

The Japanese confess to protectionism in the past but insist that they have now reformed. In their view, too few Westerners have seriously set out to please the quality-conscious Japanese consumer, and too many have given up in dismay when they learned how hard it was.

I am largely sympathetic to complaints that Japan is now being penalized for its success. Its trade partners insist that large surpluses are proof of Japanese protectionism. Could it possibly be that other countries are simply not turning out enough things that the Japanese can't make better and cheaper for themselves? Many Japanese suspect Westerners of preferring to see Japanese competitiveness decline rather than put in the effort to increase their own. One importer makes a medical analogy that is increasingly popular in Japan. "Mr. America is partly in the hospital," he says. "Europe is sick. The Europeans are trying to bring the healthy Japanese into their bed."[38]

Nevertheless, several factors should temper our sympathy. With unemployment at a postwar record, Western politicians' instinctive loyalty is to their jobless constituents, and if Europeans and Americans are beastly to the Japanese, they are equally so to each other. American lumbermen are up in arms over cheap Canadian logs, and the British coolly refuse to let cut-rate French turkeys into their market until after the Christmas season.

Furthermore, Western countries have begun to discriminate against imports because they threaten the very survival of basic industries. For the Japanese, imports pose nothing like the same threat of joblessness or industrial decline. Their protectionist policies, which grew out of a real need to shelter the fledgling industries of the postwar era, were designed to foster continuing growth as much as to protect existing industry.

Europe and America have generally abided by the rules of free trade except when imports were a menace to existing jobs. New industries have mainly had to fend for themselves. The Japanese have behaved more like an underdeveloped country; they have restricted trade not only to protect existing industries but to build up powerful new ones.

There is a profound psychological difference between quietly breaking the rules in order to grow faster than anyone else and breaking them only in desperation to stave off collapse. For the Japanese to give up protectionism means only that they forgo the possibility of greater future prosperity; for Europeans and Americans it can mean losing jobs and industries they have had for generations. In neither case is protectionism good for the world economy, but virtue has a lower price tag for the Japanese. At a time when North America and Europe are floundering in the worst recession in years, it is not very hard for Japan to strike a pose as virtue vilified.

Moreover, when the Japanese see a challenge to what is *already* theirs, they are quick to react. Recently Korean and Taiwanese steel exporters were sharply rebuked when imported steel crept above a menacing 2 percent of the Japanese market. At the time Japanese steelmen were taking 15 to 20 percent of the U.S. market. In agriculture—the one sector where free trade would not be just an inconvenience but a real threat to the Japanese—they are as stoutly protectionist as anyone else. What agriculture is to Japan, steel, electronics, machine tools, cars, and shipbuilding are to the West.

Finally, it will be years before the effects of Japan's past protectionism fully wear off. Japanese companies are entrenched in America in a way that American companies will perhaps never be in Japan. Foreigners have been playing against a stacked deck for so long that it will take time just to catch up. Also, even if the will to facilitate imports is present at the top levels of government—as it appears to be—it will take time before the new mood percolates down to the bureaucrats who actually stamp the papers. Government workers are more independent of politicians in Japan than they are in America, and a few diehard protectionists may have to be publicly disgraced before the maker of battery testers we saw earlier is willing to take another shot at the Japanese market.

Trade is currently Japan's most contentious foreign policy issue, mainly because it has raised hackles all around the world. What the Japanese cannot sell to the industrialized West they try to sell to their neighbors. Here, too, they are facing discrimination, as Taiwan and South Korea struggle to reduce their trade deficits and the ASEAN countries worry about the flood of Japanese consumer goods. Except for the Eastern bloc, to which Japan supplies badly needed high-tech equipment, and OPEC, from which it imports prodigious quantities of oil, practically everyone has a bone to pick with Japan over trade or investment. The sympathy with which it listens to complaints from less efficient trade partners will have a great impact on its future.

As a subject of international dispute, the issue of Japan's defense is, for the time being, a bilateral matter with the United States. However, depending on choices it will make over the next ten years, Japan's military posture could provoke the same widespread tension its trade patterns do today.

Japan's close military association with America is a curious legacy of the Second World War. That it should become a major commercial partner of the United States was always in the cards; that it should shelter so snugly under the eagle's wing is a historical accident.

After their bloody slog across the Pacific the Americans were determined to put an end, once and for all, to Japan's capacity and even desire to make war. In the hope of turning the Japanese into a peace-loving people, the occupation forced one democratic reform after another onto the prostrate nation. The shining symbol of America's intentions for Japan was Article IX of the Constitution drafted by General MacArthur's men: "The Japanese people forever renounce war as a sovereign right of the nation and the threat or the use of force as a means of settling international disputes.

"In order to accomplish the aims of the preceding paragraph, land, sea and air forces, as well as the other war potential, will never be maintained. The right of belligerency of the state will not be recognized."

There is some question who first thought of a war-renunciation clause, but the Americans promoted it, and the Japanese, newly converted to fervent pacifism, embraced it. In 1947, when the Constitution went into effect, both sides thought that Article IX denied the Japanese the right to rearm at all, even for self-defense. Japan's defense needs were to be met by the U.S.-Japan Mutual Security Treaty, which was signed in 1951.

The American interpretation of Article IX began to change as it became clear how rapidly Japan was turning its back on the past and shifting its attention to peace and reconstruction. As early as 1948 the U.S. National Security Council recommended the formation of a 150,000-man paramilitary police force for Japanese defense, and in 1950 Secretary of State John Foster Dulles vainly tried to persuade Prime Minister Shigeru Yoshida to engage in limited rearmament.

MacArthur, who had faced the Japanese in combat, was originally opposed to any kind of rearmament, but his views changed when a former ally, the Soviet Union, began to appear as a threat to the West. In 1949 the NATO alliance was born, China fell to the Communists, and the Soviets got the bomb. Americans in Japan lost some of their enthusiasm for rooting out ex-militarists and instead began to wonder if the hardworking Japanese couldn't be recruited to fight on our side of the cold war. After the Korean War broke out in 1950 MacArthur ordered the establishment of a 75,000-man National Police Reserve. In short order, Article IX was reinterpreted as a ban only on *aggressive* war, and MacArthur's policemen were renamed the National Safety Force in 1952 and got their present name, the Self-Defense Force (SDF), in 1954.

The Japanese armed forces have always been of dubious legality. For years they were challenged by the Communist and Socialist opposition as unconstitutional, and to the layman's eye, Article IX reads like a flat ban on all armed forces. If it had to, today's SDF could certainly fight a war, and it would be hard to argue that its guided missile destroyers are not "war potential."

The Japanese have tied themselves into knots trying to make the SDF look like anything but a war machine. The name changes were strictly semantic contortions, and even today Japan does not have an army, navy, and air force, but ground, maritime, and air self-defense forces. The old wartime ranks like general or private have been replaced with bureaucratic titles. Not even a tank is called a tank; it is a "special vehicle."

As befits its defensive role, the SDF is hemmed about with regulations meant to forestall the slightest hint of aggression. Its men cannot be sent overseas under any circumstances and thus cannot take part in UN peacekeeping missions. It would take a revision of the law even to allow an SDF man to take part in an overseas sporting event or to authorize the transport of civilian equipment for an Arctic expedition in an SDF icebreaker.[39]

Because Japan officially does not have a military, it cannot, by definition, have military secrets. Thus it is the only major power with neither spies nor spy catchers. It does have a law, dating from 1954, under which soldiers and government employees can be punished with a year in prison and a tiny fine for passing on *American* military secrets. Foreigners and private Japanese citizens are free to find out whatever they can and tell whomever they like. Japan, whose close military ties with the United States require the exchange of sensitive information, is therefore a congenial place for Soviet agents. Recent spy scandals have prompted talk of stiffer penalties, but memories of prewar thought control may be too fresh to allow passage of really effective security laws.

The SDF is shrouded in gobbledygook and hobbled with restrictions mainly to soothe the Japanese, who are still largely pacifist. They have not forgotten the terrible fix their military leaders got them into and have been deeply suspicious of any signs of recidivism. When Japan's Defense Academy was reestablished, cadets could not appear in public without being pelted with rocks. Even today the SDF must recruit door to door to attract qualified high school graduates but still cannot fill its quotas. Because civilian SDF bureaucrats are only beginning to outgrow their status as second-class citizens, the Japan Defense Agency has never been able to hire topnotch men. It is still an agency rather than a full-fledged ministry because it would take a bruising legislative battle to make the change.

From the beginning the SDF has campaigned to be thought of as kindly neighborhood policemen rather than trained killers. Troops have regularly been used to clean up after typhoons or land slides, in what has been very effective PR for the military. It may have been too effective. In a 1979 poll only 38 percent of Japanese civilians thought that the main role of the SDF in the future would be to protect national security. The rest were split over disaster relief and other nonmilitary functions.[40]

Japanese leaders have thus faced strong political and emotional opposition to rearmament. The well-known Japanese "nuclear allergy" has given rise to three nonnuclear principles: Japan refuses to manufacture nuclear weapons, possess them, or allow them to be introduced into its territory. It has also passed laws prohibiting the export of arms. In the 1950s and 1960s Japan sold small quantities of sidearms and even several munitions plants to customers in Southeast Asia, but this trickle of exports was stopped by a blanket prohibition passed in 1976.

In the same year the government announced that "for the interim" it would not let military spending exceed 1 percent of GNP, and it has so far managed to stay within that limit.* The 1 percent figure was not the result of sober analysis of the country's defense needs; it is nothing more than an expression of what is politically acceptable in Japan today. Nor is there anything immutable or historic about it. In the 1950s Japan spent nearly 2 percent of GNP on arms, and this guideline can be changed, just as the ban on arms exports could be repealed.

Thus, proportionately, Japan spends only a third or a quarter of what the major NATO allies spend on arms. However, because its economy is so large, its defense spending, at $10 or $11 billion a year, is eighth in the world, after the United States, the Soviet Union, China, Britain, Saudi Arabia, France, and Germany. Japan now has about 270,000 men in arms with 155,000 in the army. It has 800 tanks, 650 armored personnel carriers, 50 frigates and destroyers, 40 minesweepers, and about 470 combat aircraft. It is a small force by industrial nation standards; but its new Japanese-designed tanks are said to be among the best in the world, and Japan is now licensed to build the F-15 Eagle, America's premier fighter. The defensive character of the force is underlined by the absence of a single bomber or any warships larger than a frigate. The SDF is supposed to repel small-scale attacks and hold off a major assault until America sends in

---

*Japan and the NATO countries use different methods to calculate military spending. According to the NATO formula, Japan actually spends 1.6 percent of its GNP on arms.

the marines. The 46,000 U.S. troops still stationed in Japan would come to its assistance and would also serve as a tripwire for American involvement should any of them be endangered.

For a generation Japan has been content with its limited army and the U.S. commitment to its defense. For some time after the war socialist-pacifist sentiment was so strong that many Japanese argued that armed attack against their country was an impossibility, because the only potential threats were from China and the Soviet Union. They reasoned that socialist nations were by nature peace-loving and thus inherently incapable of aggression. This fanciful notion began to fade with the Sino-Soviet split of the early 1960s. If there was still any life in it ten years later, the Chinese knocked it dead after they normalized relations with Japan in 1972; they urged their new friends to rearm, with nuclear weapons if necessary, in order to counter the Soviet menace.

In the decade since then Japan or, at any rate, its politicians have drifted steadily toward more open advocacy of increased military might. There are a number of reasons for this shift, not least of which are the decline of the United States and the growing strength of the Soviet Union. The U.S. Seventh Fleet used to dwarf the Russians in the Pacific, but no longer. At the height of the Vietnam War the United States had 200 warships in the Pacific; now, with the shift in concern toward the Persian Gulf and the Middle East, it has only 55.[41] In the meantime, the Soviets have built up their Pacific fleet from practically nothing to a very respectable force of 80 surface ships and 100 submarines.

Jimmy Carter hardly bolstered Japanese confidence in America. His 1977 pledge to withdraw U.S. troops from Korea sounded to the Japanese like the first step in abandoning Asia. When he reversed his decision a year later, it was seen as a sign of weakness and indecisiveness. On the campaign trail in April 1980 Prime Minister Masayoshi Ohira himself said, "[The United States is] not a superpower anymore. The days are gone when we were able to rely on America as a deterrent."[42] In a newspaper poll the same year 60 percent of the Japanese queried did not think the United States would come to the rescue if Japan were attacked.[43]

Lately the Soviets have given the Japanese some nasty scares. In 1976 the pilot of a MIG-25 defected to Japan by flying his plane right through its air defenses and landed at a civilian airport only a few minutes away from a major air self-defense force base. The military didn't learn about the MIG until it was on the ground in spite of the fact that it landed in far northern Japan, the most likely target for Soviet aggression and thus the best defended. The Japanese have since improved their air defenses and in 1981 "scrambled" 939 times to intercept unidentified aircraft—most of them Soviet.[44]

The 1979 invasion of Afghanistan sent shivers down Japanese spines and two years later, the Soviets reinforced the northern Habomai islands, which they had seized from Japan at the end of the war. The Habomais are so close to the Japanese mainland that Soviet soldiers on maneuvers can be seen with the naked eye. Though the weapons are mainly aimed at the Chinese, the Soviets have deployed SS-20 missiles in Siberia that could hit Japan.

Next to Koreans, Japanese dislike the Russians more than anyone else in the world and have never forgiven them for attacking Japan in the waning days of the Second World War. The Soviets, with American encouragement, violated a mutual nonaggression pact signed only a few years earlier—an act of treachery as despicable to the Japanese as the attack on Pearl Harbor is to Americans. If America can no longer be counted on to defend them from the villainous Russians, some Japanese leaders are inclined to take on the job themselves.

Another impetus for rearmament is Japan's resurgent pride as a nation. A few Japanese have never been happy with their dependence on the United States, and as it begins to dawn on the Japanese that they really are a major world power, they are increasingly tempted by the military trappings appropriate to their new status. The platform of the ruling Liberal Democratic party has long called for rearmament and revision of Article IX,[45] but until recently those planks were kept under the rug. Japan's newly elected prime minister, Yasuhiro Nakasone, is an avowed hawk and has spurred debate on both issues.

Finally, the United States is putting great pressure on Japan to rearm. America has been pleading with all its allies for help in holding the line against the Soviets, but it has been most impatient with Japan. American demands have been quietly encouraged by Japanese politicians who want to rearm but who prefer not to look too promilitary to their constituents. They can point to American intransigence as a justification for policies they know to be politically unpopular but that they privately favor.

Americans have pressed the Japanese on many issues. They often point out that the mutual security treaty requires the United States to fight any nation that attacks Japan but places no such obligation on Japan if the United States is attacked. They complain that Japan spends only about $100 per capita each year on defense—about the same as Portugal—while the United States spends $760 per capita. Furthermore, in 1960, when the security treaty with Japan was last revised, Japan's GNP was only 8 percent of that of the United States. Now it is 50 percent, and American officials talk angrily of the "free ride" Japan has been getting in defense.

Americans also insist on linking defense with trade problems, arguing that if Japan spent more money on arms, it would have less to use for boosting productivity and developing new technology. Access to U.S. markets, American officials have hinted, may depend on adequate Japanese defense spending. When the military budget goes before the Japanese parliament, American pressure can be so intense that some lawmakers have wondered whether the real threat comes from the United States or the Soviet Union.

I think that the United States is making a serious mistake in urging Japan to rearm. First of all, there is no assurance that a stronger SDF would ease America's defense burden. Japan lies at a point on the globe where the interests of the United States, China, and the Soviet Union converge. Any change in Japan's defense posture affects that of the other three. The Soviet Union has historically reacted to force with force, to threat with threat, and there can be no doubt in what direction Japan's increased firepower would be pointed. American conservatives may see Soviet forces as a wildly disproportionate reaction to the minimal threat of invasion from the West, but Russian leaders would inevitably see a rearmed Japan as a potential enemy and would churn out yet more ships and planes to keep it at bay. Another armed camp on Soviet borders is just as likely to make the Pacific more dangerous as it is to make it safer.

Increased defense spending is not, moreover, a solution to America's trade problems with Japan. Government contributions to Japan's commercial success are more organizational than financial, and enormous resources would have to be devoted to the SDF to affect Japanese industry materially. Also, as Japan rearms, there will be a push to amend the laws that prevent arms sales abroad. Exports would permit larger production runs, which would lower the unit price of military hardware to the SDF. It now costs Japan roughly twice as much to manufacture American equipment under license than it would to import the finished product.[46] Japanese arms makers have paid a steep price for their new skills and would love to test them in foreign markets. Feelings in Japan still run strongly against getting into the arms trade, but if that mood were to change, Japanese companies could scoop up orders for weapons just as they did for stereos and motorcycles.

"As long as their volume is small, we've got the edge," says McDonnell Douglas's Tokyo representative. "But if anyone ever said, 'You can export to anyone and everyone,' that industry would really blossom, and it would be like Hondas all over again."[47]

This is precisely the kind of problem the United States is already at a loss to solve. Furthermore, Japan is fertile soil for a cozy military-industrial complex. Business and government already cooperate admirably, and Japan's top military contractors are, without exception, mainstays of the civilian economy as well. In America the top ten arms producers get about 35 percent of all arms orders. In Japan only three companies get nearly 80 percent of the business.[48] The members of Japan's arms industry could probably expect even more government support for foreign sales than car- or steelmakers.

Another reason America should not press for rearmament is that Japan is still a largely pacifist country. The Japanese public—correctly, I believe—sees no realistic military threat from any quarter. All of Japan's neighbors are satisfied victors of the last war; no nation has even a frivolous claim on a single inch of its territory. The only conceivable threat would be a Soviet invasion, which can be imagined only as part of an all-out war between East and West. In such a war nuclear weapons would decide the issue, and Japan's SDF, no matter how well armed, would be a minor factor.

Anything like the doubling of the defense budget that Americans are clamoring for would have to be rammed down the taxpayer's throat. One Japanese author who favors rearmament is annoyed rather than pleased when he writes, "Article IX is to the Japanese constitution what the right to life, liberty and the pursuit of happiness is to the American constitution . . . it has become the very essence of the Japanese regime or polity."[49]

Although there has been a steady shift toward greater acceptance of the SDF, Japanese opinion polls consistently show an abhorrence of nuclear weapons and only the faintest desire for more conventional weapons. In a poll reported by the *Asahi* newspaper in March 1981, 71 percent reported that they did not want Japan to have nuclear weapons. Of the respondents, 22 percent wanted the government to spend more money on arms, 61 percent thought present arms spending was sufficient, and 7 percent wanted to abolish Japan's armed forces entirely.[50] Other polls have shown that about 70 percent of all Japanese are opposed to revising Article IX of the Constitution.[51]

Few countries in the world are so opposed to arms and warfare as Japan. In a world that spends somewhere between $500 and $600 billion every year preparing for war, genuinely peaceful nations need all the encouragement they can get.

Lurking in the background of the defense debate is the possibility of a resurgence of fanatical militarism. This is an issue on which well-informed people are strongly divided, but my feeling is that a new fascist Japan is only a remote possibility.

There is no question that Japan is restoring some of its prewar symbols; the debate centers on what these changes mean. For example, when I was a child, I don't think my school even owned a Japanese flag, and though we often sang the school song, we never sang the national anthem. Now, when children graduate from public school, each makes a ceremonial bow to the flag, and on special occasions they sing the national anthem. Alarmists see these changes as a dangerous step back toward nationalist indoctrination in the schools. It is hard for me to see it as anything more than healthy patriotism.

The resurrection in 1966 of Empire Day as National Foundation Day caused great controversy at the time because it, too, harked back to an era when the emperor was a Shinto god and all Japanese were taught to believe in the divine destiny of Japan. The new holiday prompted no such return to the past, and the fight to abandon it ended long ago. In 1979 the emperor got another boost when imperial eras were reinstated as Japan's official calendar. Under this system years are numbered not from the birth of Christ—an insignificant event for the Japanese—but according to where they fall in the reign of the emperor. Thus 1926, when the current emperor began his rule, was the first year of the Shōwa era, and 1975 was the fiftieth year of Shōwa. The present era will end when Hirohito dies and his son, the crown prince, assumes the throne and starts his own era.

However, there are more disturbing trends in Japan, which are perhaps best understood by contrasts with Germany, the other major militarist power of the Second World War. The young people of Germany are overwhelmingly convinced that Adolf Hitler was an evil man who led his nation astray. German authorities picked up where the Nuremberg trials left off and have to this day continued the prosecution of war criminals. In 1982, when a stridently anti-Nazi drama about Hitler youth was shown on German TV, it captured fifty percent of the available viewing audience.[52] It is against the law to promote National Socialism in any way, and Germany continues to make reparation payments to the state of Israel. No one seriously fears the resurgence of fascism.

In Japan it is increasingly fashionable to view Pearl Harbor as a measure to which the nation was forced by American economic warfare. For most Japanese, the Tokyo war crimes trial was a mystery at best and victor's justice as worst. When Nobusuke Kishi, a class A war criminal who served several years in prison for his role in the Tojo Cabinet was released and reentered politics, he was elected prime minister. The Japanese have certainly not tried to hunt down any war criminals the Americans might have missed. On the contrary, it was recently revealed that in 1978 fourteen class A war criminals, including Hideki Tojo, were secretly enshrined in Yasukuni as "martyrs."[53] That the deification was undertaken secretly shows the opposition it might have aroused, but as a *fait accompli* the ceremony was accepted with only a murmur of protest. Recently the local government of the municipality where Tojo was executed announced plans to build a monument to the wartime leader.[54]

For a few years after the war Japan payed reparations to a number of Asian nations, and administration of these payments was one of the Bank of Tokyo's main reasons for setting up branches in Asia. However, payments were never made in good grace, and Japan wriggled off the hook as quickly as possible.

Today it is hard to find much evidence of remorse or a sense of guilt for Japan's aggressive past. The Japanese movie industry, for which the war was at one time an untouchable subject, is now making films that emphasize the courage rather than the folly of the war in the Pacific. Even those Japanese who are staunchly opposed to rearmament seem far more interested in avoiding another horrible defeat than in atoning for past offenses.

Many of the Asian nations overrun during the Second World War have long wanted an official statement of Japanese remorse, but only

Korea and China seem to have ever gotten one. In 1965, when normal relations were esablished with Korea, the Japanese foreign minister expressed formal regret for "the unfortunate events of the past." In 1972, as a condition for normalizing relations, Prime Minister Tanaka had to sign a joint communiqué that said, in part, "The Japanese side is keenly aware of Japan's responsibility for causing enormous damage in the past to the Chinese people through war, and deeply reproaches itself."[55] The Japanese had, after all, killed more than 10 million Chinese between 1931 and 1945 in what can only be described as a purely aggressive war of conquest.

Far from being remorseful, a few Japanese are downright proud of Japan's military traditions. On a recent trip to a provincial town I found myself idly following the words of a song blaring from the loudspeaker of a sound truck. With a start I realized that the rousing tune was a World War II battle song about how noble it is to die for the fatherland. The truck belonged to the extremist Patriotic party, which advocates rapid rearmament and a tough stance toward the Soviets over the northern islands.

Japanese war veterans have always sung the old regimental battle songs when they got together for sake and nostalgia, and the "empty orchestra" tapes in many bars include a selection of war songs. However, it is only recently that political extremists have played them publicly and tried to use them to stir up nationalism. Any such attempt a decade or two ago would have been met with outrage and even violence. Today the Yasukuni Shrine has become a focus for promilitary politicking, and at the entrance to the grounds visitors are likely to be harangued by right-wing extremists armed with bullhorns.

These changes have come at the same time as the open shift in the defense debate from *whether* Japan should rearm to *how much* it should rearm. Bolder nationalists have begun to feel that the time has come to raise such previously taboo questions as whether Japan should have military conscription or even build nuclear weapons. All this has begun to worry people, both in Japan and abroad. Foreigners who have been in Japan long enough to see the long-term changes don't always like what they see. "It's little things," says an American whom I have known since childhood and who is still living in Japan. "It's hard to put your finger on it, but there's a shift in attitude that makes me uncomfortable."

A Japanese political scientist of admittedly leftist leanings once talked to me about Japan's future. "Democracy," he said, "has shallow roots here. It never made any real headway before the war, and what we have now was handed to us by the Americans. It's not something the Japanese had to fight for, and I don't think they value it enough." I asked him if he thought that meant Japan could easily give up democracy.

"Today's Japanese," he said, "first learned they were living in a 'democracy' when they got the 1947 Constitution from the Americans. Ever since then Japan has been getting richer and richer, and most people think, 'Hey, this democracy is all right. I can afford a car and a trip to Hawaii.' They think democracy has more to do with economic prosperity than with anything like representative government or rule by the people. That's why I'm worried by the world recession. If things get bad in Japan, a lot of people would figure that democracy had let them down and would be willing to try something else."

The "something else" this man fears is militant nationalism. He thinks there is still enough follow-the-leader spirit in Japan for the country to follow a dictator. He is not the only Japanese I know who worries about militarism, but ironically, such talk reassures me as much as it disturbs me. I think Japan is becoming increasingly libertarian; civilian rule is firmly entrenched, and the Japanese desire for peace remains strong. I think we can count on the extreme watchfulness of people like my leftist friend to keep Japan from careering down the road to fascism. I believe the nation no longer has the stomach for aggressive war.

Right-wing fanaticism is also discredited by the company it keeps. Some of its firmest supporters are the leaders of organized crime, who claim to be the only Japanese to remain true to samurai values. This close association between gangsters and ultraconservative politicians is perhaps unique to Japan and hardly helps win broad support for increased arms spending.

Nevertheless, there are a few people besides gangsters who agree with novelist Yukio Mishima's complaint that "the Japanese people began to decline in morality in 1876 with the decree abolishing the wearing of swords for men."[56] Japan's xenophobia, race consciousness, and strong group orientation all make it more vulnerable than more heterogeneous and cosmopolitan societies to right-wing extremism. A strong emphasis on weapons and national defense can only heighten this vulnerability.

However, what I think would be the greatest tragedy of full rearmament is not what it might make Japan do but what it could prevent Japan from doing. With one foot in Asia and the other in the West, Japan could be a regional leader, a spokesman for Asia. That it is not is due to Japan's selfish insularity, its warlike past, and America's postwar dominance in the area. As America lowers its profile, Asian nations are looking for new leadership. Japan could provide that leadership, but only if it overcomes its preoccupation with strictly national concerns, lays to rest the ghosts of the Second World War, and wins the trust of its neighbors. None of these conditions will be easily met. If Japan becomes a military power, they may never be met.

Just how carefully Japan must manage its affairs was highlighted by the sharp international controversy that arose over a proposed revision of high school textbooks. In the summer of 1982 the Japanese Ministry of Education released advance copies of a newly approved social studies text that had clearly been given a nationalist slant. It had kind words for the authoritarian prewar Constitution, which defined the citizen's primary duty as devotion to the emperor, and revived the prewar custom of using special honorific language even when referring to emperors of the distant past.

What caused the greatest flap, however, was a revised account of the Second World War. Japanese atrocities were glossed over, and all references to the Rape of Nanking were removed. What had previously been called an aggressive attack on China became an advance into China. Korean resistance to Japanese colonization was downplayed, and passages referring to the forced conscription of Koreans to work in Japanese mines were dropped.

Reaction to the new text was immediate. The Japanese Teachers' Union accused the Ministry of Education of rewriting history, and in an editorial that was representative of most of the Japanese press, the influential *Asahi* asked, "Do they think that by expunging such words as 'aggression' from the textbooks, that the historical fact of aggression will fade away? This is just like the double-talk forced upon us during the war, when Americans were dogs, Englishmen were devils, and a retreat was 'a successful shift in our positions.'"[57]

But it was abroad that reactions were most spectacular. North and South Korea were united on a foreign policy issue for perhaps the first time in thirty-five years, and both made official protests to the Japanese government. For days on end the textbook controversy was front-page news in the South, and protesters took to the streets to denounce Japan. Anonymous callers threatened to blow up the Japanese consulate in Pusan, and a few days later its windows were smashed. Taxi drivers in major cities put signs in their windshields saying they would not pick up Japanese passengers, and stores posted warnings that Japanese customers would not be served. Newspapers ran grisly photos showing Japanese wartime atrocities, and the Foreign Ministry vowed that getting the new texts withdrawn would be top priority in relations with Japan. A coalition of religious groups announced that for the first time it would conduct a memorial service to commemorate the slaughter of Koreans after the Tokyo earthquake of 1923.

In China the new textbooks were excoriated with official vigor, and an invitation to the Japanese minister of education to visit Peking was canceled. The *People's Daily* claimed that the Chinese masses had smashed Japanese militarism once already and boasted that if provoked, they would do it again.[58] It, too, ran pictures—of corpses piled high during the Rape of Nanking.

Hong Kong shops and taxi drivers refused to serve Japanese customers, the Vietnam News Agency blasted Japan for reviving fascism, and the text revisions were denounced by Singaporean legislators. Throughout Asia the cry went up against Japanese militarism.

The controversy raged for months. Some Japanese Cabinet ministers and party leaders only added fuel to the fire by trying to brush off foreign protests as intervention in Japan's domestic affairs. The Foreign Ministry ruled that the protests were not out of line and accused the Ministry of Education of being high-handed and arrogant. The affair was not resolved until Prime Minister Suzuki, during a trip to China that was nearly canceled on account of the row, promised that the offending passages would be corrected.

Cynics have argued that the regional outburst over the texts may not have been all it appeared to be. They point out that American pressure on Japan to rearm has been so strong that some Asian leaders are privately resigned to the inevitable. The public outrage may have been orchestrated, in part, to embarrass the Japanese and soften them up for increased requests for aid.

Nevertheless, the violence of the popular reaction to Japan's attempt to sanitize the past is an indicator of how Asians might react if their neighbor were to rearm seriously. A courtesy call by the Japanese flotilla on Singapore, which many residents still recall was renamed Shōnan during the Japanese occupation, would not be taken as a gesture of neighborly diplomacy. Some Asian fears may be overdrawn, but Japan, as a former imperialist power and present economic colossus, is not trusted in the region.

The textbook controversy throws a harsh light on an important decision. Japan faces a choice. It can submit to the wishes of the United States and build forces capable of waging war. Its gunboats would then police the sea-lanes of Asia and play games of chicken with Soviet cruisers. Its neighbors, who have not forgotten the Greater East Asia Co-Prosperity Sphere, would tremble at the thought of a new, militarist Japan and treat it with a combination of deference and dread. They themselves would probably feel compelled to spend more money on arms. Japan could conduct an independent foreign policy but would find itself even more politically isolated in Asia than it is now. It would be tempted once more to be the lone wolf in world affairs. Its assimilation into the Asian community would be slowed, and it would lose all hope of a position of trust and leadership.

Its other choice is to rearm just enough to get the Americans off its back and to go on performing economic miracles. Japan has come the closest of any nation in the world to solving the problems of crime, unemployment, inflation, and poverty. With these domestic problems under control, it could devote its energies to the world around it. Japanese wealth and goodwill could be a powerful force for peace and development. An independent, lightly armed Japan could conduct a foreign policy that embraced interests far beyond its own. As it gently distanced itself from strictly American interests, its heightened credibility could allow it to act as an honest broker in international conflicts.

Prime Minister Nakasone seems to be trying to give his country just such an outward-looking foreign policy. Though he is urging rearmament at a quicker pace than the Japanese or their neighbors might like, he also appears to be genuinely concerned about winning the trust and esteem of the region.

If the Japanese can be persuaded to work at solving some of the world's problems rather than concentrating on their own narrow concerns of resources and markets, they could do a great deal of good. The "wet" Japanese pride themselves on their sensitivity and their concern for the feelings of others. Could they not learn to put some of this abundant sensitivity to work in some of the many conflict-torn corners of the earth?

Until the Japanese feel at home in the world, they will be too inward-looking and self-conscious to embrace it. Until they can see the prosperity of the planet as something more than an economic indicator for potential export sales, they will keep on brooding about what it means to be a homogeneous people on an island nation. In terms of the contribution they could make to peace and progress, they will remain, as one scholar puts it, "the world's least developed human resource."[59]

It may be a difficult transition from economic animal to peacemaker, but Japan has the material resources to play a noble role in international affairs if it can only marshal the spiritual resources. Playing the gendarme of Asia so that America can rattle more sabers in Europe and the Middle East will do nothing to broaden Japan's interests or make it more worthy of its neighbors' trust.

Ever since Japan was hauled into the modern world by impatient Americans, it has acted alone. The sense of group solidarity that has bound the Japanese to each other has shut out the barbarian *gaijin*. Japan has never willingly thrown in its lot with another country or pretended that its interests could coincide with those of a foreign power. Its objectives have been its own, and it has gained them—or lost them—alone.

Japanese have never stood shoulder to shoulder with another people and bled for the same cause. For nations to become allies they must have common goals that transcend nationalism; no Japanese ever gave his life to make the world safe for democracy, to rid the world of tyranny, to fight communism, or even to advance the cause of fascism. The only causes for which Japanese soldiers ever died were the greatness of Japan and the glory of the emperor. During the Second World War Germany and Japan shared common enemies but did not fight for common goals. British spies wasted a lot of time looking for a common German-Japanese war strategy that did not exist.

Japan's postwar relations with the United States approach the closeness of an alliance, but American friendship was forced upon a supine Japan and ran counter to its nature. On only one occasion has modern Japan voluntarily entered into a real alliance with another power. That was in 1902, when it signed a mutual defense pact with Britain. It was under cover of this agreement that Japan attacked Russia in 1904.

Japan is, of course, slowly joining the human race. Its urgent need to "internationalize" has become a common theme in debates about its future. Japanese insularity is solemnly condemned by intellectuals, editorial writers, and businessmen. There is now a well-established group of sophisticated Japanese who understand that Japan is a great power and can no longer pursue its own narrow interests as if it were an underdeveloped country. Earlier I quoted a commentator who admits that the Japanese do not think of foreigners as fully human.[60] In the same article he warns, "We must change, and change quickly, because there's not much time left."[61]

Some Japanese are changing. Kiyoshi Nasu, who was born in America and was for years a U.S. correspondent for the *Mainichi* newspaper, has fully understood the dangers of Japan's lingering xenophobia. At one time he tried to launch a campaign to build a Statue of Peace in San Francisco Bay, as a sister to the Statue of Liberty in New York Harbor. The French, he argued, celebrated 100 years of America by building a memorial to one of the great principles on which the nation was founded. What could be more fitting, he asked, than for the nation that is remembered for Pearl Harbor to build a Statue of Peace to celebrate America's 200th birthday?[62] Nasu's idea never got the support it needed, but it reflects a new generosity in the thinking of some Japanese.

Kōnosuke Matsushita had similarly outward-looking goals for the PHP Institute, which he founded immediately after the war. Peace, happiness, and prosperity for mankind are the goals of the institute, which encourages research and publications "to improve the quality of life worldwide."[63] The institute's English-language magazine, *PHP*, is a forum for opinion on how Japan can best serve the world.

As Japanese companies increase their presence abroad, they have begun to search for ways to build bridges to the West. Some of the larger companies have endowed chairs in Japanese studies at prestigious universities. The Nissan Motor Company, for example, recently announced a $3 million grant to Oxford University for the establishment of an institute of Japanese studies.

Older Japanese have not forgotten America's generosity after the war. "We all expected the American occupation soldiers to live off the land the way we did in China," a retired businessman once told me. "To our surprise, they not only brought food for themselves, they brought food for us as well." As a public school student in Japan I drank many gallons of powdered milk that came from America. All my classmates knew where it came from, too. All told, America spent more than $2 billion putting the Japanese economy back on its feet.

It was in a spirit of remembrance for America's past generosity that a group of Japanese banks recently formed a consortium to guarantee repayment of a bond issue that the city of Detroit was struggling to raise. It was a gesture of friendship toward a city that has been blighted by imported automobiles, but Americans are not gracious recipients of foreign aid. The people of Detroit seem to have resented the Japanese gesture as much as they benefited from it.

Perhaps they were better disposed toward the decision by Japan's largest brokerage house, Nomura Securities, to buy 30,000 shares of General Motors stock for its mutual fund. The president of Nomura Securities International, a longtime booster of U.S.-Japan relations, explained that "if Japanese people become shareholders of General Motors and if American people become shareholders of Toyota, hopefully that will soften the conflict of trade between our two countries."[64]

There is an increasing number of Japanese with a broad perspective on the world, but they continue to be exceptional. Many of Japan's leaders still operate according to outmoded assumptions about its fragility that grew out of the horror and misery of war. Just as Israel's hard-line leaders trade on the Holocaust to justify their excesses, Japan's leaders have pursued their selfish policies with the conviction that their nation's survival was at stake. Their minds are still a prisoner of the hunger mentality of the past; they are constantly haunted by their dependence on foreign resources. Many have only now begun to realize that Japan is no longer in desperate straits. It can open its markets without being swamped by imports and it can afford to pause from the single-minded pursuit of its own interests to consider the interests of others. It can hardly afford not to.

Nevertheless, what still guides its relations with America and the rest of the world is an abiding sense of isolation, a conviction that Japan is misunderstood and can only be misunderstood. "The fundamental character of international interchange," writes a Japanese scholar, "lies in a cruel and merciless collision of mutually suspicious and distrustful cultures."[65] Could an American or an Italian or even a Russian have written those words? Those who go out into the world armed with suspicion and distrust, expecting cruelty and merciless-ness, are likely to find what they are looking for.

In its search for a constructive role in world affairs Japan needs all the help it can get. No nation on earth has a greater influence on Japan than the United States. We should be encouraging the builders of the Statue of Peace, the publishers of *PHP*, the guarantors of De-troit debt—not the advocates of militarism.

CHAPTER ELEVEN

LOOKING AHEAD: LESSONS FOR AMERICA

Not long ago, when I was working in New York, I paid a visit to one of my old customers, Hayashi-san. After a pleasant chat he introduced me to Tanabe-san, an agreeable fellow in his mid-twenties, fresh from Tokyo head office. We exchanged business cards, and I went on my way.

A few days later I was working late in the office and found I needed a trifling piece of information about Hayashi-san's company. It was a detail I didn't want to bother him with, but it was a perfect excuse to call the junior man, Tanabe. To my surprise, Hayashi-san picked up the phone; Tanabe had gone home. Sometime later I was working on a deal with Tanabe and realized, a few minutes after five o'clock, that I had forgotten to explain something to him. This time it was a secretary who told me Tanabe had left for the day.

The next time I saw Hayashi-san, I kidded him about his benevolent new policy of sending the men home at five. "Are you talking about Tanabe?" he asked. "I just can't seem to get through to that boy. He's polite and works hard, but he goes home at five o'clock. I hear that head office has quite a few youngsters like him these days. Things have sure changed since I joined the company."

Hayashi is twenty-five years older than Tanabe. He grew up through the misery and poverty of the postwar period and began his career in the late 1950s. He is the classic Japanese workaholic. For him, work and company come first; he is one of the men who built the miracle. Tanabe is a man of a different era. He has never been hungry in his life and has always been able to take prosperity for granted. Hayashi and Tanabe stand on opposite sides of one of the widest generation gaps in the world.

Japan has developed so quickly from bombed-out wilderness to industrial giant that the people who have lived through both eras are still trying to catch up with the changes. While Tanabe was growing up, per capita GNP grew tenfold in real terms, and Japan surged into prominence as a genuine threat to American economic supremacy. The men and women now entering the work force are the heirs to a new Japan. It was Hayashi's generation that built the new Japan, but it is their children—Tanabe's generation—whose lives have been changed by it.

Many older Japanese have not shaken off their postwar habits of hard work and devotion to the group, but younger Japanese are pursuing goals that are more personal and divergent. Executives now find they must compete with home, family, hobbies, and vacation time for the loyalty of their employees, as Japanese lose their eagerness to make work the center of their lives. The nation now has other goals besides sheer GNP growth, and in an era of increasing disagreement over social alternatives "notorious MITI" can no longer call the shots. Japan is still a nation of remarkable coherence and unity of purpose, but diversity is on the march.

The management techniques that motivated the postwar Japanese are far from changing the face of business around the world; they are already on the wane even in Japan. For solutions to American problems we will have to look elsewhere for inspiration—perhaps to our own traditions, to the values that shaped America's own achievements.

Japanese commentators—at least those of an age to be publishing their views—are nearly unanimous in decrying the flabby attitude of young Japanese toward work. They moan about the decline in "fighting spirit" and the absence of guts and desire. They fret about what all this means for the future of Japan. What they are really complaining about, whether they know it or not, is the growing reluctance of young Japanese to buy into a system that glorifies job and company as the most important things in life.

This change in attitude is convincingly analyzed by Tamotsu Sengoku, head of the Japan Youth Research Center. Like Shichihei Yamamoto (see Chapter 3, page 72), he sees the strength of Japanese companies in the informal, emotional, dripping "wet" group structure that parallels the formal corporate structure. He warns that without these absorbing group ties, companies will lose their Japanese dynamism:

> [Today's young workers] are clearly members of the corporation but they are not members of the informal group—the very group that has made the Japanese corporation unique. This informal group structure has played such a decisive role in motivating Japanese workers that it can be called the very essence of Japanese management. It explains why after-hours QC conferences and the refusal to take paid vacation have been voluntary, not required behavior. Younger workers are trying to escape from the constraints of this group dynamic; they are willing to meet only the explicit requirements of the formal organization—and then just enough to keep their jobs. . . .
>
> What we are seeing is a white-collar revolution; the Japanese corporation is turning into an American-style corporation.[1]

For many younger Japanese, a job is simply a job. They are opting out of Yamamoto's virtual blood-kin group. They have their own lives to live and are not interested in joining the intense fellowship of the workplace. Sengoku is worried that Japanese are becoming increasingly "dry" and less concerned about camaraderie and human relations.

Otsukiai, the very lifeblood of corporate solidarity, is one of the first casualties when loyalty goes into decline. One writer marvels that some new workers actually have the gall to ask the boss point-blank if an after-hours drink is an obligatory part of the job.[2] The men who built the miracle would have leapt at the chance to cozy up to the boss over a few drinks. For them, to spurn the offer of *otsukiai* is to profane the sacred rites.

Sengoku has little sympathy for the young: "The fact that they don't care about human relations or the wishes of others shows that their basic psychological needs are different from ours. When it gets to that point, we can only conclude that they are no longer Japanese."[3] These are harsh words. But they show how deeply some Japanese resent the matter-of-fact coolness of the young.

The zeal for work has been closely tied to zeal for the group, and as one American scholar points out, "the willingness of the Japanese to subordinate the desires of the individual to those of the group is markedly weakening as generations come on the scene who have no experience of poverty, war and occupation."[4] Older Japanese are afraid that if youngsters lose their devotion to the company, they will pursue their own limited interests and productivity will suffer. One personnel manager warns that "establishing the loyalty of younger employees is the crucial challenge for Japanese companies in the 1980s."[5]

Companies may suffer in spectacular new ways as group ties weaken. In 1982 two Japanese drug manufacturers, Green Cross and Nippon Chemiphar, were punished for faking the clinical data necessary to get new products approved. In both cases ex-employees blew the whistle on their former colleagues.[6] The fact that Yamamoto calls anyone who betrays the group "a great criminal" (see Chapter 3, page 82) doesn't seem to have stopped them. This is strange new behavior in a country where a former politician's chauffeur kills himself rather than testify against the boss and where the judge in a bribery case officially recognizes that loyalty to the group can be a powerful motive for breaking the law.

Not only are young Japanese losing their taste for blind loyalty, but companies are less able to reward them for it. As times change, the hallowed institutions of lifetime employment and automatic promotions are beginning to crumble. Back when the economy was growing in leaps and bounds, excess workers could always be shifted to another division. When the population was young, older men could march steadily toward the top without overbalancing the corporate structure. Now, as Japan's population ages and as GNP growth slows, companies are looking for ways to ease out redundant workers and promote on merit rather than seniority.

Not even the titans of Japanese industry can escape the new mood. Recently, workers at the Nissan Motor Company became so uneasy about the growing number of robots on the assembly line that they began to lose confidence in the lifetime employment system. In March

1983, in what some Japanese analysts called a new chapter in labor relations, Nissan put into writing what had until then been an informal agreement: No workers will lose their jobs to robots.[7] Informal agreements are no longer enough for some unions; they want the company to commit itself on paper.

Some first-tier managers are trying to preserve the traditional corporate family structure by hiring fewer "regular" employees. The elite will still enjoy job security and regular promotions, but they will be vastly outnumbered by subcontractors, "temporary" employees, women, and other lesser mortals.

Some of the most radical changes in Japanese society could be brought about by a rapidly aging population. Today there are 8.5 active workers for every retired person, whereas the ratio is 5.5 to 1 in the other industrialized nations. This high proportion of workers has sharpened Japan's competitiveness, but the ratio is dropping quickly. Japan's Economic Planning Agency predicts that because of rapid increases in life expectancy, there will be only 2.5 workers for each retiree by the year 2000, a figure that is likely to be the lowest in the world.[8] This shift to a top-heavy population will wreak havoc on strict seniority systems and will upset the political balance. Powerful blocs of elderly Japanese are likely to demand changes in Japan's stingy retirement system just when the shrinking pool of active workers is least able to pay for them.

For now, as the prospects and even the psychological appeal of *marugakae* ("total embrace") diminish, more Japanese are flirting with the unthinkable: They are leaving the old-line companies to change jobs, go into business for themselves, or opt out of the rat race entirely. A new word has appeared for those who take the plunge: *datsusara*. Literally it means "to escape from the world of the salaried man." A decade or two ago it would have meant failure; now it has an air of boldness and adventure.

Some of the new start-up ventures have little in common with the big-name companies. A startling example is Namco, a producer of video games. Its president is not interested in hiring the good corporation men who march off the Tōdai assembly line. Instead, he advertises for "reformed juvenile delinquents and C students," whom he is convinced are more likely to think creatively. He could be right; one of the C students he hired was Tōru Iwatani, the inventor of Pac-Man.[9]

The Japanese corporation is not changing in a vacuum. Society as a whole is losing some of its discipline and predictability, and even prestigious Tōdai has learned it must bend with the times. Until a few years ago the university needed to accept only as many students as it had places since everyone who was accepted was sure to come. Now 4, 5, or even 6 percent of the men and women for whom the pearly gates are opened have better things to do than attend Tōdai. That even a few Japanese—for whatever reasons—should turn up their noses at the sure prospect of a main-line career shows that young people are discovering new goals and new routes to success.

Compared to their parents' generation, Japanese youngsters are downright disorderly. Though adult crime rates have stayed low, juvenile arrests have increased steadily, and in 1981 they surpassed adult arrests for the first time.[10] On a recent trip to Japan I was astonished to hear that rowdy junior high school kids have taken to beating up their teachers. When I attended Japanese schools, it took suicidal bravery to let fly even a smart-alecky remark; we never would have dreamed of punching out *sensei*. Still, in 1981, 943 teachers were attacked by their students, nearly double the number from the year before.[11] This may be only mild misbehavior by American standards, but it is a shocking statistic for a nation that has so respected authority and hierarchy. To lash out at the figure that most clearly embodies those values is to reject the very basis of Japanese society.

Teachers are not the only targets of violence. In 1980 there were 1,025 cases of children laying hands on their parents, likewise a dreadful new development for the Japanese. Significantly, the most frequent victim is the "education mom,"[12] as children begin to snap under the strain of examination hell. Fathers are more dangerous prey. One, who spent three months sleeping in his car because he was afraid to come home, finally killed his son.[13] Some Japanese speculate that children are unruly because their fathers spend so much time on the job and in *otsukiai* and that things will change as Japanese men work less and spend more time with their families.

Nevertheless, if having Dad around the house is good for the kids, it may not be good for the marriage. In a recent survey of what wives thought would happen if their husbands worked shorter hours and took more vacation, the typical response was "if my husband didn't work as much, he'd loll around the house all day, make more work for me, and be a pest. If he didn't go into the office, he'd just goof off since he doesn't know how to do anything else. He'd get lazy and develop bad habits."[14] Another study showed that the more meals a Japanese businessman ate at home, the more dissatisfied with his wife he was likely to be.[15] Domestic relations are going to have to change to keep up with new work patterns. Until Japanese men stop treating women as if they were servants, their wives will want them underfoot as little as possible.

One Japanese woman I know foresees another problem. She points out that modern conveniences are freeing women from the worst drudgery of housekeeping and that many are cultivating much broader interests than their husbands are. "What are couples going to talk about when the man finally retires?" she asks. "He may know everything there is to know about aluminum siding but nothing about anything else. Who's going to want to live with a man like that? Japanese men had better watch out or their wives are going to leave them out of sheer boredom."

Whether or not wives start running out on their husbands, Japan is certainly in for more dizzying changes. Like those of the recent past, they will stem from one momentous fact, namely, that Japan has become an advanced, industrial nation. This remarkable achievement raises awkward questions about the future.

For thirty-five years Japan had a single, unifying goal: *oitsuke, oikose* ("catch up and pass [the West]"). Probably no other nation on earth has ever set out on a national project—GNP growth—and stuck to it as doggedly as the postwar Japanese. For decades the prospect of a standard of living that matched the West was the pillar of flame that led to the promised land. Pollution scares forced a short detour, but as soon as environmental abuses were corrected, the Japanese got right back on course. Now, clearly, Japan has won the race for economic growth, and more and more Japanese are beginning to wonder what comes next.

There are no easy answers. A former vice-minister of MITI puts it this way: "Japan's economy was like a train on a perfectly straight track. You didn't have to be a genius to drive that train. But the era when there were no crossroads is over. Now we are going to enter a difficult period."[16] Japan has followed the Western nations right into their own camp. Imitation is no longer the answer; from now on Japan must make choices.

As Japan loses its cultural and economic role models, it loses national consensus. The authors of a recent Hudson Institute report point out that "the goals of Japanese society on a whole are becoming much more heterogeneous compared to an era when catching up to the West in terms of per capita income dominated all other goals."[17]

This means that it has become harder for MITI and the other planning agencies to do their job. Industrial policy is most effective when all participants in the economy agree on the same basic goals. Now that Japan faces a variety of social alternatives, industry is less united in following MITI's directives. Also, as Japan continues to loosen its trade, licensing, and financial regulations, government planners are losing statutory power over the economy. In the past jawboning could always be backed up by enforcing the rules; now there are fewer rules to enforce.

Older Japanese seem to long for the old days, when goals were clear and work came first. They are not entirely comfortable in the new Japan. They are unable to accept its promise of increased freedom and leisure; instead, they are transfixed by the thought of once more falling behind.

As one professor points out, ever since the war the entire nation has been goaded on to ever-increasing effort by the conviction that Japan was a pitiful, backward country. "Now that people no longer think they are far behind," he writes, "what will it take to drive and motivate them? What new goals can we find to fill the vacuum?"[18] It doesn't seem to have occurred to him that some Japanese may be tired of being driven and motivated.

Another man of the old school complains: "It seems to me that the days of workaholism are a thing of the past. We congratulate ourselves for the time being on not having caught the 'British disease' or the 'American disease,' but the day may not be far off when we suddenly find that our productivity and absenteeism rates are just as bad as theirs."[19]

Japanese can be absurdly alarmist when it comes to sniffing out the first symptoms of the dread "American disease." One *sensei* writes that for ten years he has regularly taken the bullet express train between Nagoya and Tokyo, a distance of more than 150 miles. A decade ago, if the train arrived even three minutes late, the conductor would get on the PA system and apologize three times for the delay. Now the train has to be ten minutes late for the conductor to apologize even once. The writer admits that trains are no more likely to be late than they were ten years ago; the only difference is in how often the conductor apologizes. Still, he is worried: "Doesn't this suggest that even if only gradually the spirit of workmanship is breaking down in our country, too?"[20]

Why are the Japanese in such a dither about the "British disease" and creeping Americanization? Why are they so disturbed by the changes they see in new generations?

Partly it is simple nostalgia for the values of the past. The Japanese who built the miracle have lived their lives as if they were constantly skirting the abyss. It is not always easy for them to understand why younger Japanese have lost the hunger mentality and the crisis consciousness. Middle-aged Japanese shake their heads in wonder at the luxuries their children take for granted. Americans like to moralize about how tough things were during the Depression, but they are no match for the Japanese who lived through the war. The Japanese suffered terribly and are quick to say so when they feel their children are not manifestly grateful for the abundance of the present. I suspect there is more than just a touch of envy in their moralizing.

Older Japanese are also worried because they think succeeding generations are losing the very qualities that built Japan's greatness. The time may not be far off when Japanese workers—no less than Western workers—will feel like fools singing the company song. Younger Japanese may prefer to go their own way rather than spend their free time warbling to each other in *karaoke* bars. They may decide that Japan is now rich enough to permit a little rest and recreation; they may decide to take three weeks of annual leave instead of three days. And when they do, they may not want to spend their vacation at the company beach house.

I think there is no question that this is the direction in which Japan is moving. It is a natural consequence of prosperity that Japanese should welcome rather than worry about. It's hard to maintain a hunger mentality when there is no more hunger or a crisis consciousness when the crisis has passed. A decade or more ago farsighted MITI men were writing papers on the future of postindustrial Japan, in which they wondered whether people would learn how to use their increasing free time. Younger Japanese seem to be learning nicely.

Still, as we noted in an earlier chapter, Japan is only taking its first steps toward learning how to relax and enjoy life. It is hardly in danger of sinking into the self-indulgent morass that the alarmists see just over the horizon. Succeeding generations of Japanese will lead more balanced lives than their elders, but they will continue to work hard. They may not be made of the stuff that made the miracle, but they will not have to be. It will not take the same dedication to stay with the leaders as it did to catch up with them.

Forward-looking Japanese companies are already beginning to wonder whether management style should change to accommodate new attitudes. "It all boils down to this," a middle-aged trading company executive once told me. "Younger Japanese don't want to work as hard as we did. Does that mean that if they don't do as much for the company, the company shouldn't do as much for them? I don't know."

Japanese are coming to America to find out. A young man sent by his firm to attend Stanford Business School was asked by the *Wall Street Journal* why he was studying American management just when Americans were scrambling to learn Japanese management. He explained that workers in Japan were increasingly inclined to work less and play more. He added that this was a new problem in Japan but an old one in America, and he hoped to learn how American companies had dealt with it.[21]

Not all Japanese, therefore, are fighting the inevitable. They realize that workers will be less willing to slaughter their individuality, to sacrifice for the company and for the nation. A few managers are already preparing for the future, perhaps even looking forward to it.

Ultimately those Japanese who talk as if group loyalty and the hunger mentality must survive intact for Japan to prosper are underestimating their own powers. Their lingering fears are just another version of the conviction that the Japanese are a unique people, who depend on their uniqueness for their very existence. Japan has flourished in spite of tremendous upheaval and social change; even if a few of its traditional qualities begin to disappear, others will arise to take their place.

What, then, can we learn from the Japanese? I have argued that Japan was propelled into prominence by a unique combination of cultural and historical factors that make it a very difficult place in which to search for easy answers. I have also suggested that some of these factors have begun to fade in importance and that the management and industrial strategies that have guided Japan since the war are likely to lose their effectiveness within Japan, let alone solve problems elsewhere.

Nevertheless, the ingredients to Japan's tremendous successes are not all culture, history, and national character. Many are tangible, practical considerations that are eminently portable from one economy to another. They are not, on the other hand, particularly Japanese.

At the most obvious level, Japanese have discovered how to build some things better than we do. On average, American workers are still the most productive in the world, but in a few industries, notably steel and automobiles, the Japanese clearly surpass us. In terms of plant layout, inventory control, and production engineering, Japan is second to none. In these areas, what works there will work just as well in America if American companies and unions have the will to adopt new techniques.

In the "softer" areas of management much of Japan's success is due to clear thinking and sensible behavior that is hardly unique to Japan but to which many Japanese companies have stuck with admirable consistency. In a recent book Thomas Peters and Robert Waterman have studied America's best-run companies with an eye for the traits that have made them great. [22] Not surprisingly they have found that America's best companies have a lot in common not only with each other but also with the best Japanese companies: an almost obsessive concern for quality rather than cost, unflagging eagerness to satisfy the customer, simple procedures, and a task force rather than a bureaucratic approach to problem solving. They also have found that America's best companies are not those that have diversified but those that have, like Japanese companies, concentrated on the business they know best.

Of equal importance is a solid personnel policy. Good American managers fashion a corporate culture that stimulates "unusual effort on the part of apparently ordinary employees."[23] Workers who are treated like adults, made to feel important, and rewarded for achievement are much more likely to make the extra effort that sets a company apart from its competitors.

There is nothing especially Japanese about any of this. What the best companies—Japanese, American, or any other—have in common is a commitment to the basic rules of good business. There is no deep mystery about what has made IBM, Procter & Gamble, 3M, and Delta Airlines successful. Peters and Waterman don't pretend that there is; they describe the components of management success in a section of their book titled "Back to Basics." As one reviewer says of their list of precepts, "in our heart of hearts we've known all along that that's the way to do things."[24]

All nations have more in common with each other than they have differences. It is only at the margin that culture makes a person Japanese, Turkish, or Italian rather than American. So it is with business culture. It is only at the margin that Japanese management is genuinely Japanese, and there its impact has been substantial; but what is genuinely Japanese may have no place in America.

Stripped to its essentials, the best Japanese management is simply good management: common sense, human relations, and doing a few things well. There is nothing revolutionary about doing the simple things right; there is nothing easy about it either. Robert Hayes of Harvard writes that the way for America to regain the competitive edge against Japan is "by always putting our best resources and talent to work doing the basic things a little better, every day, over a long period of time. It is that simple—and that difficult."[25] If Japanese companies can remind Americans of what, in our heart of hearts, we have always known, then they will have taught us a valuable lesson indeed.

Of course, there are differences between the best American and Japanese companies. Americans are aggressively informal, encourage argument and contradiction,[26] and may prize innovation so highly that it is risky for employees not to innovate.[27] Furthermore, although the best American companies encourage loyalty and cohesiveness, they are very careful to reward individuals and to treat them as standouts in their own right.[28]

Americans can be good team players, but they look for personal rewards as well. As one Japanese writer puts it, "The aggressive American executive thinks of the corporation as an arena in which he can develop his own powers, while the Japanese is dependent on the organization and finds personal success only in the success of the company."[29] This may overstate the contrast, but it is true that a satisfied American worker will say that he loves his job, not that he loves his company.

Where good Japanese management parts company with good American management is the point at which it begins to invade a worker's life to a degree Americans would find intolerable. Most Americans would be wearied by the endless *otsukiai* that the Japanese thrive on. They would feel smothered by the "total embrace" that

Japanese find fulfilling. They wouldn't stand for a supervisor who tried to supervise their personal lives.

Many Japanese have been happy to let the company arrange their weekends, their hobbies, their vacations, their marriages—in short, their lives. Americans have a tough core of individualism that refuses to hand over such broad control. Americans are diverse, have competing loyalties, cherish their autonomy, and are suspicious of authority. This makes them not only an unruly, undisciplined people but an independent, self-reliant, and resourceful people as well.

They can also make mistakes. The nation as a whole has coasted for too long on its earlier achievements and is now paying the price for complacency. Some American managers have been too shortsighted, too eager to reap quick profits rather than lay the groundwork for future returns. Americans have failed to enter world markets as aggressively as they should have. Content to play in their own huge backyard, U.S. companies have missed opportunities abroad.

But it may have been our greatest error to think that management was a precise science that could be mechanically applied. Some American executives have been led astray by the belief that a company's divisions could be run with the same cold efficiency as a stock portfolio, that problems could be analyzed in the abstract by professional managers. Business schools have promoted a dependence on numbers that ignores such intangibles as a passion for quality and service. Even employees are reduced to a variable in the investment formula. The "personnel management systems" of some American companies are inhuman creations that squeeze out all loyalty and sense of workmanship. Plenty of companies claim that people are their most important asset or that the customer always comes first, but many act as if employees were replaceable parts and customers were mere nuisances.

Lately, in the face of slumping profits and stiffening competition, businessmen may be reworking a few of their old strategies. Some are beginning to wonder if America doesn't have too many finance wizards and lawyer hotshots who think that any company can be run with the same bag of tricks. There seems to be renewed appreciation of people who have spent their careers in engineering or production and who know the industry inside out. Even the temples of abstract management—the business schools—may lose some of their authority as the mavericks within their ranks begin to warn that discounted cash flows and ratio analysis are no substitute for savvy and imagination.

Two professors at Harvard Business School have attacked what they call the "false and shallow concept of the professional manager."[30] They go on to say: "The key to long-term success—even survival—in business is what it has always been: to invest, to innovate, to lead, to create value where none existed before. Such determination, such striving to excel, requires leaders—not *just* controllers, market analysts, and portfolio managers."[31]

Americans should be rethinking their own management philosophies and studying the strategies of the many excellent companies within their midst. It is an illusion to think that Japanese management will be the secret to America's renewal, especially when the very techniques that make it unique are rapidly losing their grip even in Japan. American executives are tempted to study Japan because they know that their own performance is not all that it should be. A willingness to learn from others is an encouraging sign of humility. However, after cutting through the tangle of cultural differences to learn a few useful lessons, Americans will find that what they learned from the Japanese they could have learned much more quickly from each other.

At the national level as well, the Japanese economic model may not be appropriate for America. To begin with, there is wide disagreement on how essential MITI and other policy-making bodies have been in Japan's development. Likewise, even among those who believe that public policy was a key ingredient to Japan's successes, there is no consensus on whether similar strategies would be effective elsewhere.

In the United States, government has limited the free play of market forces only by setting broad guidelines for economic behavior. It has regulated the economy rather than planned it. There is some question whether the government even knows what the private sector is doing, much less whether it could guide and coordinate it. The United States does not have Japan's tradition of close cooperation between public and private sectors. And left to itself, American industry was once an unstoppable power.

Chalmers Johnson, author of what is becoming the standard English-language work on the role of MITI, emphasizes the extent to which Japanese planners drew on their country's known strengths in fashioning industrial policy. He concludes:

> This suggests that other nations seeking to emulate Japan's achievements might be better advised to fabricate the institu-

tions of their own developmental states from local materials. It might suggest that what a country like the United States needs is not what Japan has but, rather, less regulation and more incentives by the government for people to save, invest, work, and compete internationally. . . . [T]he United States might be better advised to build on its own strengths and to unleash the private competitive impulses of its citizens rather than add still another layer to its already burdensome regulatory bureaucracy.[32]

Moreover, Japanese industrial policy, like Japanese management, will lose its effectiveness as the economy becomes too complex and diverse to march in step to MITI's tune. Once again America would be ill-served by copying techniques that may have outlived their usefulness even in Japan.

Ever since 1853 the flow of influence across the Pacific has been almost entirely west to east. This is now changing. Americans have finally recognized Japan's importance to the world, and the front-page attention it has won in the last decade will not easily be lost. No world forum, no global business strategy, no assessment of industrial technology can ever again ignore Japan. This does not mean that Japan is, or will be, a model for America. We should learn all we can about Japan and should never fail to include it in our calculations, but it is not a beacon by which we should steer our course.

Recently I had dinner with an old friend from work. We swapped tales about Tokyo and New York and laughed about the crazy times we'd had trying to make sales to Japanese customers. But the conversation turned to the U.S. economy, and we lost some of our merriment. "What do you think?" I asked him after we had brooded over unemployment and trade deficits for a while. "Do you think we need to learn how to be more like the Japanese?"

"Hell, no," he said. "We don't need to be more like the Japanese. We need to be more like us."

What does it mean to be more like us? That's the question we should be asking ourselves, not how we should go about being more like someone else.

After all, we were the first to build modern factories, to understand quality control, to build an economy that spanned a continent and circled the globe. We are the people who invented all the things the Japanese are selling us. We were once undisputed masters of the game they now play so well. Only fifteen years ago American industry was such a powerhouse that Europeans were afraid we would swallow them up.[33]

What did it take to become number one? It took courage, vision, and a lot of plain hard work. It took the qualities we once were famous for: honesty, self-reliance, and determination to do the job right. America's successes were a product of our own sturdy virtues; we didn't have to take lessons from anybody to be the best.

The United States still has vast resources and enormous strengths if only we have the will to mobilize them. We have been out in front for so long that we have forgotten what it takes to come from behind. Our wealth has been so great that we have been tempted to think we had only to redistribute it, not to roll up our sleeves and make more.

Maybe it takes a crisis for America to flex its muscles. If so, the crisis is gathering. Our supremacy is being threatened in one field after another, and we are slowly waking up to the challenge. We should not be whimpering about unfair competition or running to Uncle Sam for protection. We should be working, investing, innovating, taking risks, and thinking big. America is still number one, and it is up to us to keep it that way.

By all means, let us learn from the Japanese, from the Europeans, from anyone who is working hard to be the best. But let's not forget that America has its own special powers and possibilities. It is these that should guide and inspire us.

NOTES

All translations from the Japanese, unless otherwise indicated, are by the author.

INTRODUCTION

1. Richard Lynn, "IQ in Japan and the United States Shows a Growing Disparity," *Nature* (May 20, 1982), p. 222.

2. Edwin O. Reischauer, *The Japanese* (Cambridge: Harvard University Press, 1978), p. 124.

3. Roy Andrew Miller, *Japan's Modern Myth* (Tokyo: John Weatherhill, 1982), p. xi.

4. Lafcadio Hearn, quoted in Pat Barr, *The Deer Cry Pavilion* (New York: Harcourt, Brace & World, 1968), p. 227.

CHAPTER 1 | UNIQUENESS

1. Isaiah Ben-Dasan, *The Japanese and the Jews*, trans. Richard L. Gage (Tokyo: John Weatherhill, 1972), p. 106.

2. Edward Seidensticker, *This Country, Japan* (Tokyo: Kodansha International, 1979), p. 326.

3. Urban Lehner, "Are the Japanese the Rudest People or the Most Polite?," *Wall Street Journal*, July 23, 1982, p. 1.

4. *Ibid.*, p. 18.

5. "Testing Time for Drugs," *Economist* (August 7, 1982), p. 70.

6. Quoted in Masao Miyoshi, *As We Saw Them* (Los Angeles: University of California Press, 1979), p. 13.

7. Basil Hall Chamberlain, *Japanese Things* (Tokyo: Charles E. Tuttle Co., 1971), p. 382. Originally published in 1904 as *Things Japanese*.

8. Shōsaburō Kimura, in Kimura et al., *Shin Nihonjin-ron [New Nihonjin-ron]* (Tokyo: Kōdansha, 1980), p. 39.

9. George Thomas Kurian, *The Book of World Rankings* (New York: Facts on File, Inc., 1979), p. 45.

10. Jack Seward, *Japanese in Action* (Tokyo: John Weatherhill, 1968), p. 13.

11. Kiyoshi Nasu, *Kuzureyuku Nichibei Kankei [Declining U.S.-Japan Relations]* (Tokyo: Takai Shōhō, 1978), p. 45.

12. From the diary of a member of the expedition to open Japan, quoted in Pat Barr, *The Coming of the Barbarians* (New York: E. F. Dutton & Co., 1967), p. 42.

13. Hidetoshi Katō, *Nihonjin no Shūhen [Around the Japanese]* (Tokyo: Kōdansha, 1975), p. 150ff.

14. David S. Kung, *Heisa-koku Nippon [Japan: The Closed Country]* (Tokyo: Mainichi Shinbunsha, 1980), p. 68.

15. *Ibid.*, p. 81.

16. Yoshio Sugimoto and Ross Mouer, *Nihonjin wa "Nihon-teki" ka [How "Japanese" Are the Japanese?]* (Tokyo: Tōyō Keizai Shinhōsha, 1982), p. 11.

17. Nasu, *op. cit.*, p. 45.

18. Tsuneo Iida, *Yutori to wa Nanika [What Is Affluence?]* (Tokyo: Kōdansha, 1982), p. 57.

19. Kung, *op. cit.*, p. 57f.

20. David Riesman and Evelyn Riesman, *Conversations in Japan* (New York: Basic Books, 1967), p. 319.

21. Ryō Takahashi, *Nihonjin no Hana [The Japanese Nose]* (Tokyo: Kōdansha, 1980).

22. Hisashi Suzuki, *Kaseki Saru Kara Nihonjin Made [From the Fossil Apes to the Japanese]* (Tokyo: Iwanami Shoten, 1971).

23. Kenichi Takemura, "How Do the Japanese View Foreigners?," *PHP* magazine (October 1981).

CHAPTER 2 | HIERARCHY

1. Mikiso Hane, *Peasants, Rebels, and Outcasts* (New York: Pantheon Books, 1982), p. 141f.

2. Quoted in Margaret Taylor, "It Doesn't Have to Be Like That," *Japan Christian Quarterly* (Spring 1974), p. 88.

3. Sumiko Iwao, "The Feminine Perspective in Japan Today," Kenneth A. Grossberg, ed., *Japan Today* (Philadelphia: Institute for the Study of Human Issues, 1981), p. 17.

4. Chie Nakane, *Japanese Society* (Harmondsworth: Penguin Books, 1973), p. 34.

5. *Ibid.*, p. 36.

6. Murray Sayle, "When Confucius Flies Co-pilot," *Far Eastern Economic Review* (May 12, 1982), p. 102f.

7. Shōzō Kurokawa and Bernice K. Hirai, *Joseirashii Beiei Kaiwa [American Women's Conversational English]* (Tokyo: Natsume Shuppansha, 1977), *passim*.

8. Chie Nakane, *Tateshakai no Rikigaku [The Dynamics of a Vertical Society]* (Tokyo: Kōdansha, 1978), p. 58.

9. Nasu, *op. cit.*, p. 65f.

10. Hane, *op. cit.*, p. 225ff.

11. Nihon Shiosu Kyōkai, *Nihon Kigyō no Kaigai Shinshutsu [The Overseas Expansion of Japanese Companies]* (Tokyo: Tōyō Keizai Shinhō Sha, 1973), p. 84.

12. Nasu *op. cit.*, p. 51.

13. "Japanese Men's Prostitution Tours in Asia," *Japan Quarterly* (April–June 1981), p. 149.

14. Urban Lehner, "Japan's Refugee Problem," *Wall Street Journal*, September 2, 1981, p. 20.

15. Narufumi Yano, *Tōkyō Honsha o Furimukuna [Don't Look Back to Tokyo Head Office]* (Tokyo: Daiamondosha, 1978), p. 60.

16. Masao Miyoshi, *Accomplices of Silence* (Berkeley: University of California Press, 1974), p. 57.

17. Quoted by William Wetherall, in Changsoo Lee and George De Vos, *Koreans in Japan* (Berkeley: University of California Press, 1981), p. 281.

18. Hiroyuki Araki, *Nihonjin no Kōdō Yōshiki [Patterns of Japanese Behavior]* (Tokyo: Kōdansha, 1973), p. 3.

19. Nasu, *op. cit.*, p. 47.

20. William Geist, "A Clash at the Club," New York *Times*, October 13, 1981, p. B2.

21. Lee and De Vos, *op. cit.*, p. 23.

22. *Ibid.*, p. 32.

23. Quoted in *ibid.*, p. 279.

24. Hane, *op. cit.*, p. 139ff.

25. Wetherall, *op. cit.*, p. 412.

26. *Ibid.*, p. 413.

27. Hiroshi Wagatsuma, "The Social Perception of Skin Color in Japan," in Irwin Scheiner, ed., *Modern Japan, an Interpretive Anthology* (New York: Macmillan Publishing, 1974), p. 60.

28. John K. Emmerson, *Arms, Yen & Power* (New York: Dunellen, 1971), p. 156ff.

29. Miyoshi, *As We Saw Them, loc. cit.*, p. 63.

30. *Ibid.*, p. 60.

CHAPTER 3 | THE GROUP

1. Araki, *op. cit.*, p. 39.

2. Kimura, *op. cit.*, p. 45.

3. *"Yoroku"* ["Afterthoughts"], *Mainichi Shinbun,* June 30, 1982. (Translation is from English edition *Mainichi* of July 4, 1982.)

4. William Caudill and Helen Weinstein, "Maternal Care and Infant Behavior in Japan and America," in William P. Lebra and Takie S. Lebra, eds., *Japanese Culture and Behavior* (Honolulu: University Press of Hawaii, 1974), p. 229ff.

5. Nakane, *Japanese Society, loc. cit.,* p. 144.

6. Shichihei Yamamoto, *Nihon-Shihonshugi no Seishin [The Spirit of Japanese Capitalism]* (Tokyo: Kōdansha, 1979), p. 36.

7. *Ibid.,* p. 51.

8. *Ibid.,* p. 47.

9. Takeo Doi, *The Anatomy of Dependence,* trans. John Bester (Tokyo: Kodansha International, 1973), p. 39.

10. Toshinao Yoneyama, *Nihonjin no Nakama Ishiki [Japanese Group Consciousness]* (Tokyo: Kōdansha, 1976), p. 51.

11. Yamamoto, *op. cit.,* p. 50.

12. Henry H. Schulte, ed., *Facts on File Yearbook 1976* (New York: Facts on File, Inc., 1977), entry for March 5, 1976.

13. Yamamoto, *op. cit.,* p. 48f.

14. Walter McQuade, "The Shape of Cars to Come," *Fortune* (May 17, 1982), p. 77.

15. Yoneyama, *op. cit.,* p. 31.

16. Lehner, "Are the Japanese the Rudest People . . . ," *loc. cit.,* p. 1.

17. Katō, *op. cit.,* p. 59.

18. Kurian, *op. cit.,* p. 377.

19. *The Chrysanthemum and the Sword* (Tokyo: Charles E. Tuttle Co., 1954), p. 222ff.

20. Reischauer, *op. cit.,* p. 140.

21. Yutaka Sakisaka, *Haji no Kōzō [The Structure of Shame]* (Tokyo: Kōdansha, 1982), p. 80.

22. *Ibid.,* p. 67.

23. Eikan Kyū, *Kaisha Shakai Nippon [Japan: The Company Country]* (Tokyo: Nippon Keizai Shinbunsha, 1975), p. 44f.

24. Sakisaka, *op. cit.*, p. 160f.

25. Quoted in *ibid.*, p. 145f.

26. Yamamoto, *op. cit.*, p. 164.

27. Sakisaka, *op. cit.*, p. 103.

28. Hideaki Kase, *Nihonjin no Hassō, Seiyōjin no Hassō [Japanese Thought, Western Thought]* (Tokyo: Kōdansha, 1977), p. 94f.

29. Tillman Durdin, "Tel Aviv Massacre Distresses Japan," New York *Times*, June 8, 1972, p. 4.

30. Kung, *op. cit.*, p. 81.

31. Shintarō Ishihara, in Japan Center for International Exchange, *The Silent Power* (Tokyo: Simul Press, Inc., 1976), p. 78.

32. Kung, *op. cit.*, p. 114.

33. Tracy Dahlby, "Come Along, It's Time to Join the Human Race," *Far Eastern Economic Review* (June 23, 1978), p. 65.

34. Seidensticker, *op. cit.*, p. 332.

CHAPTER 4 | CONFORMITY

1. *"Kyōiku no Hiroba"* ["Forum on Education"], *Asahi Shinbun*, June 8, 1982, p. 10.

2. Yutaka Furutani, "Spartan-like School Praised," *Mainichi Daily News*, July 12, 1982.

3. William K. Cummings, *Education and Equality in Japan* (Princeton: Princeton University Press, 1980), p. 214.

4. For a stinging criticism of Japanese education, see Chapter 11 in Miller, *op. cit.*

5. *"Seiji no Kage Koku-suru Kyōkasho Mondai"* ["Textbook Controversy Lengthens Government Shadow"], *Asahi Shinbun*, June 26, 1982, p. 5.

6. Donald Richie, "The Asian Bookshelf," *Japan Times*, July 31, 1982.

7. Tetsuko Kuroyanagi, *Totto-chan, the Little Girl at the Window*, trans. Dorothy Brittain (New York: Kodansha International, 1982).

8. Richie, *op. cit.*

9. "Wit, Soul of," *Economist* (October 16, 1982), p. 124.

10. "Moneybags," *Economist* (July 10, 1982), p. 65.

11. Robert Trumbull, "Japan Mourns Lan Lan, Who Conquered Public," New York *Times*, September 5, 1979, p. 8.

12. Yutaka Sasayama, "Follow the Plastic Warrior," *Japan Quarterly* (April–June 1982), p. 253f.

13. Robert Whiting, *The Chrysanthemum and the Bat* (Tokyo: Permanent Press, 1977), p. 41f.

14. Seidensticker, quoted in Miller, *op. cit.*, p. 217.

15. *Ibid.*

16. Remarks by Yoshio Teresawa at a conference on Japanese decision making, Columbia University, October 7, 1982.

17. Miyoshi, *As We Saw Them, loc. cit.*, p. 185.

18. John Lewis, "They Fall Among Thieves," *Far Eastern Economic Review* (May 1, 1981), p. 26.

19. Kenichi Takemura, quoted in Arthur Golden, "Group Think in Japan Inc.," *New York Times Magazine* (December 5, 1982), p. 136.

20. Paul Bonnet, *Fushigi no Kuni Nippon, No. 5 [Japan: Land of Wonders, No. 5]* (Tokyo: Daiamondosha, 1980), p. 108.

21. Araki, *op. cit.*, p. 53.

22. Henry Scott Stokes, "Suzuki, Under Growing Criticism, Says He'll Quit as Japan's Premier," New York *Times*, October 13, 1982, p. 1.

23. Paul Bonnet, *Saikin Nippon Jijō [Latest Developments in Japan]* (Tokyo: Daiamondosha, 1981), p. 78.

24. Frank Gibney, *Miracle by Design* (New York: Times Books, 1982), p. 108.

25. Clyde Farnsworth, "Washington Watch," New York *Times*, May 17, 1982, p. D-2.

26. Eikan Kyū, *Kaisha Shakai Nippon [Japan: The Company Country]* (Tokyo: Nihon Keizai Shinbunsha, 1975), p. 22f.

27. Araki, *op. cit.*, p. 80.

28. Takehiko Kenmochi, *Hikaku Nihongaku no Susume [A Plea for Comparative Japanese Studies]* (Kyoto: PHP Kenkyūjo, 1980), p. 40f.

29. Iida, *op. cit.*, p. 40.

30. Gregory Clark, *Nihonjin, Yuniikusa no Gensen [The Japanese Tribe: Origins of a Nation's Uniqueness]*, trans. Masumi Muramatsu (Tokyo: Saimaru Press, 1977), p. 62f.

31. "Japan's High-Tech Challenge," *Newsweek* (August 9, 1982), p. 53.

32. Terry Truco, "Japan's Strange View of European Culture," *Wall Street Journal*, August 6, 1982, p. 15.

33. Richard Casement, "Tomorrow's Leaders," *Economist* (June 19, 1982), survey, p. 6.

CHAPTER 5 | REASON, FEELING, AND RELIGION

1. Sakisaka, *op. cit.*, p. 113f.

2. Hiroshi Takeuchi, in Kimura, et al., *op. cit.*, p. 144f.

3. Bundō Yamada, *"Umi no Soto kara Nagameta Nihonjin-zō"* ["How the Japanese Look from Across the Water"], *OCS News* (September 24, 1982).

4. Sakisaka, *op. cit.*, p. 200.

5. Quoted in Casement, *op. cit.*, p. 9.

6. Yamamoto, *op. cit.*, p. 121.

7. Miyoshi, *Accomplices of Silence, loc. cit.*, p. xv.

8. Sakisaka, *op. cit.*, p. 186.

9. For a vigorous attack on what he calls the antimyth of silence, see Miller, *op. cit.*, Chapter 5.

10. Yamada, *op. cit.*

11. Whiting, *op. cit.*, p. 47f.

12. Susan Scully, "In Japan, a Pain-Killer Is a Culture-Killer," *Mainichi Daily News*, June 25, 1982.

13. *Ibid.*

14. Arch B. Taylor, "Clash of Cultures—Japanese Polytheism vs. Biblical Monotheism," *Japan Christian Quarterly*, Summer, 1982, p. 140.

15. John Turrent, "Nishiarai Daishi Offers Rites of Four-Wheeled Passage," *Japan Times*, July 30, 1982.

16. Yasuo Kiriyama, quoted in an ad for his book *Shugorei o Mote [You Need Guardian Spirits]* (Tokyo: Hirakawa Shuppansha, 1982). Ad appeared in *Asahi Shinbun*, summer of 1982.

17. Marvin Tokayer, *Nihon ni wa Minshushugi wa Nai [There Is No Democracy in Japan]*, trans. Sōichi Hakozaki (Tokyo: Nisshin Hōdō, 1976), p. 149.

18. *Ibid.*, p. 154.

19. Arch B. Taylor, *"Nihonshiki Hassōhō"* ["The Japanese Way of Thinking"], unpublished manuscript, p. 7.

20. Ben-Dasan, *op. cit.*, p. 107ff.

CHAPTER 6 | THE CORPORATION

1.M. Kikkawa, *Nippon Amerika e Jōriku su [The Japanese Are Landing In America]* (Tokyo: Ushio Shuppansha, 1980), p. 227ff.

2. Sharon Johnson, "Campuses Reflecting Rising Japanese Influence," *New York Times Magazine* (April 28, 1982), p. 51.

3. Bonnet, *Fushigi no Kuni Nippon No. 5, loc. cit.*, p. 206.

4. Steve Lohr, "He Taught the Japanese," New York *Times*, May 10, 1981, III, p. 6.

5. Ken Tsuji, *Nihonjin wa Hataraki-sugi ka? [Do the Japanese Work Too Hard?]* (Tokyo: Asahi Sonorama, 1981), p. 28.

6. Chalmers Johnson, *MITI and the Japanese Miracle* (Stanford: Stanford University Press, 1982), p. 34.

7. Ezra F. Vogel, *Japan as Number One* (Cambridge: Harvard University Press, 1979), p. 72.

8. Paul Wilson and Tracy Dahlby, "Blackballed from the Club," *Far Eastern Economic Review* (November 7, 1980), p. 108.

9. Kenichi Ohmae, "The Long and the Short of Japanese Planning," *Wall Street Journal*, January 18, 1982, p. 22.

10. "Businessmen Feel Gods Are Asset," *Mainichi Daily News*, May 18, 1982.

11. R. P. Dore, "Industrial Relations in Japan and Elsewhere," in Albert M. Craig, ed., *Japan* (Princeton: Princeton University Press, 1979), p. 340.

12. A. H. Cook and H. Hayashi, *Working Women in Japan* (Ithaca: New York State School of Labor and Industrial Relations, 1980), p. 18f.

13. Rodney Clark, *The Japanese Company* (New Haven: Yale University Press, 1979), p. 68.

14. Tsuji, *op. cit.*, p. 111.

15. Summarized in "Aging Workers Anxious over Retirement," *Japan Times*, August 8, 1982.

16. Yano, *op. cit.*, p. 50.

17. William G. Ouchi, *Theory Z* (New York: Avon Books, 1981).

18. Steve Lohr, "The Company That Stopped Detroit," New York *Times*, March 21, 1982, III, p. 26.

19. Keitarō Hasegawa, *Ekonomikku Sūpāpawā no Himitsu [The Secrets of an Economic Superpower]* (Tokyo: Asahi Shinbunsha, 1981), p. 186f.

20. Tomotaka Ikeda, "Big Business Sees Value of Worship," *Mainichi Daily News*, April 26, 1982.

21. Norman Macrae, "Must Japan Slow?" *Economist* (February 23, 1980), survey, p. 42.

22. Hasegawa, *op. cit.*, p. 136.

23. Morse Saito, "Battling Windmills," *Mainichi Daily News*, April 26, 1982.

24. B. Bruce-Briggs, "The Dangerous Folly Called Theory Z," *Fortune* (May 17, 1982), p. 44.

25. *Ibid.*

26. Kung, *op. cit.*, p. 44.

27. Richard Pascale and Anthony Athos, *The Art of Japanese Management* (New York: Warner Books, 1981), p. 311.

28. Kikkawa, *op. cit.*, p. 230f.

CHAPTER 7 | SEX AND SEX ROLES

1. "'Urination Incident' No Relief to Diet," *Japan Times*, August 19, 1982, p. 2.

2. Golden, *op. cit.*, p. 140.

3. Saburo Iwawaki and H. J. Eysenck, "Sexual Attitudes Among British and Japanese Students," *Journal of Psychology* (March 1978), p. 289.

4. Samuel Coleman, "The Cultural Context of Condom Use in Japan," *Studies in Family Planning* (January 1981), p. 30.

5. *Ibid.*, p. 28f.

6. Paul Theroux, *The Great Railway Bazaar* (Boston: Houghton Mifflin, 1975), p. 273.

7. Shumon Miura, *Tsuma o Metoraba [If You Should Take a Wife]* (Tokyo: Sankei Shuppan, 1978), p. 16.

8. Yoshitada Kōnoike, *Ima, Nihonbyō o Ute [Fight Back at the Japanese Disease Now]* (Tokyo: Tokuma Shoten, 1980), p. 54.

9 Quoted by Margaret Taylor, *op. cit.*, p. 88.

10. Jūzō Itami, lecture at Shikoku Gakuin University, Zentsuji, Japan, December, 1981.

11. Motofusa Murayama, *Wagaya no Nichibei Bunka Gassen [The U.S.-Japanese Culture Battle in My Home]* (Tokyo: PHP Kenkyūjo, 1979), *passim.*

12. Yano, *op. cit.*, p. 212.

13. Ichiro Kawasaki, *Japan Unmasked* (Tokyo: Charles E. Tuttle Co., 1969), p. 26.

14. Kung, *op. cit.*, p. 150.

CHAPTER 8 | CULTURE AND LANGUAGE

1. Kase, *op. cit.*, p. 229f.

2. James C. Thomson, Peter W. Stanley, and John C. Perry, *Sentimental Imperialists* (New York: Harper & Row, 1981), p. 75.

3. Marius B. Jansen, *Japan and Its World* (Princeton: Princeton University Press, 1980), p. 67.

4. *Ibid.*, p. 69.

5. Thomson et al., *op. cit.*, p. 76.

6. Miller, *op. cit.*, p. 108f.

7. Thomson et al., *op. cit.*, p. 143.

8. Lee and De Vos, *op. cit.*, p. 161.

9. Miller, *op. cit.*, p. 109f.

10. Ezra F. Vogel, *Japan's Middle Class*, 1963, quoted in Japan Center for International Exchange, *The Silent Power* (Tokyo: Simul Press, Inc., 1976), p. 8.

11. Kase, *op. cit.*, p. 240.

12. Yūjirō Shinoda, *Nihonjin-yo, Sokoku Bunka o Ushinauna [Japanese! Don't Lose the Culture of Your Fatherland]* (Tokyo: Nihon Kōgyō Shinbunsha, 1980), p. 162.

13. *Ibid.*, p. 12f.

14. Kenmochi, *op. cit.*, p. 150.

15. Kase, *op. cit.*, p. 242.

16. Katō, *op. cit.*, p. 81.

17. Tadanobu Tsunoda, in Kimura et al., *op. cit.*, p. 260ff.

18. *Ibid.*, p. 273.

19. *Journal of Japanese Studies*, no. 5 (1979), pp. 439–49, cited in Miller, *op. cit.*, p. 80.

20. *Japan Foundation Newsletter*, vol. 6 (4–5, 1978), p. 1, quoted in Miller, *op. cit.*, p. 76.

21. Kenichi Takemura, *Nihon no Jōshiki wa Sekai no Hijōshiki!? [Is What Makes Sense in Japan Nonsense to the Rest of the World!?]* (Tokyo: Daiamondosha, 1977), p. 203.

22. "Japanese Go Home to 'Culture Shock,'" New York *Times*, October 19, 1980, p. 17.

23. *Ibid.*

24. Miyoshi, *As We Saw Them*, *loc. cit.*, p. 186.

CHAPTER 9 | JAPAN AT PLAY

1. Tokuhisa Tamao, "Tourism Within, from and to Japan," *International Social Science Journal*, vol. 32, no. 1, 1980, p. 129.

2. Chie Nakane, *Japanese Society* (Harmondsworth: Penguin Books, 1973), p. 129.

3. K. Saito, "Leisure Industry in Its Golden Age," *Oriental Economist*, January 1981, p. 22.

4. *Japan Quarterly*, April–June, 1982, p. 165.

5. This account of the Orioles visit is taken from Robert Whiting, *The Chrysanthemum and the Bat* (Tokyo: Permanent Press, 1977), p. 231ff.

6. Hiroshi Takeuchi, in Kimura, Kamishima, et al., *Shin Nihonjin-ron [New Nihonjin-ron]* (Tokyo: Kōdansha, 1980), p. 155f.

7. Nasu, *op cit.*, p. 67ff.

8. Tsuneo Iida, "Affluence—Japan's Undoing?" *Oriental Economist*, September 1980, p. 16.

CHAPTER 10 | JAPAN AND THE WORLD

1. Akira Tanaka, "Japan and Korea," *Japan Quarterly* (January–March 1981), p. 37.

2. Thomson, *op. cit.*, p. 295f.

3. "Chronology," *Japan Quarterly* (January–March 1981), p. 136.

4. *Asahi Shinbun*, May 10, 1982, quoted in Yamada, *op. cit.*

5. Art Pine and Urban Lehner, "Protectionist Feelings Against Japan Increase in the U.S. and Europe," *Wall Street Journal*, January 14, 1983, p. 1.

6. Statement of Michael J. Kowalsky, president, Cigar Association of America, Inc., Senate Select Committee on Small Business. *Impact of Non-tariff Barriers on the Ability of Small Businesses to Export to Japan*, 96th Congress, 2nd Session. Hearing of June 25, 1980 (Washington: Government Printing Office, 1980), p. 179.

7. *Ibid.*, p. 189f.

8. *Ibid.*, p. 185.

9. Louis Kraar, "Inside Japan's 'Open' Market," *Fortune* (October 5, 1981), p. 123.

10. Clyde Farnsworth, "U.S. Trade Chief Says Nakasone Trip Helped Ease Tensions," New York *Times*, January 21, 1983, p. D9.

11. Roy A. Werner, "Is Japan an Open Market?" *Asian Affairs* (New York) (January–February 1982), p. 151.

12. U.S.-Japan Trade Study Group, "A Special Progress Report," included in Senate Select Committee on Small Business, *op. cit.*, p. 282.

13. Statement of Julian Morris, president, Automotive Parts and Accessories Association, *ibid.*, p. 410f.

14. Frank A. Weil and Norman D. Glick, "Japan—Is the Market Open?," *Law and Policy in International Business*, vol. II, no. 3 (1979), p. 870.

15. Jack Burton and Dennis Chase, "Sun Still Not Shining on P&G in Japan," *Advertising Age*, December 20, 1982, p. 36.

16. Statement of Abraham Katz, assistant secretary of commerce for international economic policy, Senate Select Committee on Small Business, *op. cit.*, p. 12.

17. M. Borrus, J. Millstein, and J. Zysman, *International Competition in Advanced Industrial Sectors: Trade and Development in the Semiconductor Industry* (Washington: Government Printing Office, 1982), p. 83f.

18. *Ibid.*, p. 40.

19. "Japan's Trade War with the West Goes from Cold to Hot," *Economist* (April 24, 1982), p. 88.

20. Katz, *op. cit.*, p. 18.

21. Warner, *op. cit.*, p. 155.

22. Kraar, *op. cit.*, p. 119.

23. *Ibid.*, p. 122.

24. Japanese trade official Masumi Esaki, quoted in Marc Leepson, "Tensions in U.S.-Japan Relations," *Editorial Research Reports*, April 9, 1982, p. 257.

25. Urban Lehner, "The Japanese Market, Once Hostile to U.S., Is Opening to Imports," *Wall Street Journal*, May 12, 1982, p. 1.

26. Kraar, *op. cit.*, p. 123.

27. "Ombudsman Solves 60% of Trade Cases: MITI," *Japan Times*, August 21, 1982.

28. Werner, *op. cit.*, p. 156f.

29. Lehner, "The Japanese Market, Once Hostile . . ." *loc. cit.*, p. 20.

30. Art Pine, "Japan Nears a Choice of Easing Trade Curbs or Facing West's Ire," *Wall Street Journal*, January 26, 1982, p. 20.

31. U.S.-Japan Trade Study Group, *op. cit.*, p. 270.

32. Leepson, *op. cit.*, p. 257.

33. "Is Free Trade Dead?," *Economist* (December 25, 1982), p. 77.

34. "Japan's Trade War with the West Goes from Cold to Hot," *op. cit.*, p. 88.

35. Edward Meadows, "Japan Runs into America Inc.," *Fortune* (March 22, 1982), p. 56ff.

36. *Ibid.*, p. 61.

37. Hajime Karatsu, "Advice on Elimination of Trade Friction," *Oriental Economist* (March 1982), p. 14f.

38. Pine, *op. cit.*

39. Hisahiko Okazaki, "The Political Framework of Japan's Defense," in Douglas J. Murray and Paul R. Viotti, eds., *The Defense Policies of Nations* (Baltimore: Johns Hopkins Press, 1982), p. 471.

40. John Endicott, "The Defense Policy of Japan," *ibid.*, p. 450.

41. Taketsugu Tsurutani, "Japan's Security," *Orbis* (Spring 1981), p. 89.

42. International Institute for Strategic Studies, *The Military Balance 1981–1982* (Colchester: International Institute for Strategic Studies, 1981), p. 105.

43. Quoted in Derek Davies, "Return of the Rising Sun," *Far Eastern Economic Review* (March 14, 1980), p. 21.

44. Neil Ulman and Urban Lehner, "Japan's Rearmament Is Too Slow for U.S., Too Scary for Others," *Wall Street Journal*, November 22, 1982, p. 17.

45. Tetsuya Kataoka, *Waiting for a "Pearl Harbor"* (Stanford: Hoover Institution Press, 1980), p. 67.

46. "Japanese Industry Reaches for Its Gun," *Economist*, December 18, 1982, p. 72.

47. Neil Ulman and Urban Lehner, "Japan's Arms Industry Is Expanding Briskly, with Much U.S. Help," *Wall Street Journal*, November 26, 1982, p. 5.

48. "Japanese Industry Reaches for Its Gun," *op. cit.*

49. Kataoka, *op. cit.*, p. 5. The right to life, liberty, and the pursuit of happiness is set out in the Declaration of Independence, not in the Constitution.

50. Takehiko Kamo, "The Risk of Nuclear War and Japanese Militariza-

tion," *Japan Quarterly* (April–June 1982), p. 192, quoting *Asahi Shinbun* poll reported on March 25, 1981.

51. "LDP Hawks Eye Change in Article 9 of Constitution," *Japan Times*, August 23, 1982, p. 4.

52. John J. O'Conner, "TV: A Drama About Hitler Youth," New York *Times*, November 29, 1982, p. C-20.

53. Kazuko Tsurumi, "Cultural Heterogeneity and Japanese Shinto," in Grossberg, *op. cit.*, p. 70.

54. Isaac Shapiro, "The Risen Sun: Japanese Gaullism?," *Foreign Policy* (Winter 1980–81), p. 70.

55. Henry H. Schulte, ed., *Facts on File Yearbook 1972* (New York: Facts on File Inc., 1973), p. 753.

56. Quoted in Albert Axelbank, *Black Star over Japan* (New York: Hill & Wang, 1972), p. 75.

57. *"Tensei Jingo"* [*"Vox Populi, Vox Dei"*], *Asahi Shinbun*, June 27, 1982.

58. "China Doesn't Fear Japan's Militarism," *Japan Times*, August 1, 1982.

59. Kung, *op. cit.*, p. 10.

60. See page 44.

61. Kenichi Takemura, "How Do the Japanese View Foreigners?" *PHP* (October 1981).

62. Nasu, *op. cit.*, p. 204.

63. Statement of purpose from the masthead of *PHP* magazine.

64. "Japanese Businessman Makes Big Board Debut," New York *Times*, July 17, 1981, p. D-1.

65. Tadao Umesao, in Japan Center for International Exchange, *op. cit.*, p. 18.

CHAPTER 11 | LOOKING AHEAD: LESSONS FOR AMERICA

1. Tamotsu Sengoku, ed., *Nihon no Sarariiman* [*The Japanese White-Collar Worker*] (Tokyo: Nihon Hōsō Shuppan Kyōkai, 1982), p. 19.

2. Akihisa Takaguchi, *ibid.*, p. 137.

3. *Ibid.*, p. 58.

4. Chalmers Johnson, *MITI and the Japanese Miracle* (Stanford: Stanford University Press, 1982), p. 311.

5. Masayoshi Kanabayashi, "Some Japanese Balk at Overseas Jobs," *Wall Street Journal*, July 9, 1982, p. 21.

6. "Euthanasia," *Economist* (December 11, 1982), p. 82.

7. Steve Lohr, "Labor in Japan Cools to Robots," New York *Times*, March 12, 1983, p. D-1.

8. Masaru Yoshitomi, "Economic Scene," New York *Times*, July 14, 1982, p. D-2.

9. Steve Lohr, "Japan's New Nonconformists," New York *Times*, March 8, 1983, p. D-1.

10. *"Shōnen Hanzai, Hajimete Seijin Uwamawaru"* ["Juvenile Crime Exceeds Adult Offenses for the First Time"], *Asahi Shinbun*, July 17, 1982.

11. *Ibid.*

12. Hayao Kawai, "Violence in the Home," *Japan Quarterly* (July–September 1981), p. 371.

13. Yutaka Sasayama, "Uncaring Adults—Violent Students," *Japan Quarterly* (January–March, 1983), p. 51.

14. Reported in Tsuji, *op. cit.*, p. 159.

15. Reported in Sengoku, *op. cit.*, p. 214.

16. Steve Lohr, "Japan Struggling with Itself," New York *Times*, July 13, 1982, p. F-1.

17. Jimmy Wheeler et al., *Japanese Industrial Development Policies in the 1980's* (Croton-on-Hudson: Hudson Institute, 1982), p. 66.

18. Iida, *op. cit.*, p. 119.

19. Tsuji, *op. cit.*, p. 218.

20. Iida, *op. cit.*, p. 97.

21. Marilyn Chase, "Japanese Still Think There Is Something to Learn in the U.S.," *Wall Street Journal*, October 20, 1982, p. 1.

22. Thomas Peters and Robert Waterman, *In Search of Excellence* (New York: Harper & Row, 1982).

23. *Ibid.*, p. xvii.

24. Walter Kiechel, "Management Winners," *Fortune* (November 29, 1982), p. 159.

25. Quoted in Leslie Wayne, "Management Gospel Gone Wrong," New York *Times*, May 30, 1982, III, p. 21.

26. Peters and Waterman, *op. cit.*, p. 26.

27. *Ibid.*, p. 149.

28. *Ibid.*, p. xxiii.

29. Sengoku, *op. cit.*, p. 53.

30. Robert Hayes and William Abernathy, "Managing Our Way to Economic Decline," *Harvard Business Review* (July–August 1980), p. 74.

31. *Ibid.*, p. 77.

32. Chalmers Johnson, *op. cit.*, p. 323.

33. Jean Jacques Servan-Schreiber, *The American Challenge*, trans. Ronald Steel (New York: Atheneum, 1968).

INDEX

952
TAY   1885

Taylor, Jared

Shadows of the Rising
SUn

952
TAY   1885

AUTHOR
Taylor, Jared
TITLE   Shadows of the Rising
Sun

DATE DUE	BORROWER'S NAME
NOV. 1 □ 1990	Kay Senior
NOV. 2 1990	"
JUL 2 7 1999	"Sheril Morgen"